UNTIL HE RETURNS

LESSONS LEARNED IN THE WILDERNESS
(BOOK 6)

KENNETH A. WINTER

JOIN MY READERS' GROUP FOR UPDATES AND FUTURE RELEASES

Please join my Readers' Group so i can send you a free book, as well as updates and information about future releases in the series.

See the back of the book for details on how to sign up.

* * *

Until He Returns

Book #6 in the *Lessons Learned In The Wilderness* series.

Published by:

Kenneth A. Winter

WildernessLessons, LLC

Richmond, Virginia

United States of America

kenwinter.org

wildernesslessons.com

Copyright © 2020 by Kenneth A. Winter

All rights reserved,

including the right of reproduction

in whole or in part in any form.

Cover Design: Melanie Fisher-Wellman

ISBN 978-1-7328670-7-9 (soft cover)

ISBN 978-1-7328670-6-2 (e-book)

Library of Congress Control Number 2019911444

Unless otherwise indicated, all Scripture quotations are taken from the *Holy Bible*, New Living Translation, copyright © 1996. Used by permission of Tyndale House Publishers, Inc., Wheaton, Illinois 60189. All rights reserved.

Scripture quotations marked (NASB) are taken from the *New American Standard Bible*, copyright © 1960, 1962, 1963, 1968, 1971, 1972, 1973, 1975, 1977 by The Lockman Foundation, La Habra, California. All rights reserved.

Scripture quotations marked (NKJ) are taken from the *New King James Version*, copyright © 1979, 1980, 1982 by Thomas Nelson, Inc., Nashville, Tennessee 37214. Used by permission.

Scripture quotations marked (ESV) are taken from *The Holy Bible, English Standard Version*, copyright © 2001 by Crossway, a publishing ministry of Good News Publishers. Used by permission. All rights reserved.

Scripture quotations marked (CEV) are taken from the *Contemporary English Version* Copyright © 1991, 1992, 1995 by American Bible Society. Used by permission.

Scripture quotations marked (NIV) are taken from the *New International Version*® NIV® Copyright © 1973, 1978, 1984, 2011 by Biblica, Inc. ™ Used by permission. All rights reserved worldwide.

DEDICATION

Publish His glorious deeds among the nations. Tell everyone about the amazing things He does. Tell all the nations that the Lord is King.
Psalm 96:3,10

* * *

On January 17, 2004 the Lord confirmed His direction to me to write the first book of what would become the **Lessons Learned In The Wilderness** series. Very quickly He showed me that it would be a series of six books. On the day i began writing this sixth and final book in the series He told me:

Finish doing it as well, so that your readiness in desiring it may be matched by your completing it….
2 Corinthians 8:11 (ESV)

As the book releases today – January 17, 2020 – on the sixteenth anniversary of His word to begin, i dedicate this book, with gratitude:

To my Lord and Savior Jesus Christ for Your promise and Your demonstration to me through this series, and in so many other ways, that what You begin You complete (Philippians 1:6),

To my wife, LaVonne, for your steadfast love, encouragement and partnership throughout our incredible faith journey,

To our family, for your support and collaboration in the journey – even when it made no human sense,

To Bryan, for being a Barnabas who was willing to walk beside me (chapter 27),

To Robert and Leslie, for faithfully cheering us on throughout the entire journey, and

To so many other dear friends, for your encouragement and support along the way.

* * *

CONTENTS

Chapter Scripture Listing	ix
A Word of Explanation	xi
Preface	xii
1. He Will Return	1
2. Waiting Is Not Inactivity	5
3. Why All This Concern?	10
4. The Helper Comes	15
5. Let The Nations Be Glad	19
6. A Drink At Joel's Place	23
7. A Prearranged Plan	28
8. What Should We Do?	33
9. Fully Devoted Followers	37
10. He Jumped Up	42
11. In Whose Name Do You Do This?	47
12. We Must Obey God Rather Than Men	51
13. Praying For Boldness	55
14. They Gave It All	58
15. Pride Comes Before A Fall	61
16. A Miraculous Escape	65
17. If It Is Of God, You Will Not Stop It	70
18. Chosen To Serve	74
19. Grace-full	78
20. Keep Gazing Upward	82
21. The Power Of God Isn't For Sale	86
22. A Divine Appointment	90
23. A Damascus Road Encounter	94
24. The Courage Of Ananias	98
25. A Hidden Journey In The Wilderness	102
26. An Opening In The Wall	106
27. Whose Barnabas Are You?	109
28. It Is What It Is, Or Is It?	113
29. He Goes Before Us	117
30. Being Prepared For What's Ahead	121
31. Can Anyone Object?	125
32. The Little Church That Could	129
33. Lord, What About Him?	132
34. God Doesn't Share His Glory	136
35. A Sending Church	140
36. Greater Is He That Is In Us	144
37. They Judged Themselves To Be Unworthy	147
38. From Lauding To Loathing	152

39. Be Sure To Report The Praises	157
40. It Seemed Good To The Spirit	160
41. Who Was Right?	165
42. Who Is Your Timothy?	169
43. A Macedonian Call	173
44. A Merchant Believes	177
45. A Jailer Is Set Free	181
46. Are We Turning The World Upside Down?	185
47. An Unknown God	189
48. The Corinthian Church	193
49. What Does Your Baptism Mean?	197
50. The Ephesian Church	201
51. Each One Ran Their Race – Part 1	205
52. Each One Ran Their Race – Part 2	209
53. Persuaded To Go	213
54. The Right Citizenship	217
55. The Case For The Prosecution	221
56. A Divine Delay	225
57. An Appeal To Caesar	229
58. I Am Almost Persuaded	233
59. Even Though The Ship May Go Down	237
60. Even The Snake Was Powerless	242
61. Proclaim The Good News Boldly	246
Please help me by leaving a review!	250
The Complete Lessons Learned In The Wilderness series	251
Also by Kenneth A. Winter	255
Also available as audiobooks	257
About the author	258
Please join my Readers' Group	259

CHAPTER SCRIPTURE LISTING

* * *

Chapter 1 *He Will Return* (Acts 1:9-11)
Chapter 2 *Waiting Is Not Inactivity* (Acts 1:12-14)
Chapter 3 *Why All This Concern?* (Acts 1:15-26)
Chapter 4 *The Helper Comes* (Acts 2:1-8)
Chapter 5 *Let The Nations Be Glad* (Acts 2:9-12)
Chapter 6 *A Drink At Joel's Place* (Acts 2:13-21)
Chapter 7 *A Prearranged Plan* (Acts 2:22-36)
Chapter 8 *What Should We Do?* (Acts 2:37-41)
Chapter 9 *Fully Devoted Followers* (Acts 2:42-47)
Chapter 10 *He Jumped Up* (Acts 3:1-11)
Chapter 11 *In Whose Name Do You Do This?* (Acts 4:1-7)
Chapter 12 *We Must Obey God Rather Than Men* (Acts 4:8-22)
Chapter 13 *Praying For Boldness* (Acts 4:23-31)
Chapter 14 *They Gave It All* (Acts 4:32-37)
Chapter 15 *Pride Comes Before A Fall* (Acts 5:1-11)
Chapter 16 *A Miraculous Escape* (Acts 5:12-28)
Chapter 17 *If It Is Of God, You Will Not Stop It* (Acts 5:29-42)
Chapter 18 *Chosen To Serve* (Acts 6:1-7)
Chapter 19 *Grace-full* (Acts 6:8-15)
Chapter 20 *Keep Gazing Upward* (Acts 7:51-60)
Chapter 21 *The Power Of God Isn't For Sale* (Acts 8:9-24)
Chapter 22 *A Divine Appointment* (Acts 8:26-40)
Chapter 23 *A Damascus Road Encounter* (Acts 9:1-9)
Chapter 24 *The Courage Of Ananias* (Acts 9:10-19)

Chapter 25 *A Hidden Journey In The Wilderness* (Acts 9:19-26)
Chapter 26 *An Opening In The Wall* (Acts 9:23-25)
Chapter 27 *Whose Barnabas Are You?* (Acts 9:26-31)
Chapter 28 *It Is What It Is, Or Is It?* (Acts 9:32-42)
Chapter 29 *He Goes Before Us* (Acts 10:1-8)
Chapter 30 *Being Prepared For What's Ahead* (Acts 10:9-23)
Chapter 31 *Can Anyone Object?* (Acts 10:24-48)
Chapter 32 *The Little Church That Could* (Acts 11:19-30)
Chapter 33 *Lord, What About Him?* (Acts 12:1-19)
Chapter 34 *God Doesn't Share His Glory* (Acts 12:20-23)
Chapter 35 *A Sending Church* (Acts 13:1-3)
Chapter 36 *Greater Is He That Is In Us* (Acts 13:6-12)
Chapter 37 *They Judged Themselves To Be Unworthy* (Acts 13:13-49)
Chapter 38 *From Lauding To Loathing* (Acts 14:11-20)
Chapter 39 *Be Sure To Report The Praises* (Acts 14:26-28)
Chapter 40 *It Seemed Good To The Spirit* (Acts 15:1-29)
Chapter 41 *Who Was Right?* (Acts 15:36-41)
Chapter 42 *Who Is Your Timothy?* (Acts 16:1-5)
Chapter 43 *A Macedonian Call* (Acts 16:6-10)
Chapter 44 *A Merchant Believes* (Acts 16:11-15)
Chapter 45 *A Jailer Is Set Free* (Acts 16:22-34)
Chapter 46 *Are We Turning The World Upside Down?* (Acts 17:1-9)
Chapter 47 *An Unknown God* (Acts 17:16-34)
Chapter 48 *The Corinthian Church* (Acts 18:1-18)
Chapter 49 *What Does Your Baptism Mean?* (Acts 18:24 – 19:7)
Chapter 50 *The Ephesian Church* (Acts 19:17-41)
Chapter 51 *Each One Ran Their Race – Part 1* (Acts 20:1-6)
Chapter 52 *Each One Ran Their Race – Part 2* (Acts 20:1-6)
Chapter 53 *Persuaded To Go* (Acts 21:7-17)
Chapter 54 *The Right Citizenship* (Acts 22:24-29)
Chapter 55 *The Case For The Prosecution* (Acts 23:35 – 24:9)
Chapter 56 *A Divine Delay* (Acts 24:10-27)
Chapter 57 *An Appeal To Caesar* (Acts 25:1-12)
Chapter 58 *I Am Almost Persuaded* (Acts 25:13 – 26:32)
Chapter 59 *Even Though The Ship May Go Down* (Acts 27:1-44)
Chapter 60 *Even The Snake Was Powerless* (Acts 28:1-11)
Chapter 61 *Proclaim The Good News Boldly* (Acts 28:15-31)

* * *

A WORD OF EXPLANATION

For those of you who are new to my writing.

***

You will notice that whenever i use the pronoun "I" referring to myself, i have chosen to use a lowercase "i". It is not a typographical error. i know that is contrary to proper English grammar and accepted editorial style guides. i drive editors (and "spell check") crazy by doing this. But years ago the LORD convicted me – personally – that in all things i must decrease and He must increase. And as a way of continuing personal reminder, from that day forward, i have chosen to use a lower case "i" whenever referring to myself. Because of the same conviction, i use a capital letter for any pronoun referring to God. The style guide for the New Living Translation (NLT) and some of the other translations quoted in this book do not share that conviction. However, you will see that i have intentionally made that slight revision and capitalized any pronoun referring to God in all quotations of Scripture. If i have violated any style guides as a result, please accept my apology, but i must honor this conviction.

Lastly, regarding this matter – this is a *personal* conviction – and i share it only so that you will understand why i have chosen to deviate from normal editorial practice. i am in no way suggesting or endeavoring to have anyone else subscribe to my conviction. Thanks for your understanding.

PREFACE

* * *

In my first book I told you, Theophilus, about everything Jesus began to do and teach until the day He was taken up to heaven after giving His chosen apostles further instructions through the Holy Spirit. During the forty days after He suffered and died, He appeared to the apostles from time to time, and He proved to them in many ways that He was actually alive. And He talked to them about the Kingdom of God. Once when He was eating with them, He commanded them, "Do not leave Jerusalem until the Father sends you the gift He promised, as I told you before. John baptized with water, but in just a few days you will be baptized with the Holy Spirit." So when the apostles were with Jesus, they kept asking Him, "Lord, has the time come for You to free Israel and restore our kingdom?" He replied, "The Father alone has the authority to set those dates and times, and they are not for you to know. But you will receive power when the Holy Spirit comes upon you. And you will be My witnesses, telling people about Me everywhere – in Jerusalem, throughout Judea, in Samaria, and to the ends of the earth."
Acts 1:1-8

* * *

In ancient times the Phoenicians, the Carthaginians and the Romans aided by the beliefs of Greek mythology believed that Hercules had set two pillars in place to serve as a warning. We now know those pillars to be the Rock of Gibraltar to the north and debatably either the Monte Hacho in Ceuta or the Jebel Musa in Morocco to the south. These two "pillars" flank the entrance to the Strait of Gibraltar. The narrow strait connects the Atlantic Ocean with the Mediterranean Sea and separates southern Europe from northern Africa. The "pillars" were said to have been put in place to designate the edge of the world. The ancients believed that the world was flat and that sailing vessels would fall off the edge of the world if they sailed beyond the horizon. Therefore, the pillars were deemed to mark a boundary beyond which no man should go. As such a warning was inscribed on the rocks – "NON PLUS ULTRA" – meaning "nothing more beyond". These words carried the urgent warning to all that would attempt to pass by them – NOTHING MORE BEYOND. The warning was believed to be truth and remained in place until Christopher Columbus discovered the New World at the end of the 15th century. Following that discovery, King Charles V of Spain had the negative word "NON" expunged in order to change the inscriptions from being a warning of nothing more beyond to a reminder that there was MORE BEYOND. The now-modified inscription further served as a reminder of the King's mission to extend the spread of Christianity into the newly discovered lands. Thus it became even more than a reminder; it became a challenge.

The physician Luke is faithful to record here in the first chapter of Acts, the final words Jesus spoke to His disciples as He stood before them on the mount just before He ascended into heaven. It is interesting to note that even during the days after His resurrection, the disciples were still expecting Jesus as the Messiah to *"free Israel and restore our kingdom"* right then. They still had not yet realized that there was still more to be done. They couldn't see past their immediate circumstances and grasp the Father's bigger purpose and plan. Jesus' resurrection was not the end of the road; rather, it was a brand new beginning. And that new beginning would be signaled by His departure to join the Father and the arrival of the Holy Spirit. It would be marked by His instructions to them – and to each of us who are His followers.

His instructions in many respects could be defined as "more beyond". Jesus had already told His disciples the night before He was arrested that He was *"going to prepare a place for* {His followers}*"*, and *"when everything is ready"* He would return for His followers (John 14:2-3). There was "more beyond" – there was the place that He was going to prepare. But also, there was "more beyond" – He would return. And further, there was "more beyond" – there was work to be done until He returns. He told them that the Father has set the date and time for His return; it is not for us to know. They were not – and we are not – to be fixated on the date and time; rather, they – and we – are to be faithful in the work.

In many respects, it is the ultimate wilderness journey. We have no idea all the twists and turns that lie in the path ahead, any more than those disciples did. But in the Father's timing, we will arrive at the end of that wilderness journey. In the Father's ultimate wisdom, sovereignty and grace He sent His Holy Spirit to guide, enable, equip and comfort them – and us – for all that is in store in the journey beyond. And He has given us clear instruction as to what we are to be about – *"you will be My witnesses, telling people about Me everywhere—in Jerusalem, throughout Judea, in Samaria, and to the ends of the earth."* We are to let the world know that there is MORE BEYOND. Our lives, our actions and our words are to bear that inscription… until He returns. We are to be bearers of that inscription and that message until He returns – across the street in Jerusalem, down the road in Judea, outside of our comfort zone in Samaria, and to every corner at the very ends of the earth. Because the reality is for those who do not have a personal relationship with Christ, there is NO MORE BEYOND. Apart from a saving relationship with Him, our sin will destine us for an eternity separated from Him – not in eternal life, but in eternal death. Sin is in fact that negative word "NON". But through Christ's death, burial and resurrection He made the way for that negative word "NON" caused by our sin to be expunged – and in exchange He gave us more beyond – eternal and abundant life that He has gone ahead to prepare for us. Life we can only have through Him if we will but receive it. Jesus' words to each of us are MORE BEYOND – they are LIFE – abundant life here and eternal life beyond. Life that He laid down His own life to give us.

No matter where you are in your journey until He returns, there is more beyond. The cover of this book is a depiction of that Rock of Gibraltar and the ocean and the lands that extend beyond. It is also a depiction of that mount from which Jesus ascended on the day He gave them – and us – His instructions. In this book we will look at how the men and women who were there on the mount that day, as well as others that would join them, continued in that journey beyond. Let us learn from them. Let us be challenged and encouraged by them. And let us be faithful to join them in living out that message of MORE BEYOND, until He returns.

* * *

1

HE WILL RETURN

After saying this, He was taken up into a cloud while they were watching, and they could no longer see Him. As they strained to see Him rising into heaven, two white-robed men suddenly stood among them. "Men of Galilee," they said, "why are you standing here staring into heaven? Jesus has been taken from you into heaven, but someday He will return from heaven in the same way you saw Him go!"
Acts 1:9-11

* * *

During the forty days that followed Jesus' resurrection, He appeared to individuals or small groupings of His disciples on multiple occasions, but He joined with the apostles as a group at least four times. Luke records that *"He appeared to the apostles from time to time"* (Acts 1:3), so it could have been many more times than four, but Scripture records four specific appearances. The first was the night of His resurrection in the locked upper room. The second was eight days later as they were together in a room. This time Thomas was with them. The third was along the shore of the Sea of Galilee. And the fourth was this day in Acts 1 on the Mount of Olives when He ascended into heaven. The first two of these four times, He suddenly appeared in their midst and then disappeared. On the third time, He suddenly appeared on the shore preparing breakfast while Peter and six of the other disciples were out on the sea in a boat fishing. At the conclusion of that time He again disappeared. To the extent that anyone can ever become "accustomed" to having someone appear and disappear out of and into thin air, the apostles probably became less surprised by Jesus' successive sudden appearances and departures. They came to realize that He could appear before them at any time.

On this particular day, He appeared to them at some other undisclosed place and then "led them" (Luke 24:50) to the Mount of Olives. Either as they walked or upon their arrival, He told them *"now I will send the Holy Spirit, just as My Father promised. But stay here in the city until the Holy Spirit comes and fills you with power from heaven"* (Luke 24:49). The disciples knew that this time was different from the other times He had disappeared. This time He was leaving. And though they had never known when He would appear or disappear, this time had a feeling of greater permanence. He was going to another place (the Father's house) and He would stay there until the work was completed. Jesus had already explained to the disciples on multiple occasions that He needed to return to His Father in heaven. He needed to return in order to "prepare a place" in His Father's home for all of His followers (John 14:2). He would be preparing that place by accomplishing His purposes in and through His bride – the Church. He needed to return so that He could send His Holy Spirit to empower and enable His followers in all things (John 14:16-17). And He needed to return to make intercession on their/our behalf to the Father as their/our interceding High Priest (John 14:12-14). His followers knew that the day of His departure had arrived.

In addition to the apostles, there was a larger group that also made up His closest followers. In total there were about one hundred twenty believers (Acts 1:15) who walked with Jesus to the mount that day to "see Him off". i would venture that they were sad. They didn't know when they would see Him again, and they would miss Him. i would also venture they were frightened. For the last three years, many of His followers had been with Him most every day. He was always there to turn to with a question. He was the Teacher. He was the Miracle Worker. And though He had sent seventy-two of them out on their own on the one occasion (Luke 10:1-24), they still returned to Jesus when their assignment was completed. They knew He had told them that He would send His Holy Spirit as a Helper and a Guide, but they had not yet experienced the presence of the Holy Spirit – they had experienced the presence of Jesus. Thus, with hearts of sadness and uncertainty, they gathered around Jesus to say farewell.

You may have a similar tradition to my wife and me. Whenever family and guests are departing from our home, we go outside and stand at the end of the driveway or on our front porch to wave goodbye and see them off until they are out of sight. That's what His followers were doing that day.

As they stood there, He didn't disappear as He had done on several occasions. Rather, He was *"taken up into a cloud"*. Thirty-three years earlier Jesus had arrived on this earth humbly, as He was wrapped in swaddling clothes and laid in an animal's feeding trough. But today as He began to ascend into the Father's presence in heaven, He was wrapped in the Shekinah glory cloud. You may recall that was the cloud – the cloud of God's presence and glory – that led the Israelites through the wilderness (Exodus 13:21-22)[1]. And it was that cloud that filled the tabernacle with the "awesome glory of the Lord" (Exodus 30:34-38)[2]. Jesus was enveloped by the glory of God, because Jesus is the reflection of God's glory (Isaiah 60:1-3). The disciples had always been witnessing the glory of God whenever they looked upon Jesus, but as they looked upon the ascending Jesus, they saw Him "clothed" in the glory of God.

Jesus didn't "vanish" as He had on the other occasions; rather, He ascended until they could no longer see Him. Having grown up in Southeast Florida, i can remember standing outside on clear days watching the launch of the various spacecraft. We would stand there straining to see the spacecraft as it grew smaller and smaller, and the vapor trail began to disappear. We would stare until there was nothing more to see. That's what the disciples were doing that day – they were straining to get the last glimpse they could possibly get of Jesus.

Luke records that suddenly two "white-robed men" were standing there with them. Remember, it wasn't just a handful of people; there were over one hundred people. Two people can slip into a crowd that size and not be immediately noticed, but these guys were apparently pretty easy to spot. Luke is careful to write that they were "men"; he doesn't say "angels". Luke had very specifically said that "angels" announced Jesus' birth to the shepherds (Luke 2:8-15)[3]. The appearance of angels frightened the shepherds, but Luke does not record that the group was frightened by the appearance of these two men. Dwight L. Moody contended that the two men were Moses and Elijah, who would have been familiar faces to at least Peter, James and John from the day they accompanied Jesus to the Mount of Transfiguration (Luke 9:30-31)[4]. But regardless of who they were, they were heavenly messengers who the Father had sent to assure, encourage and challenge those who were staring off into heaven. The message was clear: *"someday He will return from heaven in the same way you saw Him go!"*

He will return in the same way – enveloped in the glory of God. He will not return this time as a humble baby in a stable, He will return as the King of Kings and Lord of Lords. He will return to establish His Kingdom once and for all. And He will return to the exact same place. The prophet Zechariah writes, *"On that day His feet will stand on the Mount of Olives, east of Jerusalem"* (Zechariah 14:4).

When will He return? "Someday." And i would add – that day continues to draw closer! The Father has determined the day, and as Jesus told His disciples just before He ascended, *"The Father alone has the authority to set those dates and times, and they are not for you to know"* (Acts 1:7). We don't know the "when", but we know the "how". He will return in the exact same way as they saw Him go. And we know the "where". He will return to the exact same place from which they saw Him depart. And we know the "why". He will return to judge His creation and establish His Kingdom. Therefore, in the meantime, we must be about His purpose and His mission – until that day – the day He returns.

Wherever we are in our journey – whatever circumstance we are walking through today – the Master has given us a purpose. He has given us a mission. He <u>will</u> return. Let's be found faithful in His mission until that day!

---

1. *The Journey Begins*, Ch. 12
2. *The Journey Begins*, Ch. 61
3. *Walking With The Master*, Ch. 2
4. *Walking With The Master*, Ch. 37

2

WAITING IS NOT INACTIVITY

Then they returned to Jerusalem from the mount called Olivet, which is near Jerusalem, a Sabbath day's journey away. And when they had entered, they went up to the upper room, where they were staying, Peter and John and James and Andrew, Philip and Thomas, Bartholomew and Matthew, James the son of Alphaeus and Simon the Zealot and Judas the son of James. All these with one accord were devoting themselves to prayer, together with the women and Mary the mother of Jesus, and his brothers.
Acts 1:12-14 (ESV)

* * *

Jesus ascension into heaven occurred on the Sabbath. We know it was the Sabbath because Luke records that the group, who was gathered on the mount when He ascended, traveled a Sabbath day's journey back to the upper room in Jerusalem. He would have had no reason to explain the distance if it had not occurred on the Sabbath. i think it's worthy to note that our Lord's incarnational and redemptive ministry on earth is concluded on the day of Sabbath rest, just as was the case of His initial work of creation. The first time He made all things new, He concluded the work with the Sabbath. This time He had made the way for all things to be made new. The Sabbath, or in our case the Lord's Day, is to be a reminder and an indication that when God finished His work, He rested, but it is also a reminder to us that what He begins, He completes. In both instances the Sabbath was the exclamation point at the end of the work. Luke further adds that the group *"returned to Jerusalem filled with great joy"* (Luke

24:52). Though the group would have been saddened to see Him go, they were joyful because they knew that He would return.

Let's look at who all was there. The group was made up of the eleven remaining apostles, Mary (the mother of Jesus), the half-brothers of Jesus (Mary's other sons) , the women that had traveled with Him, and other men totaling about 120 believers. It was quite a diverse group. We know that at least seven of them were fishermen (Peter, Andrew, John, James, Philip, Bartholomew and Thomas). There was one who had fought against Rome (Simon the zealot) and one who had worked for Rome (Matthew the tax collector). A case can be made that James the son of Alphaeus and Judas the son of James may have been carpenters. The other women with Mary (the mother of Jesus) would have included Mary Magdalene (the first person to whom Jesus appeared after His resurrection), Salome (the mother of James and John), Mary (the mother of James the son of Alphaeus), and Joanna (the wife of King Herod's household manager). Four of the group were Jesus' half-brothers – James, Joseph, Jude and Simon – who had most recently become followers of Jesus. Though they had known Him their entire lives, they had only come to believe on Him as the Son of God since His resurrection. Prior to His resurrection, they would have been like some church attenders today. They grew up hearing the stories about Jesus, but they had yet to truly believe on Him. But once they believed, they believed with their whole hearts. For example, we know that James would become one of the elders of the first church in Jerusalem, and would write the Epistle of James, and Jude would become an ambassador of the gospel and write the Epistle of Jude.

It is very probable that some of the others counted among that group would have been Lazarus (the one who Jesus raised from the dead) and his two sisters, Martha and Mary. It probably included Joseph of Arimathea and Nicodemus, both of whom had been Pharisees that came to be followers of Jesus. After they had received permission from Pontius Pilate to bury the body of Jesus, they would have been ostracized by the High Council of religious leaders. And many more would have been in their number.

Though each one had a unique story of how they came to follow Jesus, Luke records that they were united in one accord. There is no question that they were united in their love for Jesus. But their unity had to go beyond that. Jesus had commissioned them for His purpose to make disciples of all people. In order to do that they couldn't only be united in their love for Him, they had to be united in their love for one another. It would have been easy for them to become divided. John could have stood before the other apostles and proudly declared that he was the only one that stood at the cross with Jesus. Peter could have been denounced for his denial of Jesus. Mary Magdalene could have established her importance by reminding everyone that Jesus had appeared to her first after His resurrection. Thomas could have been marginalized for His skepticism about Jesus' resurrection. His half-brothers could have been belittled for their failure to follow Jesus before His resurrection. Mary, the sister of Lazarus, could have proudly declared that Jesus had promised that wherever the gospel was preached her actions would be remembered (Matthew 26:13). They could have all gotten into another discussion about who would be the greatest in the Kingdom! But they knew that just before He had been arrested, Jesus had told them to love one another (John 13:34-35). They could not solely love Jesus and have faith in Jesus, they needed to love one another and have faith in one another.

They returned to the upper room – the place where Jesus had washed their feet before His arrest, and the place He had appeared to them on the night of His resurrection. In both instances they would have been surprised – the first time by His unexpected arrest and crucifixion that soon followed – and the second by His unexpected appearance and resurrection. Now they were gathering again without clearly knowing what was going to happen. All they knew this time was that they were to go and wait – wait for the Holy Spirit to come upon them. That had never happened before. They had no idea what that would mean or what that would look like. But Jesus had promised. So out of their love for Him and for one another they went together to that upper room to wait.

But they didn't just stay in the upper room. Luke records that they also spent time in the Temple, praising God (Luke 24:53). i don't know about you, but i think that was pretty gutsy. The religious leaders who had Jesus arrested and crucified were still in charge. In some respects, these followers of Jesus were "marked" men and women. The disciples had scattered and fled the night of Jesus' arrest for fear of what would happen to them. Most of them had stayed away from Golgotha on the day Jesus was crucified for the same reason. But now they were boldly entering the Temple to praise and worship God while they were waiting. And the Holy Spirit had not yet come upon them. They weren't emboldened by the power of the Holy Spirit. They were emboldened by their love and faith in Jesus and encouraged by their love for one another.

. . .

They knew that waiting was not inactivity. It required obedience – obedience to the Master and His commands. Obedience is not inactive; it is proactive. Even obedience in waiting requires a conscious decision and action to stay the course and not pursue a different course. When Jesus fasted in the wilderness for forty days, Satan attempted to tempt Jesus into taking a path other than what the Father had set forth for Him. But Jesus never deviated. He never gave up on being obedient to the Father. Obedience is often difficult. It often requires a great deal of faith in order to persevere, even when common sense may say otherwise. For example, those disciples had been told to go and make disciples. To some it would have made a whole lot more sense to invest their time in developing a plan and a strategy. They could have had maps prepared and displayed on the walls that designated each person's responsibilities.

i am currently in the midst of doing something that i believe God has told me to do. I am walking by faith in obedience to what i believe He has said. i am in that "waiting room". And it is taking a whole lot more work and activity to remain in this "waiting room" than it would take to step out of the room and pursue my own way. There is nothing inactive about obedience.

Waiting requires oneness – oneness with the Master, but also oneness with one another. As we've already seen, the believers that were waiting had a lot that they could have allowed to divide them, but they worked at remaining one. There were some pretty strong personalities among them, and potentially some pretty strong opinions. But they knew that they needed to remain united in their love, their faith and their obedience.

Their waiting involved prayer – diligently seeking the Father and trusting that the Son was interceding on their behalf. Their waiting involved worship – worshipping the One who is sovereign and worthy of all worship. And their waiting involved anticipation – trusting that the One who had promised will be faithful to accomplish that which He has promised in ways that are *"infinitely more than we might ask or think"* (Ephesians 3:20).

In your wilderness journey today, you may be waiting in your own upper room. And you are finding that waiting is very hard work! It is by no means inactivity. It requires obedience, faithfulness, oneness, prayer, worship and anticipation. Trust the One who has told you to wait in that upper room. He is faithful! Just ask the one hundred and twenty!

* * *

3

WHY ALL THIS CONCERN?

During this time, when about one hundred twenty believers were together in one place, Peter stood up and addressed them. "Brothers," he said, "the Scriptures had to be fulfilled concerning Judas, who guided those who arrested Jesus. This was predicted long ago by the Holy Spirit, speaking through King David... in the book of Psalms, where it says, 'Let his home become desolate, with no one living in it.' It also says, 'Let someone else take his position.' So now we must choose a replacement for Judas from among the men who were with us the entire time we were traveling with the Lord Jesus – from the time He was baptized by John until the day He was taken from us. Whoever is chosen will join us as a witness of Jesus' resurrection." So they nominated two men: Joseph called Barsabbas (also known as Justus) and Matthias. Then they all prayed, "O Lord, You know every heart. Show us which of these men You have chosen as an apostle to replace Judas in this ministry, for he has deserted us and gone where he belongs." Then they cast lots, and Matthias was selected to become an apostle with the other eleven.
Acts 1:15-26

* * *

Ten days passed between Jesus' ascension and the arrival of His promised Holy Spirit. Scripture tells us generally that His followers spent that time gathered in the upper room and in the Temple praying, praising and worshiping God. But in the midst of that period of time, Luke records two specific incidents: the specifics of how Judas Iscariot died and how Matthias was selected to replace Judas as the twelfth apostle. We know that there are details that the Holy Spirit led the writers of Scripture not to include. And we know that everything that was included was for a purpose: *"All Scripture is inspired by God and profitable for teaching, for reproof, for correction, for training in righteousness"* (2 Timothy 3:16 NASB). Therefore, i think it is reasonable to ask why these two specific details were inserted in the midst of this time of waiting. As a matter of fact, i think it is also reasonable to ask how these details are applicable to us in our respective journeys.

Peter gives us the key to the answer right up front when he tells us that what the Holy Spirit predicted long ago had to be fulfilled.

The first prophecy that Peter referenced was in regard to Judas. He reminded the other disciples that King David recorded, *"Let his home become desolate, with no one living in it"* (Psalm 69:25), meaning that his evil deed would cause his name to become reprehensible for posterity and his final resting place would become contemptible.

In the first century A.D., the name Judas was a name synonymous with honor, and therefore a very popular name (two of the twelve disciples were named Judas). The name was given in recognition of Judas Maccabaeus, one of the great generals in Jewish history. He and his followers defeated the Syrian armies in 165 BC, restored the religious rites and rededicated the Temple in Jerusalem. Simon Iscariot would have named his son Judas in the hope that he would be a man of honor in the tradition of Judas Maccabaeus. But, as Judas' treachery became notorious, that was no longer the case. Today If you look up the name Judas in the dictionary, you will find *"one who betrays another under the guise of friendship; a deceiver or traitor"*[1]. As a result, the name "Judas" was no longer a popular choice among parents determining the name for their bouncing baby boys. Judas' name became reprehensible as a result of his treachery as foretold by the prophecy.[2]

Both Matthew and Luke give us an account of Judas' death. When Judas fully realized the consequences of his betrayal of Jesus – the condemnation of Jesus to die and the damnation of his own soul for his part in the deed – he took the thirty pieces of silver and threw them at the feet of the leading priests and elders. The priests themselves considered the money as "payment for murder" (Matthew 27:6). Matthew records that right after Judas threw down the coins, he "went out and hanged himself" (Matthew 27:5). Luke, the physician, adds that the hanging rope broke causing Judas' body to fall headfirst to the ground causing his body to split open, spilling out his intestines. It was a gruesome death brought about by his gruesome treachery. Because that land was defiled by his suicide, the priests decided to use the coins to purchase the land to be used as a graveyard for foreigners and the "dregs" of society. As the news of Judas' death spread, the field became known as "the field of blood". When Luke writes that *"Judas had bought a field with the money he received for his treachery"* (Acts 1:18), he also is saying that the payment for Judas' treachery bought the field. His treachery and the use of the ransom to purchase just such a burial site was in fulfillment of the prophecy recorded by Zechariah – *"So they counted out for my wages thirty pieces of silver. And the Lord said to me, "Throw it to the potter" – this magnificent sum at which they valued me! So I took the thirty coins and threw them to the potter in the Temple of the Lord"* (Zechariah 11:12-13). Judas' final abode – his burial place -- became contemptible as a result of his treachery as foretold in the prophecy.

The second prophecy that Peter referenced is in regard to choosing a replacement for Judas. He reminded the apostles – and us – that King David recorded, *"Let someone else take his position"* (Psalm 109:8). The night Jesus was arrested, the apostles were engaged in another discussion about which of them would be the greatest in the Kingdom. After having corrected their thinking from being rulers to being servants, Jesus told them that upon His return each of them would *"sit on thrones, judging the twelve tribes of Israel"* (Luke 22:30). Even though Jesus had only ascended to heaven a few days before, the apostles always believed and acted in a way that was consistent with their belief that His return was imminent. Therefore, they saw the selection of a twelfth apostle to replace Judas as an urgent need, so that they might be prepared for His return.

Though the Holy Spirit had not yet been sent to empower them, they still had the Word of God and prayer. Jesus had on multiple occasions made it clear that Peter was to be their leader (Matthew 16:19, Luke 22:31-32, John 21:15-17). When Peter referenced the prophecies of King David, he was not doing so on his own, he was being led by the Spirit of God, even though he was not yet indwelt by the Holy Spirit. Thus Peter responded to the leading of the Word and the Holy Spirit to fill that vacant position. Through their process, the Lord subsequently led them to select Matthias.

Now, let's come back to our original question: why all this concern with how Judas died, the field his blood-money bought, and the way he got replaced as an apostle?

. . .

First, and most importantly, what the Holy Spirit says, will be fulfilled, no matter how long it takes. Prophecy was fulfilled – even through those who rebelled against God. No matter what people may choose to do, God's promises in His Word are invincible, irrefutable and indomitable. Even when you are being betrayed His purpose will not fail. Even when you see godless action taking place around you and to you, He ultimately prevails. God has no need to panic. Not even Judas or Satan could undermine or escape the all-encompassing invincibility of God's purpose. No one and no thing can!

Second, the importance of the memory of Jesus that Matthias preserved when he replaced Judas corresponds to the importance of God's written Word in our lives. It was important that whoever replaced Judas was someone who had been a follower of Jesus the entire time from His baptism to His ascension. It was important that they had heard and witnessed Jesus' teaching and miracles firsthand. The Holy Spirit was soon to arrive to indwell those believers – and specifically the apostles. It was important that they not only be filled by His Spirit, but they also needed to be rooted in His Word (His teaching). They did not have benefit of the New Testament. They would be the writers and messengers of those truths. It was imperative that they be firsthand witnesses.

The same principle holds true for us. We too must not only be filled with the Holy Spirit; we must also be rooted in His Word. At the timeframe of this passage in the upper room, the Holy Spirit had not yet come to indwell them and the New Testament had not yet been written. But today we have both! John Piper writes, *"...if our roots are not sunk deep into the words and deeds of Jesus (preserved for us by the apostles), then it is certain that our branches will not reach very high into the sky of God's power."*

One other point that is worthy to note: this is the last time that you ever see believers casting lots to discern God's will. Remember, at this moment in time, they were not indwelt by the Holy Spirit. Once the Holy Spirit came to live within them, He led them and guided them in all truth. Jesus had told His disciples the night of His betrayal, *"When the Spirit of truth comes, He will guide you into all truth. He will not speak on His own but will tell you what He has heard. He will tell you about the future"* (John 16:13). He guides us today. We do not need to cast lots; we only need to listen to His voice and follow His leading.

. . .

The words spoken and the actions they took that night in the upper room two thousand years ago do concern us! They point us to His unfailing Word. They point us to His unchanging character. And they point us to the invincible outcome of His purpose! All of which we must hold onto – until He returns!

---

1. Merriam-Webster Dictionary
2. *Walking With The Master*, Ch. 19

4

THE HELPER COMES

On the day of Pentecost all the believers were meeting together in one place. Suddenly, there was a sound from heaven like the roaring of a mighty windstorm, and it filled the house where they were sitting. Then, what looked like flames or tongues of fire appeared and settled on each of them. And everyone present was filled with the Holy Spirit and began speaking in other languages, as the Holy Spirit gave them this ability. At that time there were devout Jews from every nation living in Jerusalem. When they heard the loud noise, everyone came running, and they were bewildered to hear their own languages being spoken by the believers. They were completely amazed. "How can this be?" they exclaimed. "These people are all from Galilee, and yet we hear them speaking in our own native languages!
Acts 2:1-8

* * *

A few years ago my wife and i had the rare privilege of spending ten days in the heart of Jerusalem for a personal spiritual retreat. We stayed in an apartment on the second floor of a home that had been transformed into a prayer center. Though it was late June/ early July, the temperature was moderate and we kept our windows open to enjoy the refreshing light breeze that was present most of the time. Throughout our time there – and since – we couldn't help but think about the disciples as they waited in their upper room for ten days in light of the experience we were having in our upper room. Here are some thoughts i captured in my journal as our time was drawing to an end:

. . .

"Today i sit in an upper room in Jerusalem. It is not 'the' upper room where the apostles gathered; but for me personally it is 'my' upper room because it is a place where the Lord has permitted me to wait before Him, to hear His voice, to experience His presence and to be renewed with a fresh filling of His Spirit. Though i know that He is able to do those things in my life wherever i am – whenever i am willing to be still before Him – it is an added blessing to do so here in Jerusalem where the Lord Himself says that He will make His home among His people (Joel 3:21). i hear the joy of children laughing and playing in the near distance mixed with the sounds of gentle breezes and the chirping of birds. i envision – as best i can – what that day will be like when our Lord returns to make His home among His people.

"We are here at the Lord's invitation – not only to spend this time with Him, but also to do so in this place. He made the way for us to be able to do so. Otherwise we could not be here. As clearly as He instructed the apostles to wait for Him, He instructed us to come to this place.

"Truly the Lord has enabled us to be still in this place, and know that He is God. There have not been any flames or tongues of fire – and i have not been given the ability to speak in other languages – or even to improve my proficiency in the English language . And yet, i have some small sense of what the apostles felt on that day – having experienced the rush of wind and been visited by and indwelt by His Spirit.

"i know that i was indwelt by His Spirit many years ago at the moment of my salvation, but He has allowed me over these past several days to experience a fresh renewing of my spirit and a fresh filling of His presence. i know that i cannot tarry here – any more than those select disciples were able to tarry in His presence on the Mount of Transfiguration (Matthew 17). The time will soon arrive for us to come "down from the mountain" or (if you will permit) from our 'upper room'. Life awaits at the base of the mountain – the day-to-day demands of life, the many opportunities of ministry, and the activities that i can allow to so easily distract me. But i know that just as He has allowed us to be in this upper room with Him, He allows us to walk down the mountain and into the day-to-day with Him, enabled, guided and empowered by His Holy Spirit.

"Yes, i know that this is one of those mountaintop experiences – and i know that i cannot live on the mountaintop even though i would like to. But it does cause me to yearn even more for His return – that day when He returns to make His home among His people."

. . .

That is the closest i will ever come to knowing how the disciples felt as they awaited the arrival of the promised Helper. And then the *"sound from heaven like the roaring of a mighty windstorm… filled the house"*. The Helper had come! He filled them to the point that they overflowed. His filling was conspicuous. People came running because they knew there was a difference in these followers. They looked different. They spoke differently. They were ignited by the Holy Spirit. And the people knew the difference wasn't of the disciples' own making. They were "just Galileans" after all!

That same Holy Spirit dwells within us if we have become followers of Jesus. Is the world around us seeing a difference as well? Is it seeing a group of people who look different, talk differently and reflect the Person of Jesus? And if we name the Name of Jesus, we don't need to wait in an upper room for the Helper to come. He entered into our lives at the moment of our salvation.

As i write this chapter, i just received an email from The Barna Group. Barna is an evangelical research group based out of Ventura, California. Based upon their polling, they shared the following facts today:

- One-quarter of practicing Christians says there is a person who they cannot forgive.
- Almost half of practicing Christians say mercy doesn't influence their thoughts or actions or they haven't thought about whether it does.
- Christians grapple with whether certain people deserve compassion or forgiveness, and they are not all that different from non-Christians when it comes to embodying merciful attitudes and actions.

Their conclusion was that the Church is struggling to embody mercy today. Our struggle is because we have relegated the Helper to the back row of our lives instead of the driver's seat. Jesus sent His Holy Spirit to enable and empower us to embody Him, His love and His mercy. If our lives don't reflect His presence or His power it is because we have quenched the igniting of His Holy Spirit. Even the early church struggled. The apostle Paul wrote to the church in Thessalonica: *"Do not stifle the Holy Spirit"* (1 Thessalonians 5:19) and to the church in Ephesus: *"Be filled with the Spirit"* (Ephesians 5:18). We would do well to heed his counsel.

The Helper has come! We are no longer awaiting His arrival. He has come like the roaring of a mighty windstorm. Jesus, ignite Your Spirit within us. Fill us to overflowing. So that the world might see You – Your Person and Your power – for the glory of Your Name!

* * *

5

LET THE NATIONS BE GLAD

> *Here we are—Parthians, Medes, Elamites, people from Mesopotamia, Judea, Cappadocia, Pontus, the province of Asia, Phrygia, Pamphylia, Egypt, and the areas of Libya around Cyrene, visitors from Rome (both Jews and converts to Judaism), Cretans, and Arabs. And we all hear these people speaking in our own languages about the wonderful things God has done!" They stood there amazed and perplexed. "What can this mean?" they asked each other.*
> Acts 2:9-12

* * *

It is telling that the very first thing that happened after the Holy Spirit arrived was that the people of the fifteen different language groups from three continents that were gathered in Jerusalem heard the disciples praising God in their own language – simultaneously. The disciples were not yet preaching the Good News; they were praising God for what He had just done. Theologians have debated for almost two thousand years as to whether the disciples were divinely and instantaneously enabled to speak in those different languages or if the people's ears were simultaneously attuned by the Holy Spirit to hear in their own language. Or was it a combination of both? Regardless, it was quite a feat! And the fact that it was the first evidence of the Holy Spirit's presence reinforces His principle purpose – to draw all people to worship God and bring glory to His Name.

. . .

You may recall that over twenty-three hundred years earlier, God had pronounced judgement on the people at the Tower of Babel by confusing their language (Genesis 11:1-9). In building their tower, they were attempting a feat in rebellion against God in order to bring glory to themselves. God is jealous for His glory and He will not share it, so He confounded their plan by confounding their language. The judgement of differing languages caused the people to scatter and each group to go their own way. But on Pentecost, when the Holy Spirit came, He united them around the praises being offered to Him. For the first time in over twenty-three hundred years they were able to simultaneously hear the same praises to God in their own heart language. At that moment – just like in heaven to come – language was no longer a divider to worship.

Throughout the Book of Acts – and for that matter, throughout Scripture – we see the followers of Christ on mission to make His Name known – just as Jesus told us to be just before He ascended into heaven. But the Holy Spirit's first act was not about mission, it was about worship. He began with the reminder, as John Piper writes in his book *"Let the Nations Be Glad"*, that *"Missions is not the ultimate goal of the Church. Worship is. Missions exists because worship doesn't."*

"Worship is ultimate, not missions, because God is ultimate, not man. When this age is over, and the countless millions of the redeemed fall on their faces before the throne of God, missions will be no more. It is a temporary necessity. But worship abides forever.

"Worship, therefore, is the fuel and goal of missions. It's the goal of missions because in missions we simply aim to bring the nations into the white hot enjoyment of God's glory. The goal of missions is the gladness of the peoples in the greatness of God. 'The Lord reigns; let the earth rejoice; let the many coastlands be glad!' (Psalm 97:1 ESV). *'Let the peoples praise Thee, O God; let all the peoples praise Thee! Let the nations be glad and sing for joy!'* (Psalm 67:3-4 NASB).

"But worship is also the fuel of missions. Passion for God in worship precedes the offer of God in preaching. You can't commend what you don't cherish. Missionaries will never call out, 'Let the nations be glad!' who cannot say from the heart, 'I rejoice in the Lord...I will be glad and exult in Thee, I will sing praise to Thy name, O Most High' (Psalm 104:34; 9:2 ESV). *Missions begins and ends in worship.*

· · ·

"If the pursuit of God's glory is not ordered above the pursuit of man's good in the affections of the heart and the priorities of the church, man will not be well-served and God will not be duly-honored. I am not pleading for a diminishing of missions but for a magnifying of God. When the flame of worship burns with the heat of God's true worth, the light of missions will shine to the darkest peoples on earth."

Apparently the sound of the wind drew the people to the place where the disciples were gathered, but it was their praise and worship of God that captured the attention of the people. The Holy Spirit was "the sound of the wind". It is He that drew the people. And that's as true today as it was then. Jesus said, *"No one can come to Me unless the Father who sent Me draws them to Me..."* (John 6:44). And the Father "draws" through His Holy Spirit. Once drawn, the people encountered God through the praise and worship that was being offered up to Him. Why? Because God inhabits the praises of His people! (Psalm 22:3)

Several years ago, on a different visit to Jerusalem than the one i referenced in the last chapter, i was with a group as we visited the Church of St. Anne, erected near the site of the Pool of Bethesda. We were not the only people inside the church admiring the beautiful early twelfth century architecture. There was a large number of people, obviously from a wide variety of countries. We heard many languages being spoken. The acoustics in the chapel were absolutely amazing. At some point, someone began to sing the hymn, "How Great Thou Art" in another language. Very quickly everyone in the church joined in singing that familiar song in their own respective language. We didn't know one another's languages, but we all knew the words and the meaning in our own language. The difference of our languages quickly got lost in the blending of our voices – and our hearts – in praise. We went on to sing two other hymns together. i can't remember which hymns they were, but i remember thinking that this is what heaven is going to be like – people from every language, people, tribe and nation gathering around the throne praising God in one voice. And we all knew that God was inhabiting our praises. It wasn't the place; it was the praise. None of us wanted to leave. You could see the reluctance on everyone's face. But soon we did. Since then, I have had other similar experiences, but that one reigns supreme in my memory. Even as i write this, the memory of that day reawakens the anticipation of what it will be like when we are all gathered together around His throne.

. . .

The disciples and the people experienced a taste that day. The Holy Spirit drew the people together. Together they heard and understood the praises being lifted up to Him. And God inhabited that praise and worship. And the nations were glad.

That same Holy Spirit dwells within us if we are followers of Jesus. He is still at work to draw all people to worship God. What do they hear when they are drawn in our direction? Are they hearing praise? Let's not lose sight – that's why He left us here… and that's why He sent His Holy Spirit… until He returns.

* * *

6

A DRINK AT JOEL'S PLACE

But others in the crowd ridiculed them, saying, "They're just drunk, that's all!" Then Peter stepped forward with the eleven other apostles and shouted to the crowd, "Listen carefully, all of you, fellow Jews and residents of Jerusalem! Make no mistake about this. These people are not drunk, as some of you are assuming. Nine o'clock in the morning is much too early for that. No, what you see was predicted long ago by the prophet Joel:
'In the last days,' God says, 'I will pour out My Spirit upon all people. Your sons and daughters will prophesy. Your young men will see visions, and your old men will dream dreams. In those days I will pour out My Spirit even on My servants – men and women alike – and they will prophesy. And I will cause wonders in the heavens above and signs on the earth below – blood and fire and clouds of smoke. The sun will become dark, and the moon will turn blood red before that great and glorious day of the Lord arrives. But everyone who calls on the name of the Lord will be saved.'
Acts 2:13-21 (referring to Joel 2:28-32)

* * *

On the day of Pentecost, the Holy Spirit came to call out a body of believers to form the church – those through whom God has chosen to work to fulfill His purpose. The day before Pentecost there was no church. The day after Pentecost there was a church. This was "Day Zero".

It is important for us to understand the context for the day that God sent His Holy Spirit – not only for the Jewish people of the day, but also for us.

Pentecost is a Greek name. The Jews called it the Festival of the Harvest. It was one of the three annual festivals that the Jews were to observe as established by God through Moses on Mount Sinai right after God had given the ten commandments (Exodus 23:14-16). The first of the three festivals was the Festival of Unleavened Bread (the Passover), remembering God's deliverance of the people from their bondage in Egypt. The second was this festival called the Festival of Harvest, celebrating the first fruits of the harvest season. The third was the Festival of the Final Harvest (or the Ingathering), celebrating the end of the harvest season. All of these were established by God for the people to acknowledge Him – His deliverance, His goodness and His provision.

From a Kingdom perspective these three festivals coincide with significant events not only for His people who were under the Law, but for those of us who are the recipients of His grace. As we see throughout the Gospels, and as we explored in *Taking Up The Cross*, in His infinite grace, God arranged for the crucifixion and resurrection of the Son to coincide with the Festival of Unleavened Bread (the Passover). As a result, that event no longer only looks back to the salvation of the firstborn of the Israelites through the sacrifice and shedding of a lamb's blood, it now serves as a reminder of the sacrifice and shed blood of the Son through whom deliverance from the bondage of sin is now available to all. With the arrival of His Holy Spirit on the Day of Pentecost (the Festival of the Harvest), God was signifying that the harvest of the fruit of salvation had now begun. He was pouring out His Spirit as the signal and the conduit of the last days – the days of harvest in which the fruit of salvation will be brought in to the Kingdom. But more on that in a moment. For the follower of Christ, the third festival, the Festival of the Final Harvest, points to the day that Jesus will return for the completion of the harvest season.

Most everyone within the sound of Peter's voice was a lifelong Orthodox Jew or a proselyte, having gathered in Jerusalem for the Festival of the Harvest. They were drawn to investigate the sound of the rush of winds and the sound of the multiple languages being spoken. Seeing the Galileans at the center of all of the uproar, some had tried to explain away what was taking place by saying that the disciples were drunk. But all of the disciples were practicing Jews. They had been seen and witnessed in the Temple for the prior week (and even longer counting their time in the Temple with Jesus). Orthodox Jews did not eat or drink before nine o'clock in the morning on the Sabbath or on a holy day like Pentecost, nor did they usually drink wine except with meals. So when Peter initially stepped forward to speak to the crowd and refute the allegation of drunkenness, he was reminding everyone that the accusation was ludicrous and a violation of the Law. i can't help but wonder if Paul had this reaction in mind when he admonished the believers in Ephesus, *"And do not get drunk with wine, for that is debauchery, but be filled with the Spirit"* (Ephesians 5:18 ESV). Strong drink may bring a temporary exhilaration, but the Spirit gives a deep satisfaction and a lasting joy. We are vessels of the Holy Spirit. He – and He alone – should be seen to be at work in and through our lives.

But coming back to the moment, Peter immediately pointed them to the prophecy of the last days as recorded by the prophet Joel in their Scriptures. Joel was writing that the day of the Lord's return would be heralded by the pouring out of the Spirit of God. This should not seem strange or contrary. They were witnessing the fulfillment of the beginnings of that prophecy. The day was coming when all of this would be fulfilled, but on this day they were seeing a glimpse of it. As the people looked and stared at a group of Galileans, they would have been incredulous. The announcement that the Holy Spirit who Joel was writing about was now being poured out upon these Galileans would have been incredible to the Jews, because they thought God's Spirit was only given to a few select people (Numbers 11:28-29). But here were one hundred twenty of the followers of Jesus – men and women – enjoying the blessing of the same Holy Spirit that had empowered Moses, David and the prophets. The last days had dawned with the arrival of Jesus – and they would come to a climax with His return. The arrival of the Holy Spirit affirmed that they had entered into the first days of the harvest – the last days as foretold by the prophets.

Joel says that one feature of the last days will be the outpouring of the Holy Spirit on people of every kind – men and women, young and old, high and low. God's people will be clothed with power; they will receive power. And the main effect of this power seems to be bold, prophetic speech. Believers of all kinds are going to be so gripped by the Spirit of God that they see the greatness of Jesus and the purpose of Jesus with extraordinary clarity and speak it with extraordinary boldness. The people were seeing that take place before their eyes – from Galileans no less.

But though Joel's prophecy pointed to a period of time that began on that day of Pentecost, it also is a prophecy that points to the return of Christ. That means that <u>we</u> are in the midst of those days – until He returns. There is a promise that in the last days the Spirit will be poured out on all flesh – all the nations will be reached. The true church of Christ will be awakened and revived and sent with extraordinary passion and zeal and prophetic power, and – right in the midst of terrorism and war and persecution and natural disasters – the flaming end-time church of Christ will finish the Great Commission, and welcome the King. God's promise through the giving of His Spirit is to empower His people again and again through the extraordinary filling of His Spirit until the witness to His name has reached all the peoples – to the end of the earth.

i have entitled this chapter "*A Drink At Joel's Place*". i was inspired to do so by a book of that same title written by my childhood pastor, Dr. Jess C. Moody. The book is a collection of essays that struggle with the question as to why the world in which we live is no longer drawn to the church in the way that the crowds were drawn to the disciples on the Day of Pentecost – "Day Zero". Moody writes, "*We are the church. The name church implies God. God means miracle. If we say we are the church and we cannot come up with a miracle, the world thinks we are phony. Maybe they are correct. If the only success they see in our lives or our churches is that which can be explained in terms of organization and management – that is, something the world could do with the same expenditure of effort and technique, they will one day repudiate us.*" Dr. Moody wrote that statement over fifty years ago. The day that the world "*will one day repudiate us*" is no longer in the future; the day has long since passed.

Dr. John Piper writes that, as the last days grow closer to their end, "*the love of many will grow cold. Yes, there will be apostasy on a large scale. Yes, people will simply forsake the faith when the world turns up the heat. But in the midst of all that unbelief and coldness and treachery, Jesus says that the gospel will be preached through the whole world as a testimony to all the nations. In the face of all that persecution and in the midst of all that deadness, the true church of God is going to have extraordinary power, extraordinary zeal, extraordinary passion and love for Jesus.*"

Piper concludes that thought by asking the question, "*What is it like to live as Christians in a time when the power of the Kingdom has already arrived but not in its fullness, and a time when the end of this age is almost over, but not yet fully over?* Regrettably, i think we all know what it is like. Because we are that generation. The Holy Spirit of God dwells within us, but we see none of His power. The apostle Paul wrote a very clear self-diagnostic for us to apply: "*When you follow the desires of your sinful nature, the results are very clear: sexual immorality, impurity, lustful pleasures, idolatry, sorcery, hostility, quarreling, jealousy, outbursts of anger, selfish ambition, dissension, division, envy, drunkenness, wild parties, and other sins like* these" (Galatians 5:19-21). Then he went on to say, *"But the Holy Spirit produces this kind of fruit in our lives: love, joy, peace, patience, kindness, goodness, faithfulness, gentleness, and self-control"* (Galatians 5:22-23). The world does not see the latter, because we have chosen to walk in the former. Gratefully, Paul went on to write the prescription that will make the difference: "{nail} *the passions and desires of* {our} *sinful nature to His cross and* {crucify} *them there. Since we are living by the Spirit, let us follow the Spirit's leading in every part of our lives"* (Galatians 5:24-25).

Those are worthy words to heed as we continue our respective journeys in the wilderness. He has placed our feet on this path for His purpose – a purpose that will only be accomplished through the fullness of the power of His Holy Spirit. Let us follow the Spirit's leading in every part of our lives and be filled with His Spirit… until He returns.

* * *

7

A PREARRANGED PLAN

"People of Israel, listen! God publicly endorsed Jesus the Nazarene by doing powerful miracles, wonders, and signs through Him, as you well know. But God knew what would happen, and His prearranged plan was carried out when Jesus was betrayed. With the help of lawless Gentiles, you nailed Him to a cross and killed Him. But God released Him from the horrors of death and raised Him back to life, for death could not keep Him in its grip.... God raised Jesus from the dead, and we are all witnesses of this. Now He is exalted to the place of highest honor in heaven, at God's right hand. And the Father, as He had promised, gave Him the Holy Spirit to pour out upon us, just as you see and hear today. For David himself never ascended into heaven, yet he said,
'The Lord said to my Lord, "Sit in the place of honor at My right hand until I humble Your enemies, making them a footstool under Your feet.' So let everyone in Israel know for certain that God has made this Jesus, whom you crucified, to be both Lord and Messiah!"
Acts 2:22-36 (quoting Psalm 110:1)

* * *

Throughout the book, *Taking Up The Cross*, we looked at the truth that Jesus was never a victim of the religious leaders, or the Roman rulers, or the crowd, or even Judas Iscariot – because Jesus was never a victim. Jesus was always the Victor! The cross was never an infliction upon the Son, it was an instrument of the Father. Jesus was not crucified because of the religious leaders' treachery, the Roman rulers' impotence, the crowd's endorsement or Judas Iscariot's betrayal, though all are accountable before God for their own actions. If those individuals had the ability or the power over God to do anything contrary to His divine purpose, then He wouldn't be very divine! If the Sovereign, Almighty God can be defeated or manipulated by any of His creation then He is neither sovereign nor almighty. As a matter of fact, He would no longer be God if His creation had power over its Creator. As Peter said, *"God knew what would happen, and His prearranged plan was carried out"* (Acts 2:23).

Many of those to whom Peter was speaking would have been in Jerusalem the day that Jesus was crucified. Some of them may have been in the group that cried, *"Crucify Him! Crucify Him!"* But most of them were probably not a part of the group that had called for His crucifixion, and yet Peter says, *"you nailed Him to a cross and killed Him"* (Acts 2:23). i would venture that with that statement he got everyone's attention. He could say it because everybody in that crowd was involved in the crime against Jesus that brought Him to His death. The essence of the crime against Jesus was not the ending of His physical life. The essence of the crime against Jesus was the rejection of the Father in Jesus' life. In essence, their acceptance or rejection of Jesus would be a referendum on their acceptance or rejection of the Father. They could not profess to follow the Father and reject the One He had sent and endorsed. So Peter recounted all of the ways that the Father had endorsed His Son for the accomplishment of His purpose through His prearranged plan.

Jesus was handed over to be crucified on the grounds of blasphemy. He claimed to be the Son of God (Luke 22:70-71). He claimed that the Father was endorsing Him as Messiah (Luke 22:67-69). But the Jewish rulers rejected this role of the Heavenly Father in Jesus' life. They called Jesus a blasphemer. Therefore, if a person rejects the true role of the Father in the life of Jesus, that person votes for the charge of blasphemy. And to cast your vote on the side of blasphemy – to reject the Father's endorsement of Jesus – is to say in your heart, *"Crucify Him! Crucify Him!"* That was true then, and it is just as true now.

When Jesus performed a miracle, a wonder or a sign, it was the Father's endorsement – *"This is My beloved Son with whom I am well pleased, hear Him!"* (Luke 9:35) Peter declared that it was the Father who did the *". . . signs through Him, as you well know."* He was "publicly endorsed" by the Father and, don't miss this, Peter emphasized that the Father Himself did the miracles through Jesus. It was the power of the Father working in and through the Son to heal the sick and still the storm and cast out demons and raise the dead. While He was on the earth, the Father gave Jesus as the Son of Man the fullest endorsement any "human" ever had. He gave him His Spirit "without limit" (John 3:34).

The Father further endorsed Jesus by planning His death for the sins of His people. The Father planned the suffering and death of Jesus so that forgiveness of sins could be preached to all the nations (Isaiah 53). The difference between the Father's plan to crucify Jesus and Pilate's plan to crucify Jesus was that Pilate was dismissing and rejecting Jesus as a mere pretender, whereas the Father was honoring His Son as the Servant of the Lord and the Savior of the world. The Father planned the death of Jesus not to disown Him or dishonor Him or reject Him, but to glorify Him as the perfect, flawless Lamb of God, who takes away the sin of the world. The Father's plan for Jesus to die was not an indictment like the plan of the Jewish leaders, but rather, an endorsement of His infinite worth so that He could save the Jew and the Gentile alike.

The Father endorsed Jesus by raising Him from the dead. Peter says "{you} *killed Him. But God released Him… and raised Him"* (Acts 2:23-24.) You voted "no" against Jesus. But the Father voted "YES" for Jesus. You denounced Him, but the Father endorsed Him. You killed Him, but the Father raised Him. Peter fully intended for the crowd to feel the clash between their rejection of Jesus and the Father's acceptance of Jesus; their defamation of Jesus and the Father's affirmation of Jesus. What matters here ultimately is not that they killed a Man, but that their words and actions bore witness to the fact that they are against God.

Now this is a shocking and stunning thing for people to hear and extremely hard to admit. These are religious people that Peter is addressing. They are moral people. They are worshiping people. They are people who know hundreds of verses in God's Word by heart. And he is telling them that their minds are totally at odds with God. They claim to know God. They claim to love God and worship God and follow God. And Peter says that they are diametrically opposed to God. They are "anti-God".

The test of whether we are "anti-God" or not is not whether we say we believe in God, or whether we say we know God, or love God, or serve God. The test is whether we embrace God the Father's endorsement of Jesus. If we say we know God but reject the Father's endorsement of Jesus as the worker of miracles; if we say that we know God but reject the Father's endorsement of Jesus as **the** Passover sacrifice that takes away sin;

if we say we know God and reject the Father's endorsement of Jesus by raising Him from the dead, then we don't really know God. In fact we are against God. We are "anti-God".

This is what cut those listening to Peter to the heart. They saw that in their zeal "for" God they had been against God. We need to understand this today! Because in our "live-and-let-live" pluralistic society hardly anyone would dare say to another person, "You claim to know God, but in fact you are "anti-God"; you are against God." Why? Because you do not embrace God the Father's endorsement of Jesus. Jesus is the test of all true knowledge of God. Are we with the Father in His endorsement of Jesus by raising Him from the dead, or are we against Him?

The Father endorsed Jesus by seating Him on His right hand and putting all His enemies under His feet. Peter quotes the prophecy of King David who foresaw that God the Father would exalt the risen Messiah to His right hand and give Him a place of rule and supremacy over every other person and power in the universe. This endorsement of Jesus exposes the ultimate horror of rejecting Him. In rejecting Jesus, not only have they rejected the One who the Father declared to be Messiah by raising Him from the dead; they have also rejected the One whom the Father declared to be the Lord of the universe by exalting Him to His right hand.

Lastly, the Father endorsed Jesus as the only One worthy to receive the Holy Spirit and pour Him out in full portion upon sinners who repent. The Father has given Jesus the privilege of pouring out the Holy Spirit and clothing His people with the Spirit's power from on high (Luke 24:49).

What is at stake here and at every point in this message that Peter was bringing to the crowd is God the Father. The Father endorsed Jesus as the Worker of miracles on the earth. The Father endorsed Jesus as the perfect Sacrifice for sins. The Father endorsed Jesus as the risen Messiah. The Father endorsed Jesus by exalting Him to be Lord of the universe. To reject Jesus is to repudiate the Father! To vote "no" on Jesus is to oppose God the Father. That's the issue. And that is what pierced their hearts! (Acts 2:37)

The question before the crowd back then is the same question before all people today. Do you join God the Father in His affirmation of Jesus, or do you stand against Him in the life of Jesus? The Father had a prearranged plan – a plan that could only be accomplished through His Son. And the Father has a plan for our lives – a plan that can only be accomplished through the Son that He sent in order for that plan to be fulfilled. Join with the Father in His affirmation of His Son, and follow His Son in the journey of your life… trusting Him to fulfill His plan for His glory… until He returns.

* * *

8

WHAT SHOULD WE DO?

Peter's words pierced their hearts, and they said to him and to the other apostles, "Brothers, what should we do?" Peter replied, "Each of you must repent of your sins and turn to God, and be baptized in the name of Jesus Christ for the forgiveness of your sins. Then you will receive the gift of the Holy Spirit. This promise is to you, to your children, and to those far away – all who have been called by the Lord our God." Then Peter continued preaching for a long time, strongly urging all his listeners, "Save yourselves from this crooked generation!" Those who believed what Peter said were baptized and added to the church that day – about 3,000 in all.
Acts 2:37-41

* * *

With this chapter, i'm going to make a transition. Throughout the first five books of the **Lessons Learned In The Wilderness** series and throughout the first few chapters of this book, i have endeavored to share truth in a way that it is applicable to you, the reader, whether you are already a follower of Christ, or you have not yet come to that place. My prayer has been that if you do not have a saving relationship with Christ that the Spirit of God would use the Truth of His Word as shared through these books in drawing you into a personal relationship with Him. That is exactly what we see occurring in the lives of the three thousand new believers recorded in these verses. The Spirit of God used the Word of God to lead the three thousand to repentance and faith. If you have not yet come to that place, i beseech you that there will never be a better time to repent of your sins and turn to God than right now. Put this book down, go before God in prayer and receive forgiveness for your sins without any further delay. Heed the instructions that the apostle Peter gave to those who were standing before him. You are one of the very people to whom he was referring – as are we all – when he said, *"this promise is... to those far away"*. He was talking about us in this generation and all the generations to follow! How we turn to Christ has not changed in two thousand years, and it will not change until He returns! So, if you have not done so, i pray even now that you will do so today!

From here on, in this chapter and for the remainder of this book, i am going to be writing as if you already are a follower of Christ. We're going to look at the instruction from the Word for believers and followers of Jesus. i'm going to transition from "what must we do" *to be saved*, to "what must we do" *as one who is already saved*.

We begin these verses with the statement that *"Peter's words pierced their hearts"*. Allow me to make a few clarifications. The listeners were convicted of their sin. The Spirit of God used the Word of God to bring conviction to their hearts. Only the Spirit of God can do that. Conviction is not brought about by eloquence of speech or the charisma of the messenger, rather through a working of the Holy Spirit. And the words that were spoken were not Peter's words! Peter knew that! Luke, the writer of this account, knew that! Peter was simply the mouthpiece. He was the conduit. The Spirit of God was speaking through Peter. Don't read this as if this fisherman had special training to deliver this message. Though he was the first to speak that day, it appears that the crowd asked the question of all the apostles which opens up the possibility that all of them may have spoken at some time that day. But even as it relates to all twelve, the only gifting they had was the presence of the Spirit of God. The Spirit was given to equip all of those who repent and believe, not just those twelve, or your pastor, or your small group leader. He was given to equip and empower you.

And again, the words that the Spirit of God spoke through Peter – and the others – was the Word of God. *"For the Word of God is alive and powerful. It is sharper than the sharpest two-edged sword, cutting between soul and spirit, between joint and marrow. It exposes our innermost thoughts and desires"* (Hebrews 4:12). It's the Word of God – that two-edged sword – that *"pierced their hearts"*. The message was not about what Peter thought; it was about what the Word of God says. The Word brought conviction that caused them to repent and turn from their religion and turn to Christ.

Repentance means i am no longer walking in the way that i was. i have turned and am now walking toward God and with God by His grace. It's a change of heart – from a heart filled with sin to a heart that has been made new by Christ.

He next told them that once they had repented, they must be baptized. Baptism is not part of repentance; it follows repentance as a testimony of the forgiveness we have received. Put another way: we are not baptized in order to be saved; we are baptized because we have been saved. A clear example that baptism is not a part of salvation, but, rather, an obedient act that follows salvation, is the new believers that came to faith in the home of Cornelius. Luke records that they had received the Holy Spirit before they were baptized (Acts 10:44-48).

Again, **baptism is an act of obedience**. Jesus said we are to be baptized (Matthew 28:19). But it must **follow** repentance, otherwise all we did was get wet! **It is an act of proof.** It is an outward expression of the sincerity of our repentance and faith. **It is an act of identification.** Through baptism we are publicly identifying with our Savior and Messiah – bringing glory to Him, just as He did when He was baptized by John the Baptist (Matthew 3:15). **It is an act of witness.** Baptism by immersion reflects exactly what has occurred in our life. As we are lowered into the water we demonstrate that our sin nature has been put to death with Christ on the cross, and as we are raised back up out of the water, we demonstrate the new life in which we walk with the resurrected Christ.

Three thousand new believers were baptized on that day. Did you ever wonder how they were able to baptize that many people in one day? In that day, as Jews prepared to bring their sacrifices into the Temple, they first needed to go through a purification ritual in a bath called a "mikveh". Thus far, archaeologists have uncovered two hundred of those mikveh pools in and around Jerusalem, of which fifty are located on the southern side of the Temple Mount. Peter and the other apostles preached to the crowd on the southern side of the Temple. In His sovereignty, the Father had already arranged for pools to be in place for those baptisms long before anyone else knew they would be needed!

Lastly, Peter told the crowd that following their repentance they would receive the gift of the Holy Spirit. The apostles had waited in an upper room for eight days to receive the gift of the Holy Spirit, but that would no longer be the case. From that day forward the gift of the Holy Spirit would immediately be given at the point of repentance. And how much of the Holy Spirit would they receive? Remember, the Holy Spirit is a Person. He's not an "it". You don't receive a portion of a Person; you receive all or nothing. And Peter said, *"you will receive the gift of the Holy Spirit"* – that's the whole Person. The same Holy Spirit who empowered Peter to speak on that day indwells every believer – whether they have been saved for one second or one hundred years.

As you walk through your personal life journey, even in the midst of a wilderness, God will bring people across your path that His Holy Spirit is convicting of sin and drawing to Himself. He will bring people across your path who are asking, "What should we do?" The answer to that question hasn't changed in two thousand years. *"This promise is to you, to your children, and to those far away...."* Until He returns, we have been entrusted with that promise – not to keep – but to share!

* * *

9

FULLY DEVOTED FOLLOWERS

All the believers devoted themselves to the apostles' teaching, and to fellowship, and to sharing in meals (including the Lord's Supper), and to prayer. A deep sense of awe came over them all, and the apostles performed many miraculous signs and wonders. And all the believers met together in one place and shared everything they had. They sold their property and possessions and shared the money with those in need. They worshiped together at the Temple each day, met in homes for the Lord's Supper, and shared their meals with great joy and generosity – all the while praising God and enjoying the goodwill of all the people. And each day the Lord added to their fellowship those who were being saved.
Acts 2:42-47

* * *

Three thousand believed, repented and were baptized. They comprised the first church – "The First Church of Jerusalem". And the Lord added to their fellowship daily. Let's take a few minutes and look back at that first church.

All the believers devoted themselves.... The word "devoted" means *"given over to"*, *"ardently enthusiastic and loyal"*, and *"placing the needs of the object of your devotion over your own"*. We often refer to sports fans as being devoted. One of my nephews attended the University of Georgia and became a loyal Georgia Bulldog. As a matter of fact, during his undergrad days, he became so ardently enthusiastic at football games that he painted his bare upper torso red, put on a red wig, sported a letter on his chest and became affectionately known as "W", as together with eleven other fans, they spelled out "GEORGIA DAWGS" in the bleachers. That could probably be described as a number of things , one of them being "devoted". There are degrees of devotion as illustrated by my nephew. But as we see in these verses, these believers were fully devoted. There wasn't anything "halfway" in their belief or their actions.

They were fully devoted to their Lord. They repented and surrendered their life to Christ and never looked back. In our day we often give the appearance that we "added" Christ to our lives. We keep on doing many of the things we were doing before we "got saved". Those around us may – or may not – see a difference that Christ has made in our lives. But those three thousand… were radically transformed. They knew that apart from the saving work of Christ all they had was a religion that made little or no difference in their lives. They knew that apart from Christ they were dead in their sin. They knew that His Spirit and His Word had "pierced their hearts" and there was no going back. Their devotion to Jesus led them to become fully devoted to His Word. Remember, at that point, there was no New Testament. It hadn't been written yet. The apostles' teaching was the spoken word of Jesus' teachings that would become our New Testament. Together with the Old Testament, the two would subsequently become the full and complete Word of God, as we know it now. They were fully devoted to God's Word – every word! And one of the teachings from Jesus' words was that they were to love one another. They took Jesus' words seriously when He had said, *"Your love for one another will prove to the world that you are My disciples"* (John 13:35). That word from Jesus meant that if they were going to be fully devoted to Him and His Word, they also needed to be fully devoted to one another.

Their devotion led to awe. Their belief and repentance was not a "one and done conversion". Rather they became a day-in, day-out community of believers – learning, applying and witnessing the fruit of Jesus' teachings in their own lives, as well as in one another's lives. They saw the power of God working through signs and wonders. The miracles and the life transformation they witnessed never became routine; rather, their awe led to increased faith… which led to greater awe… which led to even greater faith…. There was a sense of wonder and awe – and godly fear – at the stark reality of what they saw and heard.

Their awe led to selflessness. When Jesus became Lord of their lives, they were no longer the central figure in their own lives. Selfish ambition was abandoned to be replaced by sacrificial generosity. They began to understand that everything they possessed was from God. And none of their possessions were truly theirs; they were but stewards of the gifts with which God had entrusted them. When they began to see themselves as stewards they realized that the gifts that God had given them were not for self-expression or self-fulfillment, but to fill what was lacking in someone else by meeting genuine needs. They realized that even the grace that God had extended to each one of them was not meant to end with them, but was to be extended to someone else (1 Peter 4:10). Apart from selfless and sacrificial compassion, grace would merely end up in storage, not in action. It was never our Lord's intention that we fill our barns with His grace, rather, that His grace and His gifts be poured out to others (Luke 12:16–21).

Their devotion to one another and their growing selflessness bonded them in such a way that if one was in need, the others did not feel they had the right to live on in prosperity without giving up something to meet the need. Thus, they sold their possessions and used the money to meet the needs of the poor in the church.

Their selflessness led to contagious joy. Their love for one another was expressed joyfully, not grudgingly. i mentioned this in *Taking Up The Cross* but it is worthy of repeating. Tertullian was a theologian in the early church (A.D. 155 – A.D. 240). He wrote that the Roman government was disturbed by the early church. So they sent spies to infiltrate and observe worship gatherings. They came back to their Roman leaders with a report that went something like this: "These Christians are very strange people. They speak of One by the name of Jesus, who is absent, but who they expect to return soon. And my, look at how they love one another, and are ready to die for each other." Jesus said, *"There is no greater love than to lay down one's life for one's friends"* (John 15:13). And the early church took Him seriously.[1] Their love – and their joy – were contagious!

We would do well to look within our own local fellowships. If our faith community is committed, but not compelling to anyone, we should be asking serious questions about what we're committed to. Are we known for our joy and our love, or are we known solely for what we're against? John Piper writes, *"Churches are dying today because they are not doing anything which the world should look at and say: 'There is evidence that God is real and that He is glorious.' Many churches have forgotten why they exist – namely, to meet needs in the name of Jesus so that people will be moved to give*

God glory (Matthew 5:16). *And when a church forgets that it exists for others and for God, it becomes in-grown and self-satisfied, and can go on year after year like a social club with a religious veneer. But its life is ebbing away, and people are no longer saying: 'Look at all their good deeds and the humble spirit of love in which they are done; their God must be a glorious God of encouragement.'"*

Let's recap what we see in "The First Church of Jerusalem":

- They were devoted to the teaching of Jesus as told to them by the apostles (which we have in the New Testament).
- They experienced wonders and signs (which they had the faith to see).
- They lived in a state of wonder and awe as they saw day-in and day-out the stark reality of God's presence and power in healings, deliverances and the changed lives of people that the Lord was adding to the church.
- They shared their possessions freely with the needy, as though they didn't even own them.
- They spent time together worshiping as a body in the Temple.
- They spent time together fellowshipping and ministering in small groups in their homes almost every day.
- And when they gathered together with each other, they met with God. They prayed and they praised.

What caused all of this to occur? What was the driving force that made those believers free from the enslavement of their possessions, eager to meet needs, filled with gladness and generosity, and distinguished by their praise and prayer when they came together day after day? It was that joyful, trembling sense of awe that you don't trifle with God or His Word. Regrettably that is not our experience today. In our day, for most people, including most professing Christians, God is an idea to talk about, or an inference from an argument, or a family tradition to be preserved. Only for a very few is God a stark, fearsome, stunning, awesome, shocking present REALITY. He is seen as being tame.., distant.., out of touch.., and silent. Where are the churches of whom Luke could say today, "devotion, awe, wonder, selflessness, trembling – is upon every soul"? The absence of those characteristics has a direct effect on the way we seek God, the way we seek His Word, the way we accumulate possessions for ourselves, the way we ignore the needy, the way we trivialize fellowship, and the way we play more than we pray.

・ ・ ・

It is time that we prayed for an outpouring of the Holy Spirit in an extraordinary way. It is time that we prayed that the Spirit of God would pierce our hearts with the Word of God and a holy, joyful awe would come upon the church, and people, not things, would become precious beyond words. Pray that we would again become fully devoted followers of our Lord, His Word and one another… until He returns.

---

1. *Taking Up The Cross*, Ch. 34

10

HE JUMPED UP

Peter and John went to the Temple one afternoon to take part in the three o'clock prayer service. As they approached the Temple, a man lame from birth was being carried in. Each day he was put beside the Temple gate, the one called the Beautiful Gate, so he could beg from the people going into the Temple. When he saw Peter and John about to enter, he asked them for some money. Peter and John looked at him intently, and Peter said, "Look at us!" The lame man looked at them eagerly, expecting some money. But Peter said, "I don't have any silver or gold for you. But I'll give you what I have. In the name of Jesus Christ the Nazarene, get up and walk!" Then Peter took the lame man by the right hand and helped him up. And as he did, the man's feet and ankles were instantly healed and strengthened. He jumped up, stood on his feet, and began to walk! Then, walking, leaping, and praising God, he went into the Temple with them. All the people saw him walking and heard him praising God. When they realized he was the lame beggar they had seen so often at the Beautiful Gate, they were absolutely astounded! They all rushed out in amazement to Solomon's Colonnade, where the man was holding tightly to Peter and John.
Acts 3:1-11

* * *

For a moment, imagine you have miraculously been transported back to this period of time in Jerusalem. Imagine you have been in the city for about a year beginning with the days leading up to the Passover until this day. Until that moment, you had never heard of Jesus. The day you arrived in Jerusalem, you stood in the midst of a crowd as Jesus proceeded along the streets in the midst of the throng riding on the colt of a donkey.

Those standing around you were laying down palm branches ahead of His path as they shouted, "*Hosanna!*" You turned to one of the people beside you and asked who this was riding the colt and why everyone was extending such honor to Him. The person looked at you in amazement that you had no idea who this Man was. He explained that this was Jesus of Nazareth. He was a Miracle Worker. He had made the blind to see, the deaf to hear and the lame to walk. He had even raised a man from the dead who had been in the grave for four days. Some say He is the Messiah who will lead Israel to throw off the oppressive rule of Rome and lead it to again become a great nation. This person wasn't certain about that claim, but there was no question that God's Spirit was with Him.

After Jesus passed by where you were standing, you fell in behind Him with the rest of the crowd to see what He was going to do. Jesus' journey ended at the Temple where He dismounted. He then entered the Outer Court and quietly walked around, looking, but not saying anything. He then made His way through the Beautiful Gate into the hall of prayer. There were a number of people begging at the gate. Some were lame. Some were blind. Each had been brought by family members or friends in the hopes that their friend or loved one would receive charity – or possibly a miracle of healing. Jesus looked on the people with compassion. He didn't ignore them, but He didn't stop to heal them. He continued on into the Temple and spent time in prayer. He and His disciples then quietly left.

The next day was Monday, and while you were at the Temple, Jesus returned. There was no large crowd or procession that day. But as He entered the Temple this time, He overturned the merchants' tables and stalls and drove them out into the Stoa (the area designated for merchants outside the Temple). A great commotion ensued and you saw that those who were begging by the Beautiful Gate obviously feared that they would be overrun by the people as they fled the Temple. Gratefully no one was harmed, but it caused the beggars to be wary in the days ahead.

The following day was Tuesday. Jesus again returned. This time, He remained in the Court of the Women for the entire day. A crowd continuously gathered around Him as He taught. Some of those who normally sat by the Beautiful Gate were brought to Jesus by family or friends, and He healed them! Those who remained at the Gate mourned the fact that they could not make their own way to Jesus. Perhaps their family or friends would help bring them to Jesus when He returned the next day. But Jesus didn't return the next day. As a matter of fact, Jesus never returned to the Temple. The religious leaders had Him crucified on Friday. The following Monday there was talk at the Temple that Jesus had risen from the dead. The religious leaders all said that was a lie. They said that His disciples had moved His body to make people think He was alive. But others, in hushed tones, talked about how Jesus had said He would rise from the dead after three days.

Seven weeks later, there was another commotion in Jerusalem. A sound like a roaring wind had been heard coming from an upper room in the heart of the city. Soon those who had been followers of Jesus began to praise God in languages other than their own, and all the visitors were able to hear the praise in their own language. You even heard it in your language! Several of Jesus' disciples gathered a crowd on the southern steps leading into the Temple and began to preach that Jesus was alive. And as they taught from the Scriptures, three thousand people became believers and were baptized. In the weeks and months that followed, growing numbers of these disciples of Jesus would come to the Temple to pray.

Today, about a year after Jesus was last in the Temple, two of the disciples that you had seen with Him – Peter and John – arrived to take part in the three o'clock prayer service. As they approached the Temple, a lame man was carried in. You recognized the lame man. He had been placed by the gate each day. He was there that day when Jesus had healed those who had been brought to Him. He had looked for Jesus every day after that, until He heard He was crucified. His hope had been crucified with Jesus. As Peter and John passed by him, he asked them for money. But he asked everyone for money – some would give, and others would look the other way.

Peter and John stopped, looked at him intently and said, *"Look at us!"* The lame man turned and looked at them *eagerly*. Peter said to him, *"I don't have any silver or gold for you."* The man's heart sank. *"But I'll give you what I have. In the name of Jesus Christ the Nazarene, get up and walk!"* The lame man didn't really know who these two were, but he knew who Jesus was! And he knew Jesus had healed the lame! Peter reached out and took the man's right hand, and immediately he jumped up! He stood, he walked, he leapt and he praised God! He knew he had been healed by Jesus! Jesus had been his hope. Jesus was his hope. Jesus had healed him.

• • •

Peter and John thought back to a conversation they had once had with Jesus. One of the disciples had asked Him, *"why was this man born blind?"* (John 9:2) Jesus had replied, *"This happened so the power of God could be seen in him"* (John 9:3) The same was true of this man who was born lame. But he had not been born lame so that others would see the power of God displayed through Jesus while He was in the Temple; he had been born lame that the people would see that same power of God displayed through the followers of Jesus! Everyone knew who this man was. Everyone knew he had been born lame. Everyone knew that he had just been healed. And everyone rushed to see Peter and John.

The prophet Isaiah wrote, *"And when He comes* (referring to Jesus), *He will open the eyes of the blind and unplug the ears of the deaf. The lame will leap like a deer, and those who cannot speak will sing for joy!"* (Isaiah 35:6) Jesus made the blind to see, the deaf to hear, the lame to walk and the dumb to speak. And Jesus said, *"Anyone who believes in Me will do the same works I have done, and even greater works, because I am going to be with the Father"* (John 14:12). And because Jesus was going to be with the Father, He had sent the Spirit that would empower and enable them to do the works that Jesus had done. Notice that Peter did not say, "in the name of Peter, get up and walk". He said, "in the name of Jesus". This man was made to walk to bring glory to the Son and to the Father – not to bring glory to Peter.

So it begs the question, if God could use Peter and John in that way, could He also use us? There are some who would say that the gifts of miracles and signs was limited to the apostles. To me, that contradicts what Jesus said up above in John 14:12, when He said, "<u>anyone</u> who believes in Me…." i also believe that in days past and in our current day there are charlatans that claim to have the gifts of miracles and signs who are attempting to bring glory – and profit – to themselves. Jesus taught that whatever He does will always be done in a way that brings glory to God and not the person. So here's the thing. The same Holy Spirit that entered into Peter and John and the other disciples gathered in that upper room, entered into the three thousand who believed later that day – and entered into you on the day you repented and believed. Does that mean God's Spirit will work through you in bringing about a miracle or a healing? i believe that it means He could, if He chooses to do so. God still works in miraculous ways. He is doing so every day – all around the world. It may appear to be less obvious in western culture – but perhaps that is more a reflection of the condition of our belief and our faith than it is of Him. But if each of us is honest, we will admit that we have seen God do the miraculous in our midst as well. i do, however, believe it is more conspicuous in other cultures around the world because their hearts haven't grown cold and their faith is more like that of a child. Peter and John knew that the Spirit of God within them was able to heal that man. They knew it as surely as they knew anything.

But also remember, it was the Father's perfect timing – that He had ordered from before the beginning of time. Jesus could have easily healed this man on one of His visits to the Temple – but that wasn't the Father's plan. It certainly didn't mean that Jesus was unable. It meant the Father had a different plan!

What's the take-away for us? Peter and John were not only empowered by the Spirit of God, they were guided by the Spirit of God. They were watchful and responsive to His activity. The Father initiated the activity, not them. We must walk each moment of each day with that kind of awareness and watchfulness. Then – like Mary told the servants in Cana – ""Do whatever He tells you" (John 2:5 NLT). Trust that He will equip you and empower you to accomplish what He has directed you to do. Trust that He will turn the water into wine. Trust that He will make the lame to walk. Trust that He will speak through you the words that He would have you say. If we do, we will see Him do what only He can to cause others to "jump up" and give Him the praise and the glory!

* * *

11

IN WHOSE NAME DO YOU DO THIS?

> *While Peter and John were speaking to the people, they were confronted by the priests, the captain of the Temple guard, and some of the Sadducees. These leaders were very disturbed that Peter and John were teaching the people that through Jesus there is a resurrection of the dead. They arrested them and, since it was already evening, put them in jail until morning. But many of the people who heard their message believed it, so the number of men who believed now totaled about 5,000. The next day the council of all the rulers and elders and teachers of religious law met in Jerusalem. Annas the high priest was there, along with Caiaphas, John, Alexander, and other relatives of the high priest. They brought in the two disciples and demanded, "By what power, or in whose name, have you done this?"*
> Acts 4:1-7

* * *

It started with the testimony of one man who was faithful to give praise to God for what He had done. Often that's how God begins a work of salvation. It happened through the woman at the well in Sychar. It happened through the faithfulness of one young boy who gave his sack lunch to Jesus. It happened through Lazarus when he walked out of that tomb. Seeing and hearing that the man born lame was now walking, leaping and praising God, the people in the Temple were *"absolutely astounded"* (Acts 3:10) and they *"rushed out in amazement"* to where the man was *"holding tightly"* (Acts 3:11) to Peter and John. *"Peter saw his opportunity and addressed the crowd"* (Acts 3:12). He wasted no time in asking the crowd two questions to get their focus on the right Person:

"what is so surprising about this?" and *"why stare at us as though we made this man walk by our own power or godliness?"*

It would have been easy for the group to get carried away talking about the miracle and totally miss the Miracle Worker. i am mindful that sometimes we get carried away as we share our own personal stories of how we came to believe in Jesus. We spend a good bit of our time talking about our days before we walked with Christ, then another bit about what our lives are now like since following Christ, but little to no time talking about the Miracle Worker through whom our lives have been changed. Peter immediately shifted the conversation from the miracle to the Miracle Worker.

And he quickly turned their attention away from John and himself. It can be easy to fall into the trap of pride and false modesty when God has worked through us. We start to feel good about what "we've" done or what "we've" said, and we allow the conversation to linger on about how great a Christian we are for God to use us in such a great way. A good friend, mentor and former leader, Dr. Tom Elliff, tells the story that he knew God was preparing to lead him to leave the church, where he pastored for twenty years to enter into a new chapter of ministry, when people started to refer to it as "Brother Tom's church". Our God is jealous for His glory (Isaiah 42:8) and He will share it with no other. Peter was careful to not allow any of that glory to be misdirected to him. He immediately redirected the focus – and we would be wise to heed his example.

"For it is the God of … all our ancestors who has brought glory to His servant Jesus by doing this. This is the same Jesus whom you handed over and rejected before Pilate, despite Pilate's decision to release Him. You rejected this holy, righteous One and instead demanded the release of a murderer. You killed the Author of life, but God raised Him from the dead. And we are witnesses of this fact! Through faith in the name of Jesus, this man was healed – and you know how crippled he was before" (Acts 3:13-16).

Peter knew that these men had rejected the teachings of Jesus. Approximately one year earlier He had stood in that very Temple and taught and healed. Many of them (if not all of them) had heard Him firsthand. They had been eye witnesses of some of the miracles He performed. And yet they had rejected Him and His teaching. They had been complicit in His execution, either overtly or covertly through their silence. Some of them may have been in the crowd in Pilate's courtyard who had cried out, *"Crucify Him!"* Many of them were those to whom Jesus was referring when, from the cross, He said, *"Father, forgive them, for they know not what they do"* (Luke 23:34). And the Father answered His Son's prayer and extended His grace and mercy to them.

"Friends, I realize that what you and your leaders did to Jesus was done in ignorance. But God was fulfilling what all the prophets had foretold about the Messiah – that He must suffer these things. Now repent of your sins and turn to God, so that your sins may be wiped away" (Acts 3:17-19). And hundreds of those gathered there on Solomon's Colonnade believed and repented, and received God's forgiveness that day. Some of the group were probably Pharisees. Some of the group could have been a part of the Sanhedrin. But all of that group became followers of Jesus!

Be mindful that where the Spirit of God is at work, Satan will show up to oppose the work and attempt to silence the witness. That was true that day, just as it is today. The same men that had plotted to have Jesus crucified were not going to sit silently by and allow this work of God to continue. In a very short while they had seen five thousand of their people turn from religion to Jesus. The power base of the religious leaders was again being threatened. If they permitted this to occur much longer they would be left without a people to rule – and they were jealous for their own positions and power! They sent out some of the priests and Sadducees, together with the Temple guard, to arrest Peter and John, and keep them from speaking any further.

The next morning the high council had Peter and John brought before them. They demanded to know, *"By what power, or in whose name, have you done this?"* Now that was just flat out silly! They knew "in whose name" the lame man had been healed. They knew "in whose name" the message of repentance had been preached. And they knew "in whose name" Peter and John stood before them. Remember, Caiaphas and Annas, and probably the rest of the clan, knew John and knew that he was a disciple of Jesus. They knew he stood at the foot of the cross. And they knew of Peter. They had probably heard about Peter's denial. They probably felt reasonably confident that Peter would cave-in under their interrogation. After all, he had denied Jesus three times in their homes in response to the questions of mere servants. Surely Peter would be so intimidated by Annas himself that he would again deny Jesus and this "movement" would be squelched.

. . .

From a worldly perspective, it wasn't a bad plan. The council's only problem was that they weren't expecting the power and the presence of the Holy Spirit. Luke reminds us that Peter *"was filled with the Holy Spirit"* (Acts 4:8). Annas wasn't intimidating a vulnerable fisherman, he was preparing to debate the Spirit of the Almighty God! Talk about showing up unprepared! Annas was ill-equipped to have that conversation. But bear in mind, so was Peter, apart from the presence, power and filling of the Holy Spirit.

The Holy Spirit was the principal actor in all of this. Peter and John were simply supporting cast members. The Holy Spirit had made the lame man to walk. The Holy Spirit had convicted the hearts of those who believed that day. The Holy Spirit had boldly spoken the Word of God through Peter. And it was the Holy Spirit who would now take on these religious leaders. Peter and John's role in all of this was to walk according to His guidance, emptied of their own selves and filled with His Spirit. If they had attempted to do any of this on their own, they would have failed miserably – and nothing of eternal Kingdom impact would have occurred. But because everything that was done, was done in the Name above all names – the Name of Jesus – and was done under the power of His Holy Spirit, a body was healed, lives were transformed and God was glorified.

We would do well to remember that until He returns. Because at the Name of Jesus *every* knee will bow (Philippians 2:10).

* * *

12

WE MUST OBEY GOD RATHER THAN MEN

Then Peter, filled with the Holy Spirit, said to them, "Rulers and elders of our people, are we being questioned today because we've done a good deed for a crippled man? Do you want to know how he was healed? Let me clearly state to all of you and to all the people of Israel that he was healed by the powerful name of Jesus Christ the Nazarene, the Man you crucified but whom God raised from the dead....The members of the council were amazed when they saw the boldness of Peter and John, for they could see that they were ordinary men with no special training in the Scriptures. They also recognized them as men who had been with Jesus. But since they could see the man who had been healed standing right there among them, there was nothing the council could say. So they ordered Peter and John out of the council chamber and conferred among themselves. "What should we do with these men?" they asked each other. "We can't deny that they have performed a miraculous sign, and everybody in Jerusalem knows about it. But to keep them from spreading their propaganda any further, we must warn them not to speak to anyone in Jesus' name again." So they called the apostles back in and commanded them never again to speak or teach in the name of Jesus. But Peter and John replied, "Do you think God wants us to obey you rather than Him? We cannot stop telling about everything we have seen and heard." The council then threatened them further, but they finally let them go because they didn't know how to punish them without starting a riot. For everyone was praising God for this miraculous sign – the healing of a man who had been lame for more than forty years.
Acts 4:8-22

* * *

Peter and John had just been brought before the high council. Luke tells us that Peter was filled with the Holy Spirit. The Holy Spirit had already entered into Peter's life on the Day of Pentecost. He didn't need to reenter. But rather Peter did need to be filled. Being indwelt by the Spirit of God is a one-time act. For Peter, it was at Pentecost. For you and me, it was when we believed, repented and received Christ as our Savior. But being filled with the Spirit of God is a continuing decision on our part. It is an ongoing decision about who will be in control of our lives.

Peter had consciously decided that the Spirit of God would be in control – and not Peter. As followers of Christ, we, too, must continually make that choice. Who sits in the "driver's seat" of our life? Am i the one who is steering and accelerating or braking – or have i turned those controls over to the Spirit of God? In some respects, walking with Christ would be so much easier if we didn't have the choice -- if somehow our flesh nature had been removed altogether at salvation. But though our flesh nature has been redeemed at salvation, it is still with us. The Holy Spirit is doing an ongoing work of sanctifying our flesh nature – but that nature will be with us until the day we stand face-to-face before Jesus. Until then we must continually crucify our flesh nature. That's what Jesus was talking about when He said, *"If anyone would come after Me, let him deny himself and take up his cross daily and follow Me"* (Luke 9:23 ESV). The decision to deny self and take up the cross is continual. Peter is a great picture in Scripture of what we look like when the flesh nature is in control versus the Spirit of God. When Peter's flesh nature was in control, He looked at Jesus and proudly boasted that he would follow Jesus to the death. Then he proceeded to deny His Lord three times out of fear over the simple questions of a few powerless servants. The result of his flesh nature being in control was denial of his Lord and deep personal shame. But in this passage, we see just the opposite! The flesh nature has been denied – or crucified – and the Spirit of God is fully in control. We would do well to learn from Peter's example.

Being filled with the Spirit, Peter could speak with confidence and courage in the presence of people who otherwise may have intimidated him with their position and power. The Spirit of God empowered him by giving him the strength and the power. The Spirit of God enabled him by giving him the words to speak. The Spirit of God emboldened him with the confidence and boldness to be unwavering in the speaking of truth. The very fact that Peter was not intimidated amazed the religious leaders. He spoke with an authority unlike anything he had heretofore demonstrated. It was the authority they had only witnessed from two others before this – Jesus and John the Baptist. The religious leaders knew that Peter and John were disciples of Jesus – and their boldness and actions confirmed it. Jesus had told His disciples that *"a disciple is not above his teacher, but everyone when he is fully trained will be like his teacher"* Luke 6:40 ESV). Their words and their actions affirmed that they were disciples of Jesus. Boldness and clarity come when we spend time with Him, speak His truth, and are led by His Spirit. Do our words and actions affirm that we are disciples of Jesus?

It would be nice to believe that if we are filled with the Spirit of God then those around us will rightly respond to the truth we are speaking. But that's not the case. The religious leaders rejected truth when Jesus spoke it to them, and they rejected the truth that the Spirit of God spoke through Peter. As a matter of fact, their hearts were so hardened to the truth that they attempted to discredit the undeniable truth of the healing of the lame man. The religious leaders were not seeking truth; they were seeking a way to avoid the truth. Their lack of acceptance was never a problem of the mind; but a problem of the heart and will. Those who benefit – or perceive themselves to benefit – from wrong-doing and wrong-thinking will usually turn a deaf ear and a blind eye to contrary evidence of what is right and what is true. The mind selectively sees and perceives reality in order to justify what the heart desires. And as the prophet Jeremiah wrote, *"The human heart is the most deceitful of all things, and desperately wicked"* (Jeremiah 17:9).

Peter and John knew that their calling wasn't to win an argument; their calling was to stand up and bear witness. We would do well to heed that lesson. Both groups had to choose between what was popular, safe or right? Peter and John knew that standing up for the truth of the gospel was right, though it was not the safe or popular choice with the religious leaders. The Spirit of God will always lead us to stand for what is right over what is popular or what is safe. Our flesh nature, however, will always choose what is safe or self-satisfying over what is true. The high council had no difficulty rejecting the truth, but they feared the backlash from the crowd if they attempted to deny the miracle. Thus they sought a way to reject the truth but remain politically correct.

Often one of the great obstacles to our speaking out about God's truth is that we think we have to win. Or we think we have to operate with the assumptions of secular leaders. But Peter shows us that this is not what we have to do. Our calling is not to win or to borrow the assumptions of the world. Our calling is to stand up and tell it like it is in the eyes of God. Peter defined it clearly – *"Do you think God wants us to obey you rather than Him?"*

Then Peter says, *"We cannot stop telling about everything we have seen and heard."* He is a witness. As one who is filled with the Spirit, he stands up and tells it like he sees it. Let the chips fall where they will. Don't worry if the public doesn't even agree with you. Your job is not to win. Your job is to walk in the Spirit of God, proclaiming His truth and acting according to His works, no matter how the world may respond. We must obey God rather than men – and the only way we will do that is if we are filled with His Spirit. As the apostle Paul wrote, *"So I say, walk by the Spirit"* (Galatians 5:16 NIV)… until He returns.

* * *

13

PRAYING FOR BOLDNESS

As soon as they were freed, Peter and John returned to the other believers and told them what the leading priests and elders had said. When they heard the report, all the believers lifted their voices together in prayer to God: "O Sovereign Lord, Creator of heaven and earth, the sea, and everything in them – You spoke long ago by the Holy Spirit through our ancestor David, Your servant, saying, 'Why were the nations so angry? Why did they waste their time with futile plans? The kings of the earth prepared for battle; the rulers gathered together against the Lord and against His Messiah.' In fact, this has happened here in this very city! For Herod Antipas, Pontius Pilate the governor, the Gentiles, and the people of Israel were all united against Jesus, Your Holy Servant, whom You anointed. But everything they did was determined beforehand according to Your will. And now, O Lord, hear their threats, and give us, Your servants, great boldness in preaching Your word. Stretch out Your hand with healing power; may miraculous signs and wonders be done through the name of Your Holy Servant Jesus." After this prayer, the meeting place shook, and they were all filled with the Holy Spirit. Then they preached the word of God with boldness.
Acts 4:23-31 (quoting Psalm 2:1-2)

* * *

Peter and John had just returned from their time before the high council. They had been threatened to *"never again speak or teach in the Name of Jesus"* (Acts 4:18). How did they and the other believers respond? By confessing the awesomeness of God in prayer. The greatest concentration of spiritual power in that day and in Jerusalem was in that prayer gathering. Perhaps it was the greatest concentration of any time or any place. There was no doubt. There was no hesitation. There was no fear. There was no question. There was no division. The Spirit of God united them and they lifted their voices TOGETHER. The people were of one heart and one mind, and God was pleased to answer their requests.

Their prayer was founded on the Word of God as recorded by David in Psalm 2:1-2. In His Word, God speaks to us and tells us what He plans to do. In prayer, we speak to Him and make ourselves available to Him for His will to be accomplished through us. They were not telling God what to do; they were asking Him to do His will in them and through them. They were not asking for their will to move heaven; they were asking for God's will to be done on earth. They did not pray for their circumstances to be changed, or for their enemies to be put out of office. Rather, they asked God to empower them and embolden them to make the best use of their circumstances in order to accomplish what He had already determined. This was a demonstration of their faith that God has a plan, His plan is perfect, and His plan will prevail. They did not ask God for a way of escape from the path that was before them; they asked Him to enable them to walk in the path according to His purpose. Phillips Brooks, the minister who wrote the lyrics to *"O Little Town of Bethlehem"*, also wrote, *"Do not pray for easy lives. Pray to be stronger men and women. Do not pray for tasks equal to your powers. Pray for powers equal to your tasks."* They did not pray for the persecution to cease; they prayed for courage and boldness to endure in the midst of persecution.

Each of us walk through difficult circumstances at times and for seasons of our lives. You may be walking through one right now. As i write this, a member of my family is walking through a difficult and challenging time. It is an attack from the enemy. God is not the author of the circumstance. He is not the author of deceit, or illness, or hardship. But He is the *"Sovereign Lord, Creator of heaven and earth, the sea, and everything in them."* We would do well to follow the example of those gathered in prayer that day – not praying according to our will, but according to His; not praying for escape, but praying for His Spirit to enable us, empower us and embolden us through it.

The early church acknowledged that the leaders of their day – *"Herod Antipas, Pontius Pilate the governor, the other Gentiles in positions of authority, and the religious leaders of Israel were all united against Jesus."* Their evil actions had all led to the crucifixion of Jesus. Yet all of their evil intentions had been used by the Father to accomplish His perfect plan – the resurrection of His Son and His victory over death. Therefore, the church had no need to fear! Their "enemies" were already defeated foes. But wisely, they also knew that they could not allow their faith in God's divine sovereignty to become an excuse for them not to take responsibility for the action He was calling them to take. Again, the words of St. Augustine are a wise reminder, *"Pray as though everything depends upon God, and work as though everything depends upon you."*

The believers did not ask for protection; they asked for power. They did not ask for the destruction of their enemies; they asked for boldness and power to preach the Word and heal the sick. They did not ask that their own agenda or their own needs be furthered; rather, that the Name of the Father and the Son be exalted.

God's answer was to shake the place where they were meeting, and again fill them with His Spirit. He filled them to overflowing – and the result of the filling was that *"they preached the word of God with boldness."* And it didn't stop there. It also further deepened their unity (Acts 4:32) and their desire to sacrifice and share with one another (Acts 4:34).

Phillips Brooks also wrote, *"nothing lies beyond the reach of prayer except that which lies outside the will of God."* That early church prayed according to God's will and He answered in mighty power. About thirty years later, James (the half-brother of Jesus, who did not become a follower until after Jesus arose from the dead) would write this reminder to the early church, *"You do not have because you do not ask. You ask and do not receive, because you ask with wrong motives, so that you may spend it on your pleasures"* (James 4:2-3 NASB). The same God who answered the prayers of those early believers is waiting to respond to those same prayers today… and every day… until He returns.

***

14

THEY GAVE IT ALL

All the believers were united in heart and mind. And they felt that what they owned was not their own, so they shared everything they had. The apostles testified powerfully to the resurrection of the Lord Jesus, and God's great blessing was upon them all. There were no needy people among them, because those who owned land or houses would sell them and bring the money to the apostles to give to those in need. For instance, there was Joseph, the one the apostles nicknamed Barnabas (which means "Son of Encouragement"). He was from the tribe of Levi and came from the island of Cyprus. He sold a field he owned and brought the money to the apostles.
Acts 4:32-37

* * *

They felt that what they owned was not their own. The hearts of the believers had disconnected from their "stuff" and "connected" with the Spirit of God. They no longer felt entitled. They now felt blessed. They were no longer possessed by their belongings. That which they had was now seen as a means with which to minister to others. Luke writes that the believers were *united in heart and mind.* They were no longer united with their personal possessions. They were united with one another. They were united in Christ. They were "believers"! They not only believed in Jesus for their salvation; they believed in Him and trusted Him for all that they needed. Their satisfaction and worth no longer came from what they possessed; their complete satisfaction was in God through Christ.

. . .

Today as twenty-first century believers, we read that passage and immediately want to issue disclaimers. "Surely God does not intend for us to give away all that we have!" That statement in and of itself is a reflection of the condition of our hearts, our trust and our belief. The passage doesn't tell us that they all sold their possessions all at once. It says that they shared everything they had so that no need went unmet. Needs were met as they arose through the provision that God placed within the body of believers. The issue was ownership. They didn't all immediately sell everything that they had; rather, they immediately surrendered the "deed" to all that they had to the One who had provided it. Through that transaction of "surrender", they were acknowledging that they were no longer the owners. Their possessions were no longer theirs to keep – or even to give. That decision lied solely with the Owner. The possessions were His to use as He saw fit.

There are many today who want to debate whether or not we are to tithe ten percent of our income to God through His local storehouse – the church. We see the tithe established in the Old Testament as early as Genesis 14 as a starting point for giving to the Lord. Additionally, we see a multitude of offerings that were to be given over and above the tithe. The debate today surrounds whether those commands that were given to God's people under the Law still apply to those of us who are now under grace. i have heard many who profess to be followers of Christ use "grace" as a justification that we are no longer to give ten percent because we are no longer under the Law. They are using "grace" to justify their refusal to honor God with the provisions He has given. This passage in Acts 4 clearly demonstrates that we are no longer to return ten percent of what God has provided back to Him; rather, we are to return ONE HUNDRED percent. He does not own one-tenth of what we have. Grace shows us that He owns all that we have! If we are giving a tithe of our income through the local church – that's only the beginning point – not a point of debate.

These early believers knew that giving had nothing to do with percentages or amounts; it had everything to do with their hearts. About two years prior to this, many of them had been eye witnesses to Jesus' sacrifice for them on the cross. Their hearts were tightened in their relationship with Jesus and one another, and loosened in their relationship to "things". Faith in Christ creates a bond of love with people, and cuts the bond of love with possessions. We are to be freed from the love of things and firm in our love for others. Over the years, i have heard pastors and teachers (myself included) talk about "giving sacrificially". But, in light of this passage, i think we get that wrong. i can only sacrifice something i own. If i no longer own it, it is no longer mine to sacrifice. i have "abandoned" all that i am and all that i have to the Master. i no longer have any rights or say over its disposition. i am simply the caretaker for the Owner, carrying out His directive, trusting that as i do He will also provide for my needs.

Joseph, or as we better know him – Barnabas, is a great picture of abandonment. As a Levite, Barnabas would have been far from being affluent. Barnabas' act of selling a field and bringing the proceeds to the apostles was tantamount to the widow who gave the mite. He wasn't giving from his plenty; he was basically giving all that he had. Because he had surrendered it to God long before any money was ever received from a buyer! But Barnabas' abandonment was not only seen in the property that was sold, it was seen through his other actions as well. Later in Acts we see that Barnabas was abandoned to His Lord in his willingness and obedience to reach out to a new convert by the name of Saul when all the rest of the believers in Jerusalem were afraid of him (Acts 9:26-27). Through his abandonment, God led Barnabas, a Jew, to leave his home in Cypress to go to Antioch and co-shepherd the new Gentile church (Acts 11:22). From there, Barnabas and Paul were led by the Spirit of God to preach the gospel to Gentiles throughout modern-day Turkey, Syria and Cypress (Acts 13-14). But it all began with a demonstrated freedom *from* the love of "stuff" and an overwhelming love *for* Jesus.

They gave it all – not at the point that they sold their property – they gave it all before that. They gave it all when they surrendered their lives to Jesus. The sale of property, the giving of all that they owned, was merely evidence of their surrender and abandonment. Like Barnabas or the widow who only had the mite, it doesn't matter how much or how little you have. The question before every one of us is – have we given it ALL? What are we continuing to hold onto tightly? What are we refusing to let go of? The old saying is still true – "Jesus is not Lord at all, if He is not Lord over all"! Surrender your all to Him today – all that you are and all that you have. Then, when He directs you to give or to go, it will all already be His!

* * *

15

PRIDE COMES BEFORE A FALL

But there was a certain man named Ananias who, with his wife, Sapphira, sold some property. He brought part of the money to the apostles, claiming it was the full amount. With his wife's consent, he kept the rest. Then Peter said, "Ananias, why have you let Satan fill your heart? You lied to the Holy Spirit, and you kept some of the money for yourself. The property was yours to sell or not sell, as you wished. And after selling it, the money was also yours to give away. How could you do a thing like this? You weren't lying to us but to God!" As soon as Ananias heard these words, he fell to the floor and died. Everyone who heard about it was terrified. Then some young men got up, wrapped him in a sheet, and took him out and buried him. About three hours later his wife came in, not knowing what had happened. Peter asked her, "Was this the price you and your husband received for your land?"
"Yes," she replied, "that was the price." And Peter said, "How could the two of you even think of conspiring to test the Spirit of the Lord like this? The young men who buried your husband are just outside the door, and they will carry you out, too." Instantly, she fell to the floor and died. When the young men came in and saw that she was dead, they carried her out and buried her beside her husband. Great fear gripped the entire church and everyone else who heard what had happened.
Acts 5:1-11

* * *

Barnabas had just selflessly and humbly given quite a sum of money to the church. Since the church shared all things, the believers were all aware and were probably talking about his generosity. More than likely, his gift was drawing more attention to him than he would have liked. He was mature enough in his walk with Christ to realize that no glory should come to him. God had entrusted the parcel of land to him as provision for the body. God had directed him to sell the land and surrender the proceeds to the church for the ministry of the body. There was nothing glorious about that act as it related to Barnabas – all glory belonged to God. But others wanted to ascribe glory to Barnabas, and still others were envious of that glory. Envy and pride are as old as the days of the Garden of Eden. And that nature still exists within us, even as believers, if we fail to surrender it to Jesus and ask Him to take it captive. That's true today, and that was true among the believers of the early church. Though Barnabas had surrendered that nature and refused to be "puffed-up" by the recognition he received, there were others within the body that sought that recognition for themselves. After all, why shouldn't their generosity be rewarded? (Can't you just hear the serpent whispering in their ear?)

Ananias and his wife, Sapphira, were two of those early believers. They also owned property. We're not told whether God led them to sell the property, or whether they chose to do so on their own. But either way, they sold it. They chose to keep part of the money, and give the remainder to the church. Again, we don't know what, if any, God had directed them to give. If God directed them to sell the property, He would have also directed them as to what portion they should give. It may or may not have been all of the proceeds. At issue here is not the amount that they gave. The issue is that they lied. And they apparently lied in order to garner the recognition that they had seen Barnabas receive. Otherwise there was no reason to claim that their gift was the full amount of the proceeds they had received.

Ironically, the name Ananias means "God is gracious" which is a testimony to His grace and mercy. But God is also holy. When Ananias and Sapphira lied, they not only did so to the believers in the church, they lied to God. There was a purity in that initial church. That's not to say that the early believers did not sin. We can be certain that they did; they were frail sinners just like you and me. But what made this sin of Ananias and Sapphira so repulsive to the Lord was their introduction of hypocrisy and deceit into His newly formed church, through their feeble attempt to glorify their own names. God Himself has told us, "…*I, the Lord your God, am a jealous God…*" (Exodus 20:5). He is jealous for His glory and He will not share it. "*I am the LORD; that is My name! I will not give My glory to anyone else…*" (Isaiah 42:8).

Lest there be any confusion, Peter didn't do anything that caused Ananias to "fall to the floor and die". God did! God dealt with the sin of Ananias and Sapphira swiftly and severely. Too often, we presume upon God's grace without regard to the fact that He is holy and just. He does not "wink" at our sin. The forgiveness of our sin cost Him the agony and sacrifice of His only Son on the cross. He paid dearly for our sin because of His grace. And He will not allow His grace to be trivialized by our wanton disregard for His holiness. We would do well to join with those believers who, when Ananias fell to the ground, were "terrified" before God. They realized that God was not "one of the boys" to be disregarded, lied to or defamed.

Even in its infancy, Satan was attempting to defeat the church. He was fresh on the heels of the reality that he was impotent to defeat Jesus. Satan's best efforts had been defeated at the empty tomb. So now he turned his attention to Jesus' bride – the church. Satan knew that his best opportunity to defeat Jesus was through the church, and that defeat will not come from outside the church, it will come from within the church. He knows how to lie to and deceive church members – even sincere followers of Jesus. He used the soulish ambition of Ananias and Sapphira to get them to do his bidding, and he convinced them that no one would ever be the wiser. He used the same tactic in the Garden with Eve, and he still uses it today. We would do well to remember the admonition from Paul to *"put on all of God's armor so that you will be able to stand firm against all strategies of the devil"* (Ephesians 6:11). Because as Peter wrote, *"…your great enemy, the devil… prowls around like a roaring lion, looking for someone to devour"* (1 Peter 5:8). Satan lied to and through Ananias and Sapphira, and the lie led to their deaths.

But at the root of their sin was pride. The writer of Proverbs tells us, *"pride comes before destruction, and an arrogant spirit before a fall"* (Proverbs 18:18 CSB). It was pride that transformed Lucifer into Satan (Isaiah 14:12-15). It was pride that led to Adam and Eve's sin (Genesis 3:4-6). And it was pride that led Ananias and Sapphira to attempt to deceive the Holy Spirit.

The early church saw God enter into their midst through His Holy Spirit in "great power", extending His "great grace". Then, in this moment, they were moved by "great fear". As we continue in our journey until He returns, we would do well to remember the words of the writer of

Hebrews: *"Therefore, since we are receiving a Kingdom which cannot be shaken, let us have grace, by which we may serve God acceptably with reverence and godly fear. For our God is a consuming fire"* (Hebrews 12:28-29 NKJ).

* * *

16

A MIRACULOUS ESCAPE

The apostles were performing many miraculous signs and wonders among the people. And all the believers were meeting regularly at the Temple in the area known as Solomon's Colonnade. But no one else dared to join them, even though all the people had high regard for them. Yet more and more people believed and were brought to the Lord – crowds of both men and women. As a result of the apostles' work, sick people were brought out into the streets on beds and mats so that Peter's shadow might fall across some of them as he went by. Crowds came from the villages around Jerusalem, bringing their sick and those possessed by evil spirits, and they were all healed. The high priest and his officials, who were Sadducees, were filled with jealousy. They arrested the apostles and put them in the public jail. But an angel of the Lord came at night, opened the gates of the jail, and brought them out. Then he told them, "Go to the Temple and give the people this message of life!" So at daybreak the apostles entered the Temple, as they were told, and immediately began teaching. When the high priest and his officials arrived, they convened the high council – the full assembly of the elders of Israel. Then they sent for the apostles to be brought from the jail for trial. But when the Temple guards went to the jail, the men were gone. So they returned to the council and reported, "The jail was securely locked, with the guards standing outside, but when we opened the gates, no one was there!" When the captain of the Temple guard and the leading priests heard this, they were perplexed, wondering where it would all end. Then someone arrived with startling news: "The men you put in jail are standing in the Temple, teaching the people!" The captain went with his Temple guards and arrested the apostles, but without violence, for they were afraid the people would stone them. Then they brought the apostles before the high council, where the high priest confronted them. "We gave you strict orders never again to teach in this Man's name!" he said. "Instead, you have filled all

Jerusalem with your teaching about Him, and you want to make us responsible for His death!"
Acts 5:12-28

* * *

God was at work in a new way! Many of those who were alive had been born during the latter part of the four hundred years of silence between the last prophet of the Old Testament – Malachi – and the arrival of John the Baptist. During those years the people had not heard a fresh word from God. Then God Himself showed up on the scene in the form of Jesus and the religious leaders rejected Him and crucified Him. When they should have been hungry to hear afresh from God, they had become quite content with their traditions and their own religious practices. They had settled into a very comfortable rut and were dedicated to maintaining their status quo. They thought their problems were over when they crucified Jesus. They thought they would be returning to "the good old days" of tradition and no longer having their leadership challenged.

But now, two years later, these followers of the very Jesus whom they had crucified were still on the scene performing miracles that even went beyond what Jesus had done (John 14:12). They boldly proclaimed that Jesus had risen from the dead. They preached a truth that was alive about a Living Savior that didn't square with the religious leaders' dead traditions. The apostles were disregarding the warnings from the religious leaders to stop teaching about Jesus. They were refuting the doctrine of the Sadducees by openly teaching that Christ had risen from the dead. And the people were being drawn to the apostles by their teaching and through the miracles they performed. The streets were abuzz with excitement. The sick were being healed simply by the shadow of an apostle passing over them. No one had ever seen anything like this. Caiaphas and the other religious leaders were again envious and saw their positions being threatened. They wanted the miracles to stop. They wanted the sick to remain sick. They wanted the dead to remain dead. They wanted this emerging living faith to be silenced and dead tradition to again become the order of the day. They wanted these uneducated, ordinary Galileans to know their place and leave the teaching to the educated, ordained, and "approved" professionals.

But those "ordinary" apostles, now filled with the Holy Spirit, could not be silent. They could not be disobedient to their Lord's direction to make His Name known among people everywhere, beginning right there in

Jerusalem. Their mandate was to go and tell, and they could do no less. They were prepared to risk everything so that the Good News could be proclaimed through the power of the Holy Spirit. The religious leaders, who were preoccupied with protecting themselves and their way of life, could not understand these uneducated men who were willing to risk it all.

The Sadducees failed to understand that the obedience of the apostles was, in itself, the evidence and sign that the Holy Spirit had been given. Their radical obedience came from the power of the Holy Spirit. They filled Jerusalem with their teaching because, in the face of great danger, they obeyed God and not man. They obeyed God and not man because they had received the power of the Holy Spirit. They could not be silenced, regardless of the threat of persecution. Hugh Latimer, martyred for his faith in 1555, once said, *"Whenever you see persecution, there is more than a probability that truth is on the persecuted side."* The apostles were on the side of truth and by the power of the Holy Spirit, they could not be silenced.

Just as Jesus promised (Acts 1:8), the Holy Spirit came upon the disciples with unusual fullness, and the result was supernatural power leading to courageous, life-giving witness. And that power was not merely the quiet power of preaching that looked natural, it was supernatural. It was life-changing. It was manifestly supernatural – tongues of fire, the sound of wind (Acts 2:2–3), a shaking building (Acts 4:31), and remarkable healings and deliverance (Acts 5:16). The result was that *"more and more people believed and were brought to the Lord."* Acts 1:8 was unfolding: the Spirit came upon the church in an unusual way; extraordinary power was manifested; and life-giving testimony was bringing people into the Kingdom.

Power is a very dangerous thing – both for those who have it, and for those who don't, but wish they did. The danger if you have it is pride, and the danger if you don't is jealousy. And both are based on bad mistakes. Pride is based on the mistake of believing that the power is ours, or that we in our own strength fulfilled the conditions to get it. But in fact the power is God's, and if we fulfilled any conditions to get it – like faith or prayer or purity – it was not us, but the grace of God in us (1 Corinthians 15:1). On the other hand, jealousy is not just the passion to have the power that someone else has. In itself, there may be nothing wrong with that – to want God's power in your life that you see in the life of another. Jealousy goes beyond that desire and becomes the anger and the resentment that someone else has it and you don't. Jealousy doesn't just want you to have what another has; it wants them to not have it.

The root of jealousy is three-fold. First, it is "lovelessness" (1 Corinthians 13:4). If you love another person, you will rejoice if God gives them power, even if He doesn't give it to you. Second, it is faithlessness. If you have faith in the sovereign grace of God to give power according to His own divine wisdom, then you will praise Him for the times and ways of His outpouring, and not question Him or resent His choices. God knows what He is doing, and He is wise and good in giving the Spirit in power wherever He pleases. Faith may cry for it to come; but faith also does not criticize God for when and where it comes. Third, it is "truthlessness". The Sadducees would have said, "there is no resurrection. The reason we are angry that these Christians are doing works of power is that they are deceiving the people to believe what is not true. There is no resurrection and they are leading the people astray." Jesus had given His disciples the antidote for "truthlessness" when He taught them, *"You are truly My disciples if you remain faithful to My teachings. And you will know the truth, and the truth will set you free"* (John 8:31-32). The religious leaders had rejected Truth and embraced their lies.

Their jealousy turned to rage which led to persecution – in this case, imprisonment. But in this instance, God used their imprisonment as another demonstration of His power. Before we look at their escape, let's be mindful that God does not promise that He will make a way of escape from every instance of persecution. As a matter of fact, He told His disciples that they would be imprisoned, betrayed and many would be killed (Luke 21:12-16). But He has promised that He will never leave us or forsake us (Hebrews 13:5). Stephen was stoned to death even though he was filled with the Spirit and spoke with power (Acts 7:58). The apostle James was later killed by Herod (Acts 12:1). An angel of God came again and again for Paul and for Peter. But there were many times when God did not stop the beatings and lashings, or the stoning, or the shipwrecks. And there was one last time when He did not stop their instruments of death. In those instances, no angel came to rescue them, but the Holy Spirit walked with them every step of their way.

But on this day, God sent an angel to lead the apostles in the way of miraculous escape. The miraculous spiritual power of God is precious because it is God's and it comes – or does not come – according to His sovereign plan. It is a precious thing for such great power to be in the hands of an all-wise, loving God. It is God's power and not ours. It is in God's control and not ours. It comes – or does not come – according to God's perfect plan. Upon rescuing the apostles from prison, the angel of the Lord told them to return to the very place where they had been arrested. He told them to: *"Go to the Temple and give the people this message of LIFE!"* When escape and deliverance come to us and we are freed and empowered to serve others, the purpose of our deliverance will be that we **give** LIFE. And when deliverance does not come and we are left in our suffering, the purpose will be that we might **live** LIFE. If we are delivered from distress by the power of God, His purpose is that we be ambassadors of life to other people – true life, eternal life, the forgiveness of sins and a personal relationship with the ever-living God. It is a precious thing to be empowered to give life to others.

But if you are not delivered, if the angel does not come to open the door, what then? Well, then the time may have come to simply **live** LIFE. There may be nobody else to whom you are to give it. Your days of giving may be over. They will be over for each of us sooner or later. But this too is precious: When God withholds delivering power, He gives us the grace and strength to endure. Be mindful that *"in all these things we are more than conquerors through Him who loved us"* (Romans 8:37 ESV).

As we end this chapter, be mindful of these closing thoughts. The apostles did not resist arrest. Filled and empowered by the Spirit of God, they trusted Him completely. They knew that they need not take anything into their own hands. They simply needed to follow Him, trust Him and obey Him. They could trust Him for the outcome. As a result, the more the Sadducees tried to stop the miracles, the more their actions only multiplied the miracles. God's purpose would be accomplished.. His Name would be made known. By their own admission the Sadducees bore witness that Jerusalem was filled with the teaching about Jesus, and the accusers (the religious leaders) had now become the accused (Acts 5:28) – all through the obedience of uneducated men walking in the power of the Holy Spirit.

So, with our eyes open to the price and the preciousness of the power of the Holy Spirt, let us also *"give the people this message of life"* either by "giving" it or "living" it... until He returns... as His Spirit rests upon us.

* * *

17

IF IT IS OF GOD, YOU WILL NOT STOP IT

But Peter and the apostles replied, "We must obey God rather than any human authority. The God of our ancestors raised Jesus from the dead after you killed Him by hanging Him on a cross. Then God put Him in the place of honor at His right hand as Prince and Savior. He did this so the people of Israel would repent of their sins and be forgiven. We are witnesses of these things and so is the Holy Spirit, who is given by God to those who obey Him." When they heard this, the high council was furious and decided to kill them. But one member, a Pharisee named Gamaliel, who was an expert in religious law and respected by all the people, stood up and ordered that the men be sent outside the council chamber for a while. Then he said to his colleagues, "Men of Israel, take care what you are planning to do to these men! Some time ago there was that fellow Theudas, who pretended to be someone great. About 400 others joined him, but he was killed, and all his followers went their various ways. The whole movement came to nothing. After him, at the time of the census, there was Judas of Galilee. He got people to follow him, but he was killed, too, and all his followers were scattered. So my advice is, leave these men alone. Let them go. If they are planning and doing these things merely on their own, it will soon be overthrown. But if it is from God, you will not be able to overthrow them. You may even find yourselves fighting against God!" The others accepted his advice. They called in the apostles and had them flogged. Then they ordered them never again to speak in the name of Jesus, and they let them go. The apostles left the high council rejoicing that God had counted them worthy to suffer disgrace for the name of Jesus. And every day, in the Temple and from house to house, they continued to teach and preach this message: "Jesus is the Messiah."
Acts 5:29-42

* * *

There are two powerful statements in this exchange between the apostles and the high council. The first was made by Peter. "We must obey God" – not your god – not the one you have created in your own image – rather, we must obey the God of our ancestors – the One and only true God. He is the God who raised Jesus from the dead – after you in your jealousy and hatred had Him crucified. You rejected the One through whom God chose to bring repentance and forgiveness to His people – the One who now sits on His right hand as Prince and Savior. And in so doing, you have rejected God. Though you sit in seats of religious authority, you have chosen not to place yourself under God's authority – and we must obey Him rather than you. His Spirit bears witness to His truth and His authority, but you have not been given His Spirit because you have rejected Him.

As we can imagine, the high council became furious and decided to kill the apostles. After all, they had killed one Galilean, why not eradicate the movement by killing a few more?

The second statement was made by Gamaliel. He appears to have been a voice of reason. His voice appears to have been one that carried weight with Caiaphas, Annas and the others on the high council. Remember that only two years earlier this same council had met to discuss and plot the killing of Jesus. It is reasonable to presume that if Gamaliel was present for this discussion about the apostles, he was present at the discussions about Jesus. The absence of his name in conjunction with those earlier discussions would tend to indicate that he supported the popular view of the council to crucify Jesus. So, who was Gamaliel and why did he speak up here when he apparently had not done so two years earlier?

Gamaliel was considered to be one of the greatest teachers of the Law in all the annals of Judaism. When the apostle Paul was defending his pedigree in Jewish Law, he cited Gamaliel as being his teacher because the name obviously carried great weight and respect (Acts 22:3). Gamaliel was a Pharisee and, in the Talmud, he bears the titles of *"Nasi"* meaning "prince", and *"Rabban"* meaning "our master". Some believe that he was the president of the Great Sanhedrin in Jerusalem. Regardless, he held great authority and influence within the council.

. . .

Gamaliel used two examples in his statement to dissuade the other members of the high council from choosing to execute the apostles. The first was Theudas. Apparently Theudas was a zealot who lived at the dawn of the first century A.D. He gathered a following of about four hundred men who joined him in an attempted insurrection. His attempted revolt ended in his death, which in turn resulted in his now-leaderless followers scattering and going their separate ways. As a result, the whole movement fell apart. His second example was Judas of Galilee, who was also a leader of a group of zealots. It was a similar situation. In 6 A.D. he got a number of people to follow him in an attempted raid on a Roman armory. Their attempt also failed, and he, too, was killed. The result was that all of his followers also scattered.

Both of the events that Gamaliel referenced occurred twenty to thirty years earlier, which means they had occurred long before Jesus was brought before the high council as well. But Gamaliel apparently did not choose to make the same argument at Jesus' "trial" that he was making now at the apostles' "trial". That would indicate that he believed that the work of Jesus would stop with His death. Gamaliel believed that Jesus' followers would scatter. Remember, the devoted followers of Jesus at the time of His crucifixion were only about one hundred twenty men and women. Though thousands flocked to Jesus to witness and experience His miracles, only one hundred twenty really followed Him to the end. In Gamaliel's mind at the time of Jesus' crucifixion, Jesus had less followers than Theudas or Judas of Galilee. He didn't make the argument before the council then because he believed the movement would fail with Jesus' death.

But two things happened! First, Jesus did not stay dead! Though Gamaliel probably never saw the resurrected Jesus himself, he was witnessing the boldness of His followers who were now unwaveringly proclaiming His resurrection. These uneducated fisherman were speaking with a boldness and an authority unlike he had ever witnessed – and his spirit was bearing witness to the fact that they were speaking truth. Jesus was the Son of the Living God! No matter what he and the other religious leaders had tried to do, Jesus had been victorious. The shedding of Jesus' blood had not stopped the movement; it had fueled the movement! Second, there was no denying that tens of thousands of people had since become followers of Jesus – three thousand on just one day! And some of those had been Pharisees! There was a movement taking place that could not be denied, and Gamaliel's eyes were becoming opened to the truth. The Holy Spirit was at work in His life. And the pivotal point for him was this: *"If they are planning and doing these things merely on their own, it will soon be overthrown. But if it is from God, you will not be able to overthrow them. You may even find yourselves fighting against God!"* Gamaliel had already come to the conclusion that he and the other members of the high council were *"fighting against God!"* His argument and authority swayed the decision of the other council members and they decided to "accept his advice".

Biblical historians, including Josephus, tell us that Gamaliel subsequently became a follower of Jesus. Whether it occurred before his remarks to the high council or after, we can see the evidence of the Holy Spirit at work in his life. In that light, i want us to see the sovereignty of God through all of this. First, it was always the Father's plan that His Son would be crucified on the cross. Remember Jesus was not a victim; He was – and is – the Victor. Gamaliel remained blinded to these very arguments at Jesus' trial because it served the Father's purpose for him to be so. Second, it was the Father's plan that this Jewish rabbi be a part of His plan to preserve the lives of the apostles in the early days of the formation of His church. It was God's timing for Gamaliel's eyes to be opened to truth and, in the Father's sovereignty, He had ordered his steps to stand in that place with the authority and respect he commanded for just such a time. Third, God was also already at work in and through Gamaliel to help equip a young man by the name of Saul, who would by all accounts become the greatest Christian missionary who has ever lived.

So here's the takeaway for us… until He returns. "If it is of God, it will not be overthrown. You may even find yourselves fighting against God!" His plan will not be thwarted. His purpose will prevail. Trust Him. Follow Him. No matter the circumstance. No matter who stands before you. The apostles rejoiced that God had counted them worthy. Even if you are flogged, don't lose sight that our God is sovereign. He was then, and He always will be.

* * *

18

CHOSEN TO SERVE

But as the believers rapidly multiplied, there were rumblings of discontent. The Greek-speaking believers complained about the Hebrew-speaking believers, saying that their widows were being discriminated against in the daily distribution of food. So the Twelve called a meeting of all the believers. They said, "We apostles should spend our time teaching the word of God, not running a food program. And so, brothers, select seven men who are well respected and are full of the Spirit and wisdom. We will give them this responsibility. Then we apostles can spend our time in prayer and teaching the word." Everyone liked this idea, and they chose the following: Stephen (a man full of faith and the Holy Spirit), Philip, Procorus, Nicanor, Timon, Parmenas, and Nicolas of Antioch (an earlier convert to the Jewish faith). These seven were presented to the apostles, who prayed for them as they laid their hands on them. So God's message continued to spread. The number of believers greatly increased in Jerusalem, and many of the Jewish priests were converted, too.
Acts 6:1-7

* * *

The church was experiencing amazing growth. In three years, it is estimated that the church had grown to twenty-five thousand men and women. It was a supernatural movement, but it was not pure. The apostles were casting nets into the sea of the world as fishers of men empowered by the Holy Spirit. Not all of the "fish" who were drawn in were Spirit-filled believers. They all had been gripped by the power of God, but they were not all truly born again. They were all touched by the Spirit of God, but not all were transformed. They were all excited about the supernatural power they were witnessing, but not all had truly been crucified in their flesh. They were all caught up in the movement, but not all had experienced true brokenness for sin or passion for holiness. There were the likes of the deceitful Ananias and Sapphira in the Jerusalem movement (Acts 5:1-11), the power-hungry magician Simon in the Samaritan movement (Acts 8:13-24), the fearful, retreating John Mark in the missionary band (Acts 13:13; 15:38), the doctrinally confused Apollos in the Asian movement (Acts 18:24-28), the professing Christians in Ephesus who for some time concealed their black magic (Acts 19:18), and so on. None of that should come as a shock to us. The same is true today.

As we've already said, Satan was never able to defeat Jesus, so he turned his attention on trying to defeat His bride – the Church. Satan was not going to sit idly by while a movement of God was taking place. He began his effort by stirring up rumblings of discontent within the body, which then grew into complaints and accusations of discrimination. The apostles were doing absolutely everything. Everybody turned to them for everything, and they realized that they could no longer handle the demands at the level that was needed. The demands were not being adequately met. And the apostles knew that they could not neglect the Word of God in order to meet them.

The conflict came to a head between the Hellenists (the Greek-speaking Jews) and the Hebrews (the Hebrew- or Aramaic-speaking Jews), and the failure of the church to properly nurture the Greek-speaking widows. It was a two-fold threat to the movement of the gospel. First, the system the emerging church had developed (Acts 4:34) to take care of the needs within the body was not working for the Hellenist group. If that failure to properly care for the Hellenist widows continued, the church would fail in loving and caring for one another, the glory of Christ would be diminished in the eyes of the world, and the movement of the gospel could experience a serious reversal. The second threat to the movement would be if the apostles left their primary calling to the ministry of the Word in order to serve those needs. The felt needs would be met but the advance of the gospel would suffer. The "best" was being threatened by the "good", not something "bad". And that is usually the case.

The Spirit of God led the apostles to respond immediately so that Satan could not use the issue to gain a foothold in the growing church. He led the apostles to respond in a way that brought unity rather than further division within the church. The apostles instructed the church to appoint seven Hellenistic leaders (their Greek names tell us their ethnicity), who were trustworthy and full of the Spirit and wisdom, to take care of the need. They delegated the responsibility, enabling the apostles to keep on devoting themselves to the ministry of the Word and prayer. The widows were cared for and the ministry of the Word of God was not forsaken. Both were utterly crucial. Either threat could have undermined the church and ended its amazing growth. The issue was resolved by utilizing the full diversity of gifts and abilities that God had already placed within the church.

Everyone agreed with the solution, and seven men were chosen as the precursors of those who would soon become known as deacons. It is interesting to note that six of the seven men were subsequently used by God in the spread of the gospel throughout Jerusalem, Samaria and the uttermost parts. The exception was Nicolas of Antioch, who later demonstrated that his understanding of the gospel was more syncretistic, being caught up in the fusion of religious beliefs instead of truly entering into a relationship with Jesus Christ. Of the six who became passionate evangelists, all but Philip were subsequently martyred for their faith, the first of whom being Stephen, as we will see in the next two chapters of this book.

The result of the selection of these seven men was that *"God's message continued to spread. The number of believers greatly increased in Jerusalem...."* Attention to the Word of God and the mission of God was not forsaken or diminished. They did not become so inwardly focused that they forsook the mission of Christ, but they also remained faithful to the ministry to the saints. The outcome was a new breakthrough in evangelistic power. Now, even priests, who had been heretofore hostile to the gospel (Acts 4:1), were responding to the Word of God and obeying the faith. It is estimated that there were eight thousand priests attached to the Temple in Jerusalem – and now "many" of them were responding. The church had been tested. She had passed the test by nurturing the widows and guarding the Word. And God honored this triumph with new power and fruitfulness.

So, what is the application for us today? First, let us be mindful of our priorities as followers of Jesus. We must never lose sight that we have been charged by our Lord to be His witnesses – to make disciples. It is easy for us to allow other activities to consume our attentions and our energies. We must be as passionate as the apostles to stay rightly focused. But second, we must never lose sight of the ministry opportunities that God places before the body. The same Holy Spirit who placed within the early church seven men who were uniquely equipped to carry out their specific ministry function has also equipped the body today to carry out His ministry purposes. We must remain watchful and obedient to His direction. God has uniquely equipped us for His purpose and He has chosen us for His service. God raised up those seven men, including Nicolas, for that hour. We must pray that there are no obstacles – inside our lives or inside the church – that will hinder the work of the Spirit of God through the Word of God in our lives and in our churches, and that the same power that brought thousands into the church in the Book of Acts will do the same today – until He returns – throughout our Jerusalem and around the world.

* * *

19

GRACE-FULL

Stephen, a man full of God's grace and power, performed amazing miracles and signs among the people. But one day some men from the Synagogue of Freed Slaves, as it was called, started to debate with him. They were Jews from Cyrene, Alexandria, Cilicia, and the province of Asia. None of them could stand against the wisdom and the Spirit with which Stephen spoke. So they persuaded some men to lie about Stephen, saying, "We heard him blaspheme Moses, and even God." This roused the people, the elders, and the teachers of religious law. So they arrested Stephen and brought him before the high council. The lying witnesses said, "This man is always speaking against the holy Temple and against the law of Moses. We have heard him say that this Jesus of Nazareth will destroy the Temple and change the customs Moses handed down to us." At this point everyone in the high council stared at Stephen, because his face became as bright as an angel's.
Acts 6:8-15

* * *

Earlier Luke described Stephen as *"a man full of faith and the Holy Spirit"* (Acts 6:5), and now he describes him as *"a man full of God's grace and power"*. The former description is the cause and the latter is the effect. Stephen was *"a man full of God's grace and power"* because he was *"a man full of faith and the Holy Spirit"*. To be full of grace, which means God's favor, is the result of being full of faith. There are several expressions of grace, but all of them come as a result of faith. The apostle Paul wrote, *"For by grace you have been saved through faith"* (Ephesians 2:8 ESV). So there's grace that comes in the form of salvation and it comes by faith. Paul also wrote that he pleaded to the Lord to remove his thorn in the flesh, and in response *"He said to me, 'My grace is sufficient for you, for My power is made perfect in weakness.' Therefore,* [Paul went on to say], *I will boast all the more gladly of my weaknesses, so that the power of Christ may rest upon me"* (2 Corinthians 12:9 ESV). There's grace that overcomes, and is made perfect in weakness. And it too comes by faith. And there is grace that comes in the midst of persecution that also comes through faith. *"But even if you should suffer for righteousness' sake, you will be blessed"* (1 Peter 3:14 ESV). And finally, there is the grace of extending loving kindness toward others that comes by faith. Paul wrote that *"He might display the surpassing riches of His grace, demonstrated by His loving kindness to us in Christ Jesus"* (Ephesians 2:7). i believe this may be the kind of grace that Luke bears witness to within Stephen's life. He was full of grace toward others.

That, in fact, is part of the reason that the church chose him to be one of the men responsible for helping the Hellenist widows. But, the greatest example came as he stood before the high council at the end of Acts chapter 7. They had been stoning him, the rocks were smashing against his head and shattering his body, and yet, he looked up to heaven and cried out with a loud voice, *"Lord, don't charge them with this sin!"* (Acts 7:60) That is nothing short of graciousness and loving kindness. That is bestowing favor upon those who attack you – even kill you. How in the world could he possibly do that? How could he be so forgiving? Because he believed that God was sovereign, even over persecution and death. He wasn't busy trying to protect himself. He was willing to die if God wanted him to do so. Only by faith could he so completely trust God's grace in such a way that loving kindness was being expressed even at the point of his death.

But also, he was a man full of God's power. Because he was full of the Holy Spirit. If you're full of the Holy Spirit then you are full of God's power! Jesus promised, just before He ascended to sit at the right hand of the Father, *"you will receive power when the Holy Spirit comes upon you"* (Acts 1:8). When we are right in our hearts toward God and obedient to His Spirit, He will then be gracious toward us and express His power on our behalf. We will never know grace toward others and experience the power of God working in and through us until we are filled with His Spirit. It is a simple spiritual principle! Luke records that Stephen *"performed amazing miracles and signs among the people"* (Acts 6:8). The power of God and the grace of God were exhibited in his life because he believed God and obeyed the Spirit, and the same is true for us.

. . .

Be mindful that Stephen came to faith in Christ as a Hellenist (Greek-speaking) Jew. Those that began to debate with him were also Hellenist Jews. They came from Cyrene (northern Africa), Alexandria (Egypt), Cilicia (on the southern coast of Asia Minor), and other parts of Asia. They represented the people of other languages and ethnicities that were assembled in Jerusalem as proselytes of Judaism. They were some of the very ones who had heard the apostles speaking in their own languages on the Day of Pentecost, but even then had rejected the truth. It is very likely that one of those who was debating him was Saul of Tarsus in Cilicia (Acts 21:39), who of course would later become the apostle Paul. Stephen in many respects was a precursor to the ministry of the apostle Paul. He was sharing the gospel with people who were from the Gentile nations – the very places where Paul would take the gospel. He confronted those congregations of Jews with the truth and countered the opposition of their Jewish bigotry. He was treated with insults and violence and subsequently stoned, just like Paul would one day be. So, in a very real sense, the mantle of Stephen fell upon Saul of Tarsus that day. But Saul, one of Stephen's bitterest opponents, had no idea that it was taking place.

Since none of the Hellenist Jews were able to stand against the wisdom and power of the Holy Spirit, the only tact available to them was false witness and deceit. Those were the same weapons they had employed against Jesus. They were unable to refute the truth and power of His word so they turned to lies and false accusations. Let's not lose sight that Stephen was brought before the same high council that had tried and "convicted" Jesus, four years earlier, and had tried and released the apostles, slightly more than two years earlier.

It is interesting to note that as the high council stared at Stephen, his face began to become *"as bright as an angel's."* Only one other man in history has been described in that way, and that man is Moses (Exodus 34:29-30). The council was accusing Stephen of blaspheming Moses, and God's response was to bear witness by allowing his face to reflect the glory of God, just as He had done through His servant Moses. In essence, God was saying, "This man is not against Moses! He is like Moses – he is My faithful servant! His face even reflects My glory – just like Moses!"

As we see in Acts 8:1, Stephen's life and ministry marked the climax of the church's witness to the Jews. From here the gospel would push out to the rest of Judea, Samaria and the ends of the earth through the scattering of the newly formed church. As we will see in the next chapter, Stephen was not a victim; rather, God accomplished His victory though his life. The victory was that the gospel was being preached with grace and power to the Jews, and now God was preparing to send that good news out to the rest of the world through other men and women who were full of faith and the Holy Spirit. The evidence of their anointing and filling would be just like Stephen's. Their lives would reflect the grace and power of the Holy Spirit's presence.

The same is true today. If we are filled with the Holy Spirit, walking with Him by faith, our lives will be "grace-full". Our faces may not become as bright as an angel's, but our lives will bear witness through the fullness of grace and the power of His presence… until He returns.

* * *

20

KEEP GAZING UPWARD

> "You stubborn people! You are heathen at heart and deaf to the truth. Must you forever resist the Holy Spirit? That's what your ancestors did, and so do you! Name one prophet your ancestors didn't persecute! They even killed the ones who predicted the coming of the Righteous One – the Messiah whom you betrayed and murdered. You deliberately disobeyed God's law, even though you received it from the hands of angels." The Jewish leaders were infuriated by Stephen's accusation, and they shook their fists at him in rage. But Stephen, full of the Holy Spirit, gazed steadily into heaven and saw the glory of God, and he saw Jesus standing in the place of honor at God's right hand. And he told them, "Look, I see the heavens opened and the Son of Man standing in the place of honor at God's right hand!" Then they put their hands over their ears and began shouting. They rushed at him and dragged him out of the city and began to stone him. His accusers took off their coats and laid them at the feet of a young man named Saul. As they stoned him, Stephen prayed, "Lord Jesus, receive my spirit." He fell to his knees, shouting, "Lord, don't charge them with this sin!" And with that, he died.
> Acts 7:51-60

* * *

Let's not get the idea that being full of grace means that we do not stand for and declare the truth. i think too often today we have bought into the lie of a false grace that declares "live and let live". We have become confused into thinking that if we are standing up for truth, we are being judgmental and "grace-less". As Stephen's life shows us, nothing could be further from the truth!

. . .

Throughout the preceding fifty verses of this chapter in Acts 7, Stephen recounts the promises and the pursuit of God from the time of Abraham through the prophets as He was at work to raise up a people through whom He would bring glory to His Name. But now Stephen confronts them with the reality that they rejected the truth from every prophet that God sent to them, including Moses – whom they were now accusing him of blaspheming – and Jesus – whom this very group had murdered. He confronted the high council with the reality that they had disobeyed the very Word of God that through their position they were charged to honor and guard. They had so compromised the truth that they had crucified the very One who was the personification of God's grace and truth (John 1:14). Instead of seeking and worshiping their Creator, they had created a god in their own image that they now served. Their god was their tradition, their position and their misguided power. And they had become so blinded by the god they created that they didn't recognize the Glory of God when He stood before them. Stephen was by no means preaching a message of "live and let live", he was confronting them with the truth of God's Word.

And, no, it wasn't popular. The Jewish leaders were infuriated. They literally shook their fists at him in rage. If it had occurred today, they would have accused him of being intolerant. But Stephen, because he was full of the Holy Spirit, did not divert his gaze to their rage or back down from his mission. He kept gazing upward toward heaven with His eyes on the glory of God and his faith directed toward the Son of God. And he told them exactly what he was seeing. He chose to go right on speaking the truth when he knew that it would cost him his life. He chose to die rather than not speak the Word of God empowered by the Spirit of God. He chose to honor the One, rather than the crowd. The Jewish leaders killed him in their feeble attempt to silence the truth. They saw it as so threatening that it was better to kill a good man than to let this truth be spread. They had thought when they murdered Jesus that they were squashing the truth. And they had been wrong! Now, they were making the same mistake. They thought that by stoning Stephen they would silence the truth.

As we saw in chapter 17 of this book, when they had earlier considered the fate of the apostles, they had been halted in their murderous intent by the wisdom of Gamaliel. No such wisdom was going to dissuade them today. They were blinded by their rage – because God in His sovereignty permitted them to be blinded. Does that mean that He loved the apostles more than He loved Stephen? Of course not! That would be like saying He loved the apostles more than Jesus because He let His Only Son die. God had a purpose in Christ's death (and subsequent resurrection) – our redemption. He had a purpose in the apostles escaping death that day – the establishment of His church. And He had a purpose in Stephen's death – the advancement of His mission.

You see, in the religious leaders' attempt to silence the truth, they had underestimated God's plan. Stephen was to be the catalyst that triggered an explosive growth of the church. It was his martyrdom that scattered the believers to the ends of the earth (Acts 8:1).

Allow me to take a side road here. Stephen was also important because of who he was and the very character of his life. He is great proof that the effect of a follower's life has nothing to do with the length of it, and the effect of a follower's ministry has nothing to do with how long it lasts – or how many that follower is able to personally lead to Christ. Stephen's ministry was short. He never had opportunity to preach to the multitudes that many others did. He was the first martyr for the Christian faith. Yet, his life – and death – was the catalyst that caused the church to move out in the next step of Christ's commission to reach Judea, Samaria and the ends of the earth with the gospel. Stephen was the trigger that God used to "shoot" the church out into the world.

And one who would subsequently become the greatest missionary of the gospel who has ever lived – a man named Saul – stood there and kept watch over the coats of the accusers. As Stephen kept his gaze turned upward toward heaven, Saul kept his gaze turned downward toward the coats on the ground. We now know that in a short while (Acts 9), God would turn Saul's gaze upward as well – and, as a result, use him as His chosen instrument to take the Good News *"to the Gentiles and to kings, as well as to the people of Israel"* (Acts 9:15).

But on this day – the day of Stephen's death – Stephen kept gazing upward full of grace and truth, as Saul kept gazing downward while truth was being denied and silenced. So the question for us, as we stand in our respective crowd is – are we gazing upward speaking truth or gazing downward in silence? This may be the very moment that God has ordained for His grace and truth to be proclaimed and revealed through the power of His Holy Spirit. Let's be careful to keep our eyes gazing in the right direction as we speak up with words of grace and truth... until He returns.

* * *

21

THE POWER OF GOD ISN'T FOR SALE

A man named Simon had been a sorcerer there for many years, amazing the people of Samaria and claiming to be someone great. Everyone, from the least to the greatest, often spoke of him as "the Great One – the Power of God." They listened closely to him because for a long time he had astounded them with his magic. But now the people believed Philip's message of Good News concerning the Kingdom of God and the name of Jesus Christ. As a result, many men and women were baptized. Then Simon himself believed and was baptized. He began following Philip wherever he went, and he was amazed by the signs and great miracles Philip performed. When the apostles in Jerusalem heard that the people of Samaria had accepted God's message, they sent Peter and John there. As soon as they arrived, they prayed for these new believers to receive the Holy Spirit. The Holy Spirit had not yet come upon any of them, for they had only been baptized in the name of the Lord Jesus. Then Peter and John laid their hands upon these believers, and they received the Holy Spirit. When Simon saw that the Spirit was given when the apostles laid their hands on people, he offered them money to buy this power. "Let me have this power, too," he exclaimed, "so that when I lay my hands on people, they will receive the Holy Spirit!" But Peter replied, "May your money be destroyed with you for thinking God's gift can be bought! You can have no part in this, for your heart is not right with God. Repent of your wickedness and pray to the Lord. Perhaps He will forgive your evil thoughts, for I can see that you are full of bitter jealousy and are held captive by sin." "Pray to the Lord for me," Simon exclaimed, "that these terrible things you've said won't happen to me!"
Acts 8:9-24

* * *

It was now about four years since the Holy Spirit had been given to the Jews. *"A great wave of persecution"* had now begun on the day that Stephen was killed (Acts 8:1). It swept over the church, and many of the believers, except the apostles, scattered throughout Judea and Samaria. The church did not cease to exist in Jerusalem; rather, as it scattered elsewhere, it still continued to grow. Thus, the apostles remained in Jerusalem for a season to shepherd that still growing church through her infancy, despite the threats that were specifically made against them by the religious leaders and the persecution that was now being directed toward the believers. It is very possible that the initial persecution was primarily being directed toward the Hellenistic Jewish believers, as was the case with Stephen.

Philip, the second of the seven Hellenistic Jewish leaders who were selected to minister to the widows, was directed by God to go to Samaria. Jesus had at one time prohibited the apostles from going there (Matthew 10:5-6). But now, the Lord was inviting Philip to enter into the labor that He had begun through His encounter with the woman at the well (John 4). Philip was not only to declare God's Word, but he was also to demonstrate God's power through miracles.

Sadly, wherever God sows His true believers, Satan will eventually sow his counterfeits. It was as true in the first century church as it is today. It was true in the ministry of John the Baptist (Matthew 3:7) and Paul (Acts 13:6; 2 Corinthians 11:1-4, 13-15), and it was even true in the ministry of Jesus (Matthew 23:15, 33; John 8:44). The enemy seeks to devour, and if he is unsuccessful at that, he will turn his attention to deceive. Satan's instrument in this case was a sorcerer by the name of Simon. The people were amazed by the "things" that Simon did, and, as a result, they believed the "things" he said. Training in the identification of counterfeit currency always begins with studying the real thing. Recognizing counterfeit faith is best identified in the same way. Genuine truth and works will always align with God's Word and glorify Him. The enemy's counterfeit actions and lies will always bring attention to self. Simon relished in being called *"the great one"* by the crowd.

When Simon witnessed the miracles performed by Philip, he did not demonstrate a faith in the Word of God; rather, he placed his faith in the miracles themselves. His belief was like many of the people who witnessed the miracles of Jesus, but refused to acknowledge His Word. Simon's "belief and baptism" were not the result of true repentance; they were part of his attempt to manipulate and deceive in order to gain favor and power. i can relate to that. There was a time that i was going through the motions of belief. My motivation was more to win the heart of the woman i was pursuing, than to pursue Jesus as my Lord and Savior.

Let's take a momentary side road. Simon had truly not repented and believed, but there were many who had – and they were baptized by Philip. Luke tells us that they had not yet received the Holy Spirit (Acts 8:15-16) even though they had trusted in Christ. Paul, writing to the church in Ephesus, tells us, "… *when you believed in Christ, He identified you as His own by giving you the Holy Spirit, whom He promised long ago. The Spirit is God's guarantee that He will give us the inheritance He promised and that He has purchased us to be His own people…*" (Ephesians 1:13-14). So, if God gives us the Holy Spirit when we believe in Christ (like Paul says), why didn't the Samaritans receive the Holy Spirit immediately upon believing in Christ (like Luke says)? It would seem to be a contradiction – and that's the reason for this side road.

In these beginning days of the church (Acts chapters 1 through 10), we see God working in ways that were unique to that time period. The two elements we need to understand are these. First, before Jesus ascended, He told His disciples that they would receive power and then they would tell the Good News in Jerusalem, Judea, Samaria and the ends of the earth (Acts 1:8). There was an initial order to the spread of the Gospel that applied at the start, but no longer applies today – first to Jerusalem, then to Judea and Samaria, followed by the ends of the earth.

Second, Jesus told Peter, in the presence of His other apostles, "*And I tell you, you are Peter, and on this rock I will build My church, and the gates of hell shall not prevail against it. I will give you the keys of the Kingdom of heaven, and whatever you bind on earth shall be bound in heaven, and whatever you loose on earth shall be loosed in heaven*" (Matthew 16:18-19 ESV). Jesus very specifically gave the "keys to the Kingdom" to Peter. He gave Peter the unique privilege of opening the door (loosing on earth and in heaven) the releasing of the Holy Spirit. Peter was the one who preached on the Day of Pentecost and the door was opened to the Jews in Jerusalem and Judea. We see here that Peter (and John) laid their hands on these new believers and the door was opened to the Samaritans. Later in Acts 10, we see that God used Peter to open the door to the Gentiles (the ends of the earth). Once the doors were opened, they no longer need to be reopened. And the truth that Paul wrote to the Ephesians applies to us today. We are immediately identified and indwelt by the Holy Spirit at the point of our salvation.

Let's come back to Simon. There is a word in the English language today – "simony" – which means "the buying or selling of something spiritual."[1] Its origins are in this very passage. Peter confronted Simon for his sin in thinking he could buy the power and presence of the Holy Spirit. That still exists today. People attempt to gain positional or spiritual favor from God and/or recognition from man through "good works" or through the giving of financial gifts as a "quid pro quo". As i mentioned earlier, i attempted to impress and receive favor through my disingenuous actions. Within the church, we may want to appear to others to be "more spiritual" than we truly are in order to gain favor or position, and that fake façade most often quickly falls away and reveals our true hypocrisy.

Regrettably, there is no indication that Simon ever truly repented. Oh, he was "sorry", and he asked Peter to pray that he would escape the judgement of God, but he stopped short of turning from his own way and turning to Christ. He sought power and recognition, but never sought the Savior.

There are those walking through a wilderness journey today who attempt to spiritualize their circumstances in an effort to "buy" sympathy or recognition. They believe God owes them something, or the church owes them something. Their focus is on themselves and what they can "get" through the journey – not on the promises and faithfulness of God even in the midst of the trials and the hardships. An attitude surfaces that God "owes" me – based upon what i have done or what has happened to me. i sometimes see that attitude being expressed through comments on my blog posts. But here's the reality – just as it was for Simon – the power of God is not for sale! It's not earned. It's not deserved. We can only witness and experience the power of God working in us and through us when our hearts are turned and surrendered to Him – and even then, only for His purpose and glory. The power of God isn't about us – it's all about Him. And it's not for sale!

---

1. Encyclopedia Britannica

22

A DIVINE APPOINTMENT

As for Philip, an angel of the Lord said to him, "Go south down the desert road that runs from Jerusalem to Gaza." So he started out, and he met the treasurer of Ethiopia, a eunuch of great authority under the Kandake, the queen of Ethiopia. The eunuch had gone to Jerusalem to worship, and he was now returning. Seated in his carriage, he was reading aloud from the book of the prophet Isaiah. The Holy Spirit said to Philip, "Go over and walk along beside the carriage." Philip ran over and heard the man reading from the prophet Isaiah. Philip asked, "Do you understand what you are reading?" The man replied, "How can I, unless someone instructs me?" And he urged Philip to come up into the carriage and sit with him.... So beginning with this same Scripture, Philip told him the Good News about Jesus. As they rode along, they came to some water, and the eunuch said, "Look! There's some water! Why can't I be baptized?" He ordered the carriage to stop, and they went down into the water, and Philip baptized him. When they came up out of the water, the Spirit of the Lord snatched Philip away. The eunuch never saw him again but went on his way rejoicing. Meanwhile, Philip found himself farther north at the town of Azotus. He preached the Good News there and in every town along the way until he came to Caesarea.
Acts 8:26-40

* * *

Philip was in the midst of a great spiritual awakening that was spreading throughout Samaria. God was using him in a great way, and many were repenting of their sins and believing in Jesus, when an angel of the Lord told him, "*Go south down the desert road that runs from Jerusalem to Gaza.*" God was directing him to leave a work among the multitudes to go to a desolate place. That doesn't necessarily align with a successful career path from a human perspective – even if you're a pastor. Whenever we hear a pastor announce that God has called him to go elsewhere, it is rarely to a "smaller" church. And such a move would be even more puzzling, if we are serving in a place where the power and the presence of the Spirit of God is mightily at work, and many are coming to faith and the church is growing. But such was the case with Philip.

We aren't told whether or not he had a conversation with God as to the wisdom of such a move. However, with all we do know about Philip and his walk with God, i tend to think that he immediately set out on the journey to Gaza without ever questioning God. He was in Samaria because God had placed him there. The work that was occurring in Samaria was a work of the Holy Spirit of God, and not of Philip. i don't believe that Philip ever got confused about that. i don't believe he ever tried to take any credit, or saw himself as being instrumental in any way. He was a man full of faith and full of the Holy Spirit – led by, empowered by and used by God for His purpose. Therefore, it didn't matter whether the assignment was in Samaria, Gaza or Azotus. All that mattered was that he was in the place where God would have him.

During my years of serving with the International Mission Board of the Southern Baptist Convention, i had the blessing and privilege of meeting thousands of men and women who, in response to God's call, were leaving successful careers in the U.S. – in a myriad of vocations – business, education, healthcare, agriculture, etc., as well as church ministry – to go to a remote part of the world, where there were few, if any, other believers. They were going in obedience to God in order to share the Good News of Christ with a people group who, most often, had never heard the Name of Jesus. From a human perspective, it was rarely a "step up". But i rejoiced, as i heard the testimonies of these men and women, because these men and women knew that following Jesus wherever He leads is ALWAYS a step up!

Philip, like the men and women i've mentioned, had no idea who he would encounter. All he knew was that God told him to go – and God's direction is never haphazard. We constantly saw Jesus model obedience to the Father in His journeys – sometimes traveling long distances to see just one person, and sometimes to engage a multitude. But the numbers never mattered. It was all about the Father's plan – and the divine appointment that He was orchestrating. In this case with Philip, the divine appointment was with an Ethiopian eunuch – the Secretary of the Treasury for the Queen of Ethiopia.

A few years ago, almost to the day as i write this, i was blessed to travel throughout the country of Ethiopia with a group of pastors from the U.S. i was leading the group and coordinating our schedule. As i look back i can clearly see the Father's hand in assembling that group of men. Our group was comprised of a Korean pastor, a Hispanic pastor, a Chinese pastor, two African American pastors, a white pastor of Italian descent and me. Most of us did not know one another prior to traveling together. We were traveling to spend time with men and women that God was using to spread the gospel throughout Ethiopia and other parts of Central Africa. Our goal was to encourage these workers, as well as to see where God might be leading these pastors to lead their churches to join with Him in the work He was doing among the people in that part of the world. Each of these men also held (and continue to hold) positions of significant leadership in influencing other pastors and churches in doing the same. As a result, we were given an opportunity to see the work in many places within a short window of ten days. We were constantly on the move – riding on every form of transportation imaginable.

On one of the days we were flying through one of the smaller airports in the country. We had spent the day with a team of eight people who were being used by God in a great movement of the gospel among a nomadic people. We were scheduled to depart on a flight at 5:00 P.M. to go to another city to meet up with another team. There was only one plane at the airport when we arrived – the one we were scheduled to take. As it turned out, it was experiencing mechanical failure. The airline representatives continued to tell us that they were working on the problem as day became night, and night kept getting later. i became acutely aware that we hadn't allowed for this much of a delay in our schedule, and we would be forced to cancel some of the visits we had planned. As i was working through the adjustments to our schedule, i began to observe something take place that had been totally unplanned – by us!

The majority of people in the waiting room were native to the country and only spoke their native language of Amharic. None of us knew Amharic, but we were grateful that the airline representatives also knew English. As we sat there, we noticed that there was a Chinese man who was obviously injured, traveling with a companion. It turned out that he had sustained a work injury earlier that afternoon, and was on this flight to get to a hospital in our destination city in order to receive needed medical care. They only spoke Mandarin Chinese. The Chinese pastor with us was able to communicate with them as to what was happening with our delays and was able to assist them with interim care, all the while sharing the gospel in word and deed as the night progressed. Also in the waiting area was a young Korean woman who was traveling alone and was obviously distraught over the delay. The Korean pastor began to minister to her to calm her fears, and in so doing was also able to share the gospel. The Lord provided one of our pastors with the opportunity to minister to a young Amharic man who spoke English. As it turned out, he was a believer who was struggling over a decision that he needed to make regarding the direction of his life. The night before God had told him, through a dream, that He would bring someone across his path who would provide him with words of wisdom regarding his decision. The pastor who was with us was able to point him to the Word of God and challenge him in his walk with God. And on it went with all of our team, each one experiencing the hand of God orchestrating divine appointments. We finally departed on a replacement plane at 10:00 AM the next morning. We hadn't gotten much sleep, and we all felt a little gamey – but we also knew that we had been right where the Father had intended for us to be. And just like Philip, when our assignment was completed, He "snatched us away" on our plane and we found ourselves headed to His next assignment for us.

As we read about Philip in the Book of Acts, his divine appointment with the Ethiopian wasn't the exception, it was the norm. Because Philip walked in obedience as the Father directed him – wherever, whenever, and however. The Spirit of God went before him to prepare the way, to order his steps and empower him for the work. As followers of Jesus, divine appointments should be the norm for us as well, and not the exception. Whatever your journey looks like today, God has a purpose and a plan in the midst of it. It may be right where you are, or He may interrupt you and lead you somewhere else. It probably won't happen when you expect it or the way you expect it, but it will happen if you follow the Spirit's lead. He has arranged for those divine appointments throughout the path ahead. And He will continue to do so… until He returns.

* * *

23

A DAMASCUS ROAD ENCOUNTER

Meanwhile, Saul was uttering threats with every breath and was eager to kill the Lord's followers. So he went to the high priest. He requested letters addressed to the synagogues in Damascus, asking for their cooperation in the arrest of any followers of the Way he found there. He wanted to bring them – both men and women – back to Jerusalem in chains. As he was approaching Damascus on this mission, a light from heaven suddenly shone down around him. He fell to the ground and heard a voice saying to him, "Saul! Saul! Why are you persecuting me?" "Who are you, lord?" Saul asked. And the voice replied, "I am Jesus, the One you are persecuting! Now get up and go into the city, and you will be told what you must do." The men with Saul stood speechless, for they heard the sound of someone's voice but saw no one! Saul picked himself up off the ground, but when he opened his eyes he was blind. So his companions led him by the hand to Damascus. He remained there blind for three days and did not eat or drink.
Acts 9:1-9

* * *

Saul set out on a journey that day. It was a journey of his own choosing. He was on a mission – his own mission. No one sent him. He had to solicit letters of endorsement to provide to the synagogues in Damascus so that he could obtain their cooperation. No one gave him those letters. He had to solicit them. There are two possible reasons for his actions. One possibility is that he had become so caught up in the rhetoric of the religious leaders that he truly had developed a deep-seated hatred for these followers of Jesus. He had guarded the cloaks while the others had stoned Stephen. Since that day he had begun to make a name for himself as a persecutor of Christ followers there in Jerusalem. He had become a part of the threat that prompted the believers to scatter. As he saw it, the believers were a threat to the very fiber of the established religious community, and he saw this as a holy war to eliminate their influence. As such, he was willing to go fight battles that even the religious leaders themselves had no interest in fighting. They were content to be rid of the many believers who had fled from Jerusalem; Saul was not.

A second possibility was his own selfish ambition. Saul apparently was a good student and a quick learner. He was probably a graduate of the university in Tarsus – the greatest Greek university of the day. He was a student of Gamaliel, considered by most to be the greatest Hebrew scholar of the day. He obviously aspired to become an influential religious leader himself, perhaps even the high priest. This ambitious young man saw this journey as a way to prove himself to the religious leaders and garner their support so that he might more quickly rise in the ranks of leadership. Thus, either his hatred or his ambition – or both – created an eagerness in his heart to "kill the Lord's followers". He was on a mission to kill them. Let there be no confusion – Saul was not pursuing God. He was declaring war on God. And yet, God in His sovereignty, in His mercy, and by His grace was Himself pursuing Saul – not for his defeat, but for his transformation.

As he approached Damascus at midday, suddenly he saw a bright light from heaven that caused even the sun to pale. He could not stand in its presence and immediately he fell to the ground. As he did, he heard the voice of the Lord Jesus speaking to him. Though his companions heard the sound of someone's voice, they could not distinguish what Jesus was saying, and they were not blinded by the light. Without Saul having any awareness, the Father had ordered his steps that day to have an encounter with the Living Lord Jesus. None of his companions shared in that encounter – it was a personal encounter between Jesus and Saul. It was not a gradual encounter; it was sudden and momentary. In a brief moment Saul knew four things.

First, he now knew firsthand that Jesus was alive. Saul may have possibly been in the crowd the day Jesus was crucified five years earlier. He had refused to accept the testimony from the believers about the resurrection of Jesus. His disbelief had been central in his persecution of the believers. But now he knew that Jesus was alive.

. . .

Therefore, second, he knew that he had been wrong. He had denied Jesus and been a part of murdering innocent Christians. He was immediately overcome by his sin. There was no hiding his sin in this light. There was no denying his sin. Jesus had just totally illuminated all the darkness of his sin. He had no choice other than to repent – which was no small thing for this self-righteous Pharisee. Saul's encounter on that road, in some ways, is similar to the encounter that Isaiah describes in Isaiah 6, and John describes in Revelation 1. Each of them fell at the feet of Christ when they encountered His holiness and His righteousness. Each of them were overwhelmed by their own sinfulness. Each of them could do nothing but confess their sin and repent. Saul knew he was a sinner in need of a Savior and lying there in the dirt, he surrendered his life to Christ.

Third, he knew that everything about his life had to change – his mission, his pursuits, his ambition and his values. He knew everything had just changed. He could no longer chase after anything in his life that he had been pursuing – everything had been made different. He no longer sought the approval of others (the religious leaders); He sought the approval of only One (Jesus). He could no longer do anything he had been doing – all of his so-called good works and attempts at legalistic self-righteousness were all as filthy rags. He could no longer walk in those rags. He must now walk in the righteousness of Christ. His circle of friends (albeit probably a small circle) would have to change. The very ones that to this moment he had been persecuting would now become his circle of friends. He was a new person – the old had passed away (2 Corinthians 5:17).

Fourth, not only had his life just been transformed, but so had his purpose. This Hebrew of the Hebrews would become the apostle to the Gentiles. This one who had made it his life focus to scatter and persecute the sheep would now be a shepherd. This enforcer of the law would now be a proclaimer of grace. He had now been transformed into a vessel of honor to be used by the Master (2 Timothy 2:20-21).

Saul had set out on his journey to arrest others, but instead, Jesus arrested him. He had set out in a religious pursuit, but instead, he had gained the righteousness of Christ -- all because of the grace, mercy and sovereign purpose of God! His had been a journey totally contrary to God's purpose, but now God had transformed the purpose to align with His sovereign plan.

. . .

And the same is true for us. Your journey through your wilderness may have begun out of your own selfish desires or ambition. Or it may have been driven by your rebellion against God. Or it may have begun as a result of someone else's rebellion. Or it may have arisen due to a circumstance that you had no control over. The journey may in fact be a path in a relationship or a decision that will result in you being led away from God – and the best that He desires for you. The fact of the matter is that whatever prompted the journey, God can – and will – use the journey for you to have a fresh encounter with Him and to experience the transformation that He intends for your life. It was a personal journey that day for Saul – hopefully his traveling companions were transformed on another day. It's a personal journey for you as well. He is going with you – every step of the way. And He will continue to do so… until He returns.

* * *

24

THE COURAGE OF ANANIAS

Now there was a believer in Damascus named Ananias. The Lord spoke to him in a vision, calling, "Ananias!"
"Yes, Lord!" he replied. The Lord said, "Go over to Straight Street, to the house of Judas. When you get there, ask for a man from Tarsus named Saul. He is praying to Me right now. I have shown him a vision of a man named Ananias coming in and laying hands on him so he can see again." "But Lord," exclaimed Ananias, "I've heard many people talk about the terrible things this man has done to the believers in Jerusalem! And he is authorized by the leading priests to arrest everyone who calls upon Your name." But the Lord said, "Go, for Saul is My chosen instrument to take My message to the Gentiles and to kings, as well as to the people of Israel. And I will show him how much he must suffer for My name's sake." So Ananias went and found Saul. He laid his hands on him and said, "Brother Saul, the Lord Jesus, who appeared to you on the road, has sent me so that you might regain your sight and be filled with the Holy Spirit." Instantly something like scales fell from Saul's eyes, and he regained his sight. Then he got up and was baptized. Afterward he ate some food and regained his strength. Saul stayed with the believers in Damascus for a few days.
Acts 9:10-19

* * *

On April 21, 1855, God prompted a Sunday School teacher in Boston by the name of Edward Kimball to visit a young man who was attending his Sunday School class. The young man wasn't attending the class willingly. His uncle had made it a condition of his employment as a shoe salesman. The boy would only get the job if he attended the class.

Edward Kimball's visit took place at the shoe store where the young man worked. Here is Kimball's account of the visit: *"When I was nearly there I began to wonder whether I ought to go in just then during business hours. I thought my call might embarrass the boy, and that when I went away the other clerks would ask who I was, and taunt him with my efforts in trying to make him a good boy. In the meantime I had passed the store, and, discovering this, I determined to make a dash for it, and have it over at once. I found him in the back part of the building wrapping up shoes. I went up to him at once, and putting my hand on his shoulder, I made what I felt afterwards was a very weak plea for Christ. I don't know just what words I used. I simply told him of Christ's love for him, and the love Christ wanted in return. That was all there was. It seemed the young man was just ready for the light that then broke upon him."*[1] Dwight L. Moody, a shoe salesman, surrendered his life to Christ that day. God went on to use D. L. Moody as an evangelist, publisher, pastor and the founder of the Moody Bible Institute to have far-reaching impact for the Kingdom that continues to this day. And God used a humble, unknown servant who had to work up the courage to go talk to Moody to set his feet on the right path. The same could also be said of another humble, otherwise unknown, servant of God by the name of Ananias.

Ananias was a follower of Jesus living in Damascus. We don't know how Ananias came to faith in Jesus. It may have been through the ministry of Jesus Himself, or through the ministry of the seventy-two that Jesus sent out. Possibly, he was one of those who were gathered in Jerusalem on the Day of Pentecost, or soon thereafter. He apparently was one of the more mature believers, and was recognized as a respected and trusted leader of the believers there in Damascus. He, together with the other believers in Damascus, were very familiar with the persecution that the believers were experiencing in Jerusalem. Word had also apparently already reached them that Saul was coming to Damascus to persecute and arrest the believers there. Ananias was very familiar with Saul's terrible reputation when God directed him to go to Saul. It is reasonable to imagine that Ananias and the other believers were terrified as they awaited Saul and his cohort, for they knew their lives might be lost for the sake of Christ. They were awaiting his arrival to the city with great dread.

Note what Ananias did. He made a point to tell God all about Saul, as if God wasn't fully aware! *"I've heard many people talk about the terrible things this man has done to the believers in Jerusalem! And he is authorized by the leading priests to arrest everyone who calls upon Your name."* As if to say, "God, You must not know all the facts about this man. Otherwise, surely You wouldn't be sending me to him!" Ananias showed his fear and anxiety here. He did not yet have unwavering trust in God. As a matter of fact, he reminds me of me! i suspect i would have said the same thing to God – just in case He had somehow forgotten or overlooked some of the details. After all, this guy was dangerous! Didn't God know that? Over the years, i have had some honest conversations with men and women who sensed God's call to carry the gospel to some pretty difficult places. They have shared some of the conversations that they have had with God. "Um…God…don't You know that country is closed to missionaries? Don't You know that Your people are persecuted in that nation? Don't You know what could happen to me, or to my family, if we go there, God?"

But God knows all about those people, just like He knew all about Saul. He told Ananias *"Go, for Saul is My chosen instrument to take My message to the Gentiles and to kings, as well as to the people of Israel. And I will show him how much he must suffer for My name's sake.""* God knew exactly who Saul was and gave Ananias the assurance that He was still in control. As a matter of fact, providence dictated that He would use this man to do incredible things for His kingdom. Saul, the chief of sinners, the persecutor of the church, was to be God's chosen means of bringing the gospel to great and small, Jew and Gentile alike.

Ananias was obedient. He appeared before Saul and had the great honor of laying his hands on this broken man in the name of the Holy Spirit. At that moment, the scales fell from Saul's eyes and he regained his sight. As a testimony to his new found faith in Christ, he was baptized, probably by the hand of Ananias himself. We then read that *"Saul stayed with the believers in Damascus for a few days."* Whether at that point Saul was the student or the teacher, we do not know. Perhaps he sat and learned at the feet of Ananias.

At this point, Ananias disappears from Luke's account and we do not hear any more about him. His role in the drama of Acts was brief, yet very significant. We see a man who wavered when he heard God's voice, yet despite his initial hesitation, he was faithful and obedient. While at first he thought he might have to correct God, in the end he submitted himself and his very life to God's call. God then used this man to further His purposes in launching the career of one of the most influential apostles. Ananias' small act of obedience, just like Edward Kimball's, led to a great harvest for the Kingdom.

. . .

And this is the lesson of Ananias for us to learn. There will be times when God will direct us through His Word in ways that seem contrary to our own reasoning. We do not know – and may never know – the full significance of what God intends. Let's not forget that our perspective is finite and limited. God's perspective is infinite, taking in all of history in a single glance. We need to trust Him, His Word, and His voice; trusting that He will never lead us astray. It will take courage – just like it did for Ananias and Edward Kimball. Courage that can only come through the confidence that we do not go alone; His Holy Spirit, who is within us, will go before us, will go with us and will empower us... every step of the way... until He returns.

---

1. from *Twice-Born Men: True Conversion Records of 100 Well-Known Men in All Ranks of Life* compiled by Hy Pickering

25

A HIDDEN JOURNEY IN THE WILDERNESS

Saul stayed with the believers in Damascus for a few days. And immediately he began preaching about Jesus in the synagogues, saying, "He is indeed the Son of God!" All who heard him were amazed. "Isn't this the same man who caused such devastation among Jesus' followers in Jerusalem?" they asked. "And didn't he come here to arrest them and take them in chains to the leading priests?" Saul's preaching became more and more powerful, and the Jews in Damascus couldn't refute his proofs that Jesus was indeed the Messiah. After a while some of the Jews plotted together to kill him. They were watching for him day and night at the city gate so they could murder him, but Saul was told about their plot. So during the night, some of the other believers lowered him in a large basket through an opening in the city wall. When Saul arrived in Jerusalem, he tried to meet with the believers, but they were all afraid of him.
Acts 9:19-26

* * *

Luke writes that Saul stayed with the believers in Damascus for a few days following the day that Ananias laid his hands upon him, and he regained his sight. Luke also tells us that Saul arrived in Jerusalem after the believers in Damascus lowered him through an opening in the city wall. There is an important part of the narrative that the Holy Spirit chose to tell us through Saul himself, and not through Luke. Saul tells us that *"it was not until three years later that I finally went to Jerusalem..."* (Galatians 1:18). That means that three years transpired between verse 19 and verse 26. Saul also writes *"I went away into Arabia and later returned to the city of Damascus"* (Galatians 1:17). That means that somewhere between verse 21 and verse 23 Saul was in Arabia and then returned to Damascus. We don't know if that was for the full three years, but it was apparently for a long portion of it. So what was he doing and why did Luke leave a three year gap in his narrative?

Apparently, Saul only remained in Damascus initially for a matter of days – long enough for his sight and strength to be regained (Acts 9:18-19). During those initial days, Saul was already boldly proclaiming that Jesus, the One whose followers he had been persecuting, was in fact the Son of God. He did not delay in bearing witness to the grace and mercy of God. His witness was immediate – and the Jews, both believers and non-believers alike, were amazed by the conspicuous transformation in his life. But after a few days, the Lord led Saul on a wilderness journey into Arabia so that He might prepare and equip Saul for the work He had chosen for him to do. Though Saul had been an ardent student of the Word under the teaching of the religious scholars, there was much that needed to be clarified before he could effectively minister as an apostle. And if Saul was going to be His apostle to carry the Good News to the Gentiles, he needed to be taught firsthand by Jesus. Remember, the apostles did not have benefit of the written New Testament as we do – they were the writers of that New Testament under the direction of the Holy Spirit. And they were writing what they had seen and heard from Jesus. It's interesting to note that the duration of this time in Arabia is approximately three years, similar to the amount of time that Jesus spent discipling His other apostles.

Though the Holy Spirit did not lead the writers of the New Testament to tell us many of the details about Saul's time in Arabia, we know that it pleased God *"to reveal His Son to me so that I would proclaim the Good News about Jesus to the Gentiles. When this happened, I did not rush out to consult with any human being. Nor did I go up to Jerusalem to consult with those who were apostles before I was. Instead, I went away into Arabia..."* (Galatians 1:16-17). And throughout his time in Arabia, Jesus was his Teacher. Saul explained, *"I received my message from no human source, and no one taught me. Instead, I received it by direct revelation from Jesus Christ"* (Galatians 1:12). Later, Saul (now the apostle Paul) wrote to the believers in Corinth, *"I have traveled on many long journeys. I have faced danger from rivers and from robbers. I have faced danger from my own people, the Jews, as well as from the Gentiles. I have faced danger in the cities, in the deserts, and on the seas. And I have faced danger from men who claim to be believers but are not. I have worked hard and long, enduring many sleepless nights. I have been hungry and thirsty and have often gone without food. I have shivered in the cold, without enough clothing to keep me warm"* (2 Corinthians 11:26-27) Some of these details refer to his missionary journeys, but some, such as the flooding rivers, the danger of robbers, the danger in the deserts, the cold and the lack of food may very well refer to the three years in Arabia. As Jesus led Saul on his wilderness journey with Him, it is very likely that it included time at Mount Sinai (Galatians 4:25). It is also most likely that Jesus led Saul to evangelize as he journeyed through the wilderness of Arabia. Jesus often sent out His apostles to preach and perform miracles throughout His earthly ministry It would be reasonable to believe He followed a similar pattern with Saul. Thus, Saul was already a "marked man" when he returned to Damascus.

Saul is a reminder to each of us that often Jesus will take us on a wilderness journey with Him in order to prepare us and equip us for the task that He is placing before us. There are things that He can only teach us when we are one-on-One with Him in the deserts, or the floods, or the difficulties of a wilderness journey. He alone determines how long the journey will take and where it will lead. Though He is using the time in the wilderness to prepare us for what He has in store after the wilderness, He also has work for us right there in the midst of the wilderness! Through the preparation and the work, He is teaching us truths we can only learn directly from Him. Though Saul was already a bold witness before Jesus led him out into the wilderness of Arabia, he returned to Damascus as a vessel prepared and ready to be used by the Master for every good work (2 Timothy 2:21).

Also, as we have already seen, there is not much recorded in Scripture about this journey. That should serve as a reminder to us that often the wilderness journey that God leads us in, or permits us to travel, is one that is personal and private. It is an intimate journey between our Lord and us. That's not to say that we don't bear witness and bring glory to God as Saul did. But it is to say that our Lord knows us, and knows our frame, better than we know ourselves. He knows just what we need. Allow Him to draw you close in the journey. Allow Him to remove the dross from your life and refine you to be that vessel that is prepared and useful to Him.

Prior to that initial day on the road to Damascus, Saul's personal ambition had been all wrapped up in what people thought about him. He had built that ambition over a lifetime. He wanted the early Christians to fear him for his ferocity. He wanted the Jews to admire him for his piety. He wanted the Jewish leaders to respect him for his fervency. He wanted God to accept him for his solemnity. But all of that changed. Some of it changed instantly at the moment of his salvation, but some of it changed through a work of sanctification, as he journeyed with Jesus through the wilderness of Arabia. By his own admission, Saul ceased being a "people pleaser". He wrote, *"No, I am trying to please God. If I was still trying to please people, I would not be Christ's servant"* (Galatians 1:10). He realized that he stood before an audience of One – the One who had chosen him, called him, extended His undeserved mercy to him (Galatians 1:15), and led him through a wilderness to prepare him. He knew that his relationship with Christ was not because of His efforts. He knew that his "righteous" deeds were but filthy rags (Isaiah 64:6).

When Saul returned to Damascus, his preaching was so powerful that the Jews could not refute him. It wasn't ferocity, or piety or fervency that they saw. His power and authority came from the fact that, like Peter and the other disciples, he had been with Jesus (Acts 4:13).

Yes, his Lord made a way of escape through the city wall of Damascus, but perhaps even more importantly He allowed him to walk with Him through the trials and challenges of a wilderness journey – all so that the Father's mission and purpose would be fulfilled. And that same God will also lead you and i through each and every step of our way… until He returns.

* * *

26

AN OPENING IN THE WALL

After a while some of the Jews plotted together to kill him. They were watching for him day and night at the city gate so they could murder him, but Saul was told about their plot. So during the night, some of the other believers lowered him in a large basket through an opening in the city wall.
Acts 9:23-25

* * *

When Saul returned to Damascus, the Jews soon plotted together to kill him. The "hunter", Saul, had now become the hunted. Having been an ardent persecutor of Christians, he was fully aware of all of the means that were at his "hunters'" disposal. He may have actually trained some of these Jews in the best way to capture the Christians. He could anticipate the details of the next steps in the playbook of the plot against him. He had written the playbook! Saul was a brilliant man. He probably had "plays" in his playbook that these men had never thought of. It would have been very easy for him to be overconfident in his own knowledge and his own ability to thwart the plans of those who were plotting against him. He easily could have determined to rely on his own ability to overcome the problem himself.

Jesus had appeared to Saul personally on the road to Damascus. He had just returned from almost three years in the Arabian wilderness being led in a one-on-One journey with the Son of God. He was on a first name basis with the Creator of the universe. He could have begun to believe that he was invincible – kind of like a spiritual "Iron Man". He could have developed a spiritual arrogance that nothing or no one could defeat him by virtue of his spiritual position.

Do i hear you saying that either or both of those positions would have been silly for him to take? Well, i mention them both because they are positions that we, as believers, have been known to take. When we encounter a difficulty or a challenge in life, too often our first instinct is to fight it off in our own ability or make our own plans. It may be a health issue, a financial setback, a personal attack, or even a spiritual attack – and our first recourse is to try and overcome it "our way". We're not going to "bother" God with it. We can deal with it on our own. Our wit, wisdom and strength will get us through.

Or perhaps, we take the "super-Christian" approach of "name it and claim it". We believe that since we are a child of God, nothing can overtake us or overcome us because we have special privileges. And if something does overcome us, we blame God because it must be His fault, because as His child we are supposed to be exempt from life's difficulties. As a result, we do nothing, believing we will miraculously escape our problems. But Saul himself (later as Paul) counted it a privilege to suffer for the sake of Christ. As a matter of fact, he says *"everyone who wants to live a godly life in Christ Jesus will suffer persecution"* (2 Timothy 3:12).

And as the writer of the letter to the Roman believers, Paul wrote the truth that Jesus had taught him: *"The Holy Spirit helps us in our weakness. For example, we don't know what God wants us to pray for. But the Holy Spirit prays for us with groanings that cannot be expressed in words. And the Father who knows all hearts knows what the Spirit is saying, for the Spirit pleads for us believers in harmony with God's own will. And we know that God causes everything to work together for the good of those who love God and are called according to His purpose for them"* (Romans 8:26-28). The apostle John did likewise when he wrote, *"And we are confident that He hears us whenever we ask for anything that pleases Him. And since we know He hears us when we make our requests, we also know that He will give us what we ask for"* (1 John 5:14-15). And Jesus Himself said, *"But if you remain in Me and My words remain in you, you may ask for anything you want, and it will be granted!"* (John 15:7). In all three instances, the Lord tells us that if we ask according to His Word and His will, we can walk assuredly in His answer. Years ago, i heard Dr. Charles Stanley say, *"If God tells you to run your head through a brick wall, you start running and trust Him to make a hole in that wall."* The key is what

God has said – and once we know what He has said, trusting Him to make the way to bring it about.

Jesus had said that Saul was His chosen instrument to take His *"message to the Gentiles and to kings, as well as to the people of Israel"* (Acts 9:15). Saul could walk confidently knowing that as long as he continued in obedience according to the Lord's will that nothing could defeat him until that work was accomplished. And God would make a "hole" even where it otherwise seemed impossible. In Saul's situation, God made an opening in the city wall for him to escape.

As i write this, i am running head-first toward a wall. God has given me a clear promise through His Word. In recent weeks, He has been affirming His promise almost every day through His Word and in so many other ways. In my own strength and according to my own ability, it is an impossible task. i am not running toward the wall because i think it is a good idea. In my own wisdom, i think it is a terrible idea. But my wife and i believe with all our hearts that it is what God has told us to do. And He has promised that in His perfect timing and in His perfect way, He will bring it about. So the question before us is – do we trust Him at His word? And if so, are we willing to charge ahead according to His word? Do we trust that when we arrive at the wall He will make the opening? It won't happen through my own ability. It won't happen simply because i am His child. It will only happen if we are walking by faith, trusting Him at His word.

That's what Saul did. And God made an opening in the wall. The result was that the Good News was preached to the nations. God's work was accomplished in His way according to His word and for His glory. That was true two thousand years ago in Damascus, and it's true today. And it will continue to be true… until He returns.

* * *

27

WHOSE BARNABAS ARE YOU?

When Saul arrived in Jerusalem, he tried to meet with the believers, but they were all afraid of him. They did not believe he had truly become a believer! Then Barnabas brought him to the apostles and told them how Saul had seen the Lord on the way to Damascus and how the Lord had spoken to Saul. He also told them that Saul had preached boldly in the name of Jesus in Damascus. So Saul stayed with the apostles and went all around Jerusalem with them, preaching boldly in the name of the Lord. He debated with some Greek-speaking Jews, but they tried to murder him. When the believers heard about this, they took him down to Caesarea and sent him away to Tarsus, his hometown. The church then had peace throughout Judea, Galilee, and Samaria, and it became stronger as the believers lived in the fear of the Lord. And with the encouragement of the Holy Spirit, it also grew in numbers.
Acts 9:26-31

* * *

When Saul arrived in Jerusalem the believers were afraid of him. They thought his witness was a deception in order to entrap them. They had known him before he had left Jerusalem. And they knew that he had left Jerusalem in order to persecute the believers in Damascus. They knew what he was capable of. The believers, including the apostles, questioned whether he was even a believer. But on top of that, he was calling himself an apostle. What right did he have to call himself an apostle? He hadn't walked with Jesus – or so they thought. So they would not accept him into their fellowship.

· · ·

That is, until Barnabas took action. Luke tells us that Barnabas *"was a good man, full of the Holy Spirit and strong in faith"* (Acts 11:24). We have already seen that he was selfless and generous as he sold his property and gave all of the proceeds to the church (Acts 4:36-37). Barnabas was very quickly seen within the newly-developing church as a leader – but this "son of encouragement" was more than that – he was a leader-maker. He was willing to take a risk for the sake of the Kingdom. He was willing to take the risk and sell his property, and he was willing to take the risk and reach out to Saul. He was willing to put his riches and his reputation at stake for the cause of Christ. He not only reached out to Saul; he put his arm around him and drew him close.

If you have read my other books in this series, you have heard me speak of a man by the name of Bryan Evans, who was a Barnabas in my life for a number of years. God brought Bryan into my life to be a part of the journey that led to my salvation in Christ. Bryan reached out to me as a friend and a discipler. Initially, because of the place where i was walking, i saw him as somewhat extreme in his relationship with Christ, but i never questioned the genuineness of his faith. When, as a new believer, i was seeking God's direction for my life, he volunteered to meet with me each morning before the crack of dawn to pray together. As i followed the Lord's leading to enter into pastoral ministry, Bryan was there to pray for me and encourage me every step along the way. When, as a pastor, i needed someone to lead through some challenging projects, he was there to stand in the gap with me and lead. i rarely saw Bryan when he wasn't surrounded by several men in whom he was pouring his life. Bryan, like Barnabas, was a leader-maker – and though time and distance now separate us, i'm sure he still is!

Barnabas convinced Peter and James (the half-brother of Jesus) to meet with Saul. Saul tells us in Galatians 1:18 that he did not meet with any of the other apostles at that time. But over the next fifteen days, he told Peter, James – and Barnabas – about the work that God had done in his life over the prior three years from the moment of his salvation until the current time. In particular, he told them about the time that he had spent following Jesus in the wilderness of Arabia. Bear in mind, there is no indication that Jesus appeared to him bodily, or in any way other than how he appeared to him on the Road to Damascus. However, Jesus discipled Saul – in whatever way He chose to do so – in the truths that He had taught the other apostles and in the truths that a newly forming church needed to know. By the conclusion of Saul's time with Peter and James, they were convinced in the veracity of his testimony and the genuineness of his transformation, as well as his apostleship.

Saul accompanied some of the leaders of the Jerusalem church – at least, Peter, James and Barnabas – as they went all around the city, *preaching boldly in the name of the Lord*. As they preached, many of the Jews recognized Saul. In particular the Hellenistic Jews – those who had engineered the trial and death of Stephen – recognized him as one who had been one of them. They began to debate with Saul, and he may have sensed a need to take up the witness of Stephen, in whose death he had been complicit. The Jews soon began to make attempts to murder him, but God had other plans for Saul. He tells us through Luke, "*I was praying in the Temple and fell into a trance. I saw a vision of Jesus saying to me, 'Hurry! Leave Jerusalem, for the people here won't accept your testimony about Me.' 'But Lord,' I argued, 'they certainly know that in every synagogue I imprisoned and beat those who believed in You. And I was in complete agreement when your witness Stephen was killed. I stood by and kept the coats they took off when they stoned him.' But the Lord said to me, 'Go, for I will send you far away to the Gentiles!'*" (Acts 22:17-21).

Knowing the threat against Saul, the believers aided him in making his way to Caesarea so that he could travel to his hometown of Tarsus – probably to tell his family and hometown friends about Jesus. Though Scripture is silent on the point, i would conjecture that Barnabas was right there with him every step of the way. He was with Saul when the Jews were debating with him, and he was there accompanying Saul to Caesarea. Barnabas didn't "make leaders" from a distance. He was there with him – with his arm around him – walking with him through "thick and thin". Such was the son of encouragement!

We'll pick back up with Saul in chapter 32 of this book, after a seven year period of time will have passed, but in the meantime Tarsus became his "base of ministry" as he began to carry the gospel to the Gentiles. He evangelized in the regions of Syria and Cilicia (Galatians 1:21), planting churches as he went (Acts 15:41). Also it is very likely that some of the trials that he writes about in 2 Corinthians 11:24-36 occurred during this period, including at least a half dozen beatings at the hands of the Jews, as well as the Romans (at the urging of the Jews). He apparently was shipwrecked twice during that period. Those seven years were anything but a "cakewalk". Through those years, the gospel was being preached and the Kingdom advanced among the Gentiles long before he and Barnabas were reunited in Tarsus (Acts 11:25).

. . .

Though Barnabas and Saul were apart for those seven years, God had used Barnabas to encourage and help strengthen Saul in his faith. He had introduced him to the apostles, enabling Saul to go out with the endorsement of the Jerusalem church. He had been the friend and companion that Saul needed in that season – and he would be again. A "Barnabas" may not walk with us permanently, but his/her efforts on our behalf will always have lasting impact. Everyone needs at least one Barnabas in our lives. Thankfully, often God brings more than one. And He, in turn, gives us opportunity to be a Barnabas in others' lives. Be that Barnabas that God has equipped you to be, and called you to be. Step up boldly and courageously as He brings that one across your path, being that friend and that encourager that *"sticks closer than a brother"* or a sister (Proverbs 18:24). God has so ordered your journey to prepare you as a Barnabas, and to bring that one across your path who is in need of a Barnabas. Don't miss the invitation!

The seven years that followed, while Saul was in Tarsus, Syria and Cilicia, may have been a time of "peace" in Jerusalem, Judea and Samaria, but it wasn't a season of complacency. The church grew and strengthened. God raised up new workmen to continue the work. Barnabas was there to encourage those new workmen. God is still raising up new workmen today – workmen for you to encourage – and He will continue to do so… until He returns.

* * *

28

IT IS WHAT IT IS, OR IS IT?

> *Meanwhile, Peter traveled from place to place, and he came down to visit the believers in the town of Lydda. There he met a man named Aeneas, who had been paralyzed and bedridden for eight years. Peter said to him, "Aeneas, Jesus Christ heals you! Get up, and roll up your sleeping mat!" And he was healed instantly. Then the whole population of Lydda and Sharon saw Aeneas walking around, and they turned to the Lord. There was a believer in Joppa named Tabitha (which in Greek is Dorcas). She was always doing kind things for others and helping the poor. About this time she became ill and died. Her body was washed for burial and laid in an upstairs room. But the believers had heard that Peter was nearby at Lydda, so they sent two men to beg him, "Please come as soon as possible!" So Peter returned with them; and as soon as he arrived, they took him to the upstairs room. The room was filled with widows who were weeping and showing him the coats and other clothes Dorcas had made for them. But Peter asked them all to leave the room; then he knelt and prayed. Turning to the body he said, "Get up, Tabitha." And she opened her eyes! When she saw Peter, she sat up! He gave her his hand and helped her up. Then he called in the widows and all the believers, and he presented her to them alive. The news spread through the whole town, and many believed in the Lord.*
> Acts 9:32-42

* * *

Over the last fifty years, the idiom "it is what it is" has sprung forth from the fatalists in our midst who firmly believe that we are victims -- victims of our circumstances, our situations, our upbringing, our medical condition, etc. It communicates that we have resigned ourselves to the belief that our situation is immutable, and nothing or no one can change it. It is used to convey a sense of resignation, helplessness and hopelessness. "That's just the way I am." "That's just the way my spouse is." "That's just the way my kids are." "That's just how people like me are treated." "That's just the way the system works." "It's always been this way, and it will never change."

This journey with Peter is a reminder that we will never know the truth of any situation until we have heard from Jesus. In His world, the only thing that is immutable is that sin separates us from a Holy God. And He Himself made the way – the only way -- whereby we might overcome that immutable truth. He is not dead; He's alive. He is not distant. He is not silent. He is not weak. His arm has not grown short. He is mighty and He is able to save – spiritually, physically, and emotionally. Throughout His earthly ministry, Jesus healed. He raised the dead. He stilled storms. He met physical needs. He was the King of the reality that it is NOT what it is, if Jesus says it isn't. And as Peter shows us – He still is! What He began to do through His earthly ministry, He still does. He is still full of surprises – for individuals, for families, for churches, and even for nations.

John Piper writes, *"There is a pride in the predictions of human beings based on human calculations of human knowledge about human factors. There is a pride in such predictions that God does not like – even when made by Christians! It is a practical atheism. It does not allow for the Living Lord of the universe who turns things around – out of the blue!"* It's true today, and it was true in the first century. Imagine what it must have been like for the believers in the first century. Jesus was gone. The religious leaders were still in charge. They were condoning – and initiating – persecution of the church. The Romans were still in control of the country. Everyone was against these followers of Jesus! They were battling the belief that it is what it is.

Peter was in the town of Lydda – about twenty miles northwest of Jerusalem. He was there to visit the church in the town. It had either been started by residents of the town who had been in Jerusalem at Pentecost nine years earlier, or by believers who scattered from Jerusalem after the stoning of Stephen five years earlier. Peter had come to town to encourage them in their faith. He met a man by the name of Aeneas who had been paralyzed for eight years. Aeneas had heard of the healing miracles of Jesus when He was travelling the Judean hillside. But Aeneas hadn't needed healing when Jesus was in the hillside. Today was a different matter, but Jesus was no longer there. So, "it was what it was". Imagine the hopelessness of this one who had been bedridden for eight years! Then – out of the blue – Peter came passing by and said, *"Aeneas, Jesus Christ heals you! Get up, and roll up your sleeping mat!"* Instantly, Aeneas was healed! Imagine the joy. Imagine his euphoria! The whole town saw him walking around, but i would venture that was after he jumped up and down in the air! Jesus may have been out of sight, but He sure wasn't gone. It no longer "was what it was". Jesus had healed Aeneas – for the glory of the Father, and for the spread of the gospel. We read, *"the whole population turned to the Lord."* Not only was one life transformed, but an entire town! And the word spread from there... another ten miles toward the coast to the city of Joppa.

Tabitha was already a believer. She apparently had an active ministry to the widows of Joppa as a couturier. She had become ill and died. She was already being prepared for burial when the believers sent two men to fetch Peter. The entire region knew about how Jesus had raised Lazarus from the dead. Now they had heard how He had healed Aeneas through Peter, and they immediately believed that Jesus could still raise the dead. They believed that "it was NOT what it was" – because of Jesus. And God's plan was for Tabitha to "get up!" God responded to the faith of the believers and the obedience of Peter in a way that aligned with His perfect plan.

This is the only instance recorded in Scripture where Jesus worked through Peter to raise someone from the dead. Jesus hadn't called Peter to an itinerant ministry of raising the dead to life; He had called him to make disciples. In this instance, God chose for this one to be raised from the dead. His plan will not always look the same. His plan will not always be to bring about physical healing – but it will always be about bringing glory to the Father. If the healing doesn't occur on this side of eternity, it will always occur on the other side. Don't forget that Jesus sees with an eternal perspective and He works all things *"together for the good of those who love God and are called according to His purpose for them"* (Romans 8:28), and always for His glory. Trust Him to do the same thing in your circumstance and in your life.

Jesus is as much alive today as He was in the first century. He is able to do a lot more today than we are often willing to see or receive. He has surprises in store for us of which we have never dreamed. There were two characteristics that were evidenced in that early church that we have seemingly lost today. If we would see Jesus work in the same power He demonstrated that day in Lydda and in Joppa, perhaps He is waiting for us to turn to Him in the same way. Luke wrote, *"So the church throughout all Judea and Galilee and Samaria had peace and was being built up. And walking in the fear of the Lord and in the comfort of the Holy Spirit, it multiplied* (Acts 9:31 ESV). First, they walked in a holy fear of the Lord. They believed in a Lord God who is infinitely holy and infinitely powerful. They knew that He was not to be trifled with. They had seen the storms stilled. They had seen Ananias and Sapphira fall dead. You do not make light of this God. He is the "I AM that I AM", and He is greater than whatever is.

Second, they walked in the comfort of the Holy Spirit. That comfort is much like being in the eye of a hurricane. In the eye you are experiencing a calmness and a peace in the midst of mighty power. We walk in the center of a fearsome power, but as we do, we can have the calm and confidence that we are in His presence. When we walk in that place, there is no circumstance or situation that can withstand His power. "It is what it is" can't stand up to "I AM that I AM". He alone is an immutable force… and so He will be… until He returns!

* * *

29

HE GOES BEFORE US

In Caesarea there lived a Roman army officer named Cornelius, who was a captain of the Italian Regiment. He was a devout, God-fearing man, as was everyone in his household. He gave generously to the poor and prayed regularly to God. One afternoon about three o'clock, he had a vision in which he saw an angel of God coming toward him. "Cornelius!" the angel said. Cornelius stared at him in terror. "What is it, sir?" he asked the angel.
And the angel replied, "Your prayers and gifts to the poor have been received by God as an offering! Now send some men to Joppa, and summon a man named Simon Peter. He is staying with Simon, a tanner who lives near the seashore." As soon as the angel was gone, Cornelius called two of his household servants and a devout soldier, one of his personal attendants. He told them what had happened and sent them off to Joppa.
Acts 10:1-8

* * *

Approximately nine years have passed since the Day of Pentecost. Saul has just recently departed for Tarsus. God has just raised Tabitha from the dead through the ministry of Peter, and he is still about thirty miles away in Joppa. The door of faith has been opened for the Jews in Jerusalem and Judea, as well as the Samaritans, and the Father has empowered Peter to use the "keys of the Kingdom" to unleash His Spirit to dwell among those peoples (as we saw in chapter 21 of this book). God is now preparing to open the remaining door to the Gentiles, first here in Caesarea through Peter, then soon to be followed in Syria and Cilicia through Saul.

. . .

God's ways are most definitely not our ways (Isaiah 55:8). He will accomplish His purpose in His way (Isaiah 46:9-11). He has the capacity to be at work in all places at all times. He is not confined by space or time (Psalm 139:7-12). He is always at work preparing us for what He is preparing for us. And this day in Joppa and Caesarea was no exception. We'll look in our next chapter at how God was preparing Peter at Simon the tanner's house in Joppa (Acts 9:43). While at the same time, He was preparing for the work in Caesarea.

Most of the Roman soldiers in the Iudaean province were locally recruited. They tended to be more like mercenaries than professional soldiers. But the Centurion – Cornelius – led a contingent of one hundred professional soldiers that had been recruited and trained in Rome. This was an elite fighting force that was stationed in Caesarea because that is where Pilate and those who ruled the land lived. Remember that Romans, for the most part, were polytheistic pagans – worshipping many gods. Luke tells us that Cornelius was "God-fearing". He was not a Jewish proselyte, but he apparently prayed to Jehovah God and worshiped Him, albeit perhaps not exclusively. Interestingly, he was probably never taught by a rabbi as to "how" to pray to God. He prayed as best as he knew how – with a sincere heart. Also, he, uncharacteristically as an officer of the oppressing military force, gave gifts of charity to the oppressed poor. And as Luke points out, he did so generously.

In many respects, Cornelius was a model of religious respectability. On the outside he looked like many today, and on the inside he also looked like many – he did not yet have a true relationship with God. But unlike many today, he knew that his religious devotion was not sufficient to save him. Many today are satisfied that their character and good works will earn them a place in heaven, because they have no concept of their own sin or of God's grace. Cornelius, on the other hand did, and he was asking God to show him the way of salvation. God, by His grace, chose to hear the prayer of Cornelius. He will always respond to the prayer from the heart that is sincerely seeking Him.

Warren Wiersbe tells the story of John Wesley, who in many ways resembled Cornelius. *"Wesley was a religious man, a church member, a minister and the son of a minister. He belonged to a religious club at Oxford, the purpose of which was the perfecting of the Christian life. He served as a mission-*

ary, but even as he preached to others, he had no assurance of his own salvation. On May 24, 1738, he reluctantly attended a small meeting in London where someone was reading aloud from Martin Luther's writings on the Book of Romans. 'About a quarter before nine,' Wesley wrote in his personal journal, 'while he was describing the change which God works in the heart through faith in Christ, I felt my heart strangely warmed.'" At that moment, Wesley surrendered his life to Christ, trusting Him alone for salvation. He stepped from religious beliefs into a relationship with Christ. The result was a revival that swept many into the Kingdom of God!

God sent one of His heavenly "soldiers" – an angel, and Cornelius immediately snapped to attention. The angel instructed Cornelius to send for Peter. Being the good military man that he was, Cornelius immediately obeyed.

Peter was God's man for this assignment. Very possibly, there were others who were closer to Caesarea than Peter. Philip may have already made his way back up the Mediterranean coast from Gaza. Saul had just sailed out of Caesarea not that long ago, and God could have orchestrated a visit while Saul was still in the city. And yet, God's plan involved Peter. Remember, Peter "held" the "keys to the Kingdom". The Father had ordained for him to be the one to open the door of faith to the Gentiles. And God was simultaneously at work in Peter's heart to prepare him to do just that. It would take an adjustment in Peter's life. It would require him to step out of his "comfort zone". It wouldn't have been as great of a stretch for Saul, or even Philip. But God's work wasn't about the worker's comfort. That's why God does not, most often, call the equipped, He equips the called (Hebrews 13:21). That's why He empowers us through His Spirit – the same Spirit who goes before us to make a way.

Most of you who are reading this book would be considered Gentiles – just like me. i am certain that as you look back on your life, you can "see" spiritual markers where God was divinely orchestrating events that He would use in your life for you to enter into His salvation – through His saving grace. But it is worthy to point out that this moment in Caesarea – and in Joppa – God was at work preparing the way for the door of faith to be opened to us. The obedience of Cornelius put in motion the means through which the door of faith was opened to you – and to me. Obedience that was as simple as sending two servants and a soldier to bring a message to Peter. In many respects, for a person of Cornelius' rank and position that was a small thing. But the ripple effect touches you and me today.

God is still at work preparing us for what He is preparing for us. No matter how small – or large – it may seem, trust Him and take the step. We have no idea what the ripple effects will be down the way... until He returns.

* * *

30

BEING PREPARED FOR WHAT'S AHEAD

The next day as Cornelius's messengers were nearing the town, Peter went up on the flat roof to pray. It was about noon, and he was hungry. But while a meal was being prepared, he fell into a trance. He saw the sky open, and something like a large sheet was let down by its four corners. In the sheet were all sorts of animals, reptiles, and birds. Then a voice said to him, "Get up, Peter; kill and eat them." "No, Lord," Peter declared. "I have never eaten anything that our Jewish laws have declared impure and unclean." But the voice spoke again: "Do not call something unclean if God has made it clean." The same vision was repeated three times. Then the sheet was suddenly pulled up to heaven. Peter was very perplexed. What could the vision mean? Just then the men sent by Cornelius found Simon's house. Standing outside the gate, they asked if a man named Simon Peter was staying there. Meanwhile, as Peter was puzzling over the vision, the Holy Spirit said to him, "Three men have come looking for you. Get up, go downstairs, and go with them without hesitation. Don't worry, for I have sent them." So Peter went down and said, "I'm the man you are looking for. Why have you come?" They said, "We were sent by Cornelius, a Roman officer. He is a devout and God-fearing man, well respected by all the Jews. A holy angel instructed him to summon you to his house so that he can hear your message." So Peter invited the men to stay for the night. The next day he went with them, accompanied by some of the brothers from Joppa.
Acts 10:9-23

* * *

God's timing is perfect – in His preparation and His invitation. The messengers from Cornelius were already en route and would soon arrive. Peter was on the roof resting before the noon meal. He was hungry. His stomach was probably growling. He began to dream about food. So God spoke to him in a language that would clearly speak to him at that moment. God was preparing Peter to not only receive the messengers, but also, to receive their invitation – which was truly His invitation. And God completed His preparation just as the messengers arrived.

As i write this, i am mindful of a personal experience that occurred just last week. Ten days ago, God began to stir my wife's and my hearts regarding a change in direction that we believed He was wanting to make within our small group. We planned to discuss it with the leaders of our group over our weekly meal that immediately precedes our discussion time. We love the members of our group and our leaders and wanted to make sure that the change truly was being Spirit-led and not "Ken and LaVonne led". Two hours before the starting time of our group, i received a call from our leader. God was stirring his heart that we needed to make a change. He was calling to see what we thought and what that new direction might be. He also was thinking that we needed to make a change that very night. Wasn't that a coincidence? NOT! We all immediately knew that God was speaking to all of our hearts and confirming the change of direction, and had already given us the plan of what that new direction was to be. Only God can orchestrate events with such perfect timing! You, too, have probably experienced similar "coincidences" in your life. The reality is that when we are walking according to the Spirit of God, there are no "coincidences". Our steps are being ordered by a Sovereign God who has a perfect plan, and He is orchestrating events for the accomplishment of that plan. Such was the case that day in Joppa.

As Peter's dream began, he knew right away that the voice that was speaking to him was that of the Lord. It is interesting that his first response was *"No, Lord!"* That answer reminds us of the same Peter who we all know never hesitated to speak up to Jesus. Do you remember the night in the upper room when Jesus was washing His disciples' feet? He came to Peter, and he refused, saying, *"No, Lord, You will never wash my feet"* (John 13:8). Though a lot had occurred in Peter's life since that night in the upper room, his flesh nature still was given to responding in a similar way. That is a reminder to each of us that we also can quickly be influenced by our flesh nature. Our initial response too often is born out of our flesh and not out of our spirit. We, like Peter, need to make sure that our response is Spirit-led. Also, we need to be mindful that when we know that the Lord is leading us to do something, the response can never be "No, Lord". Those two words can't go together in one sentence. Either

Jesus is Lord, and the answer is "yes", or the answer is "no" because He is not our Lord.

God will always reveal His will and purpose to us in a way that will enable us to understand. He is not in His heaven hoping we will figure it out. He will make it abundantly clear in a "language" that we will clearly understand. If we are in any doubt, all we need to do is ask Him to give us eyes and ears to see and hear Him clearly. Too often, the reason we are not clear is because we don't like what He has told us to do – not unlike Peter's first response.

The distinction between foods that were clean and those that were unclean was a major point of contention between Jews and Gentiles – not only in that day, but also for the centuries that had passed before, and those that have passed since. In that light, the Lord was directing Peter in a truth that He had already taught His apostles one day in Galilee while He was with them. He had just rebuked the Pharisees for being more concerned about their food laws and ceremonial cleaning laws than they were about the condition of their hearts and truly honoring God. Then He had turned to the crowd and said, *"All of you listen," He said, "and try to understand. It's not what goes into your body that defiles you; you are defiled by what comes from your heart"* (Mark 7:14-15). Right after that, Jesus led His disciples into a house to get away from the crowd, and *"His disciples asked Him what He meant.... 'Can't you see that the food you put into your body cannot defile you? Food doesn't go into your heart, but only passes through the stomach and then goes into the sewer.' (By saying this, He declared that every kind of food is acceptable in God's eyes.) And then He added, 'It is what comes from inside that defiles you. For from within, out of a person's heart, come evil thoughts, sexual immorality, theft, murder, adultery, greed, wickedness, deceit, lustful desires, envy, slander, pride, and foolishness. All these vile things come from within; they are what defile you.'"* (Mark 7:17-23)

It is interesting to remember that Mark penned his Gospel account from the eyewitness testimony of Peter. The parenthetical note about the acceptability of "every kind of food" is an indication from Peter that he now knew that what Jesus had taught all of His disciples that day in Galilee was the same truth He had taught him through the dream this day in Joppa.

. . .

So here are the take-aways for us to carry with us in our journey… until He returns. First, we will never know the truth of any situation until we have heard from God. That which He calls clean, can never be unclean; and that which He calls unclean, can never be called clean. The world – or the religious leaders – don't set the rules, God does! Second, He will reveal His Truth, His purpose and His plan in a way that is clear, and in a way that is timely. When God has revealed a truth to you, be watchful – He is preparing to lead you into a situation where you will need to apply it! Third, the correct response to God when He directs is, "Yes, Lord!" – and never "no". He is preparing you and guiding you in what's ahead. Follow Him… because the messengers have come for you. They are at the door – and His time is now.

* * *

31

CAN ANYONE OBJECT?

They arrived in Caesarea the following day…. As Peter entered his home, Cornelius fell at his feet and worshiped him. But Peter pulled him up and said, "Stand up! I'm a human being just like you!" So they talked together and went inside, where many others were assembled. Peter told them, "You know it is against our laws for a Jewish man to enter a Gentile home like this or to associate with you. But God has shown me that I should no longer think of anyone as impure or unclean. So I came without objection as soon as I was sent for. Now tell me why you sent for me." Cornelius replied, "Four days ago I was praying in my house…. Suddenly, a man in dazzling clothes was standing in front of me. He told me, 'Cornelius, your prayer has been heard, and your gifts to the poor have been noticed by God! Now send messengers to Joppa, and summon a man named Simon Peter….' So I sent for you at once, and it was good of you to come. Now we are all here, waiting before God to hear the message the Lord has given you." Then Peter replied, "I see very clearly that God shows no favoritism. In every nation He accepts those who fear Him and do what is right. This is the message of Good News for the people of Israel – that there is peace with God through Jesus Christ, who is Lord of all…. He is the one all the prophets testified about, saying that everyone who believes in Him will have their sins forgiven through His name." Even as Peter was saying these things, the Holy Spirit fell upon all who were listening to the message. The Jewish believers who came with Peter were amazed that the gift of the Holy Spirit had been poured out on the Gentiles, too. For they heard them speaking in other tongues and praising God. Then Peter asked, "Can anyone object to their being baptized, now that they have received the Holy Spirit just as we did?" So he gave orders for them to be baptized in the name of Jesus Christ….
Acts 10:24-48

***

At the beginning of all of this, Cornelius did not have a saving relationship with God. He knew within his heart that there was one true God. He knew that the one true God was not any one of the countless gods that were recognized by his people, the Romans. The gospel had not yet come to the Romans. They were, what we would call today, an "unreached people group" – without knowledge of the gospel, or access to the gospel from within their own people. There was a growing desire within Cornelius' heart to know this one true God, and he began to search. He knew that he must search outside of his Roman people group.

Cornelius was like every one of us. His Creator created him with the innate need for relationship with Him. Cornelius was a successful officer within the greatest army that existed in the world at the time. The Romans dominated the known world. Cornelius had great reason to be content with what he had achieved in life. And yet, he knew that there must be more. God not only created him with the need; He also gave him a desire to seek that "something more". As Cornelius responded to that desire and began to diligently seek the one true God, He directed his steps – because God *"rewards those who sincerely seek Him"* (Hebrews 11:6). God directed him to seek the "Jehovah God" of the Jews. Cornelius began to pray to Him – not yet truly knowing Him. God answered his prayer and led him, in an extraordinary way, to the truth whereby he could enter into a personal saving relationship with the one true God. Then through this one, and the family and friends gathered with him, God opened the door of the gospel to the entire unreached people group (the Romans) and all of the unreached people groups that were or forever would be (the ends of the earth). As i've said before, God wasn't just hoping he would figure it out! He, who created him with the need to know God, gave him the desire to seek Him, and directed his path to find Him through His messenger, having also directed the steps of His messenger to seek him. Peter said, *"I see very clearly that God shows no favoritism. In every nation He accepts those who fear Him"* (verse 34-35). God was prepared to work wonders to bring Cornelius to the gospel – and the gospel to Cornelius.

Luke writes in verse 31 that Cornelius told Peter that the angel said to him, *"Cornelius, your prayer has been heard, and your gifts to the poor have been noticed by God! Now send messengers to Joppa, and summon a man named Simon Peter...."* This implies that the prayers were for God to send him what he needed in order to be saved. God accepted his prayer and his "groping for truth" in his life, and worked wonders to bring the saving message of the gospel to him. Paul describes this "groping for truth" when he says, "{God} *made from one man every nation of mankind to live on all the face of the earth, having determined their appointed times and the boundaries of their habitation, that they would seek God, if perhaps they might grope for Him and find Him, though He is not far from each one of us*" (Acts 17:26-27 NASB).

Through his journey to seek God, Cornelius shed any objection that he had toward God. He had shed the objections of false religion, self-sufficiency, selfish ambition, and pride. Through Peter's journey to follow His Lord, he had shed his objections of religious pride, ethnic bigotry and personal prejudice, such that he came to Cornelius *"without objection"*. Most importantly, God Himself had no objection! The Father sent the Son to redeem a lost world to Himself – peoples of every tribe, language and nation. There was, however, one objection – and that objection existed within, of all places, the body of believers – the church! Those who were the recipients of God's grace had somehow come to believe that they were uniquely qualified to receive God's grace, while others (the Gentiles) were not. Their objection was a direct contradiction to the idea of grace. Grace is unmerited favor extended to all. No one can have a corner on grace, or it ceases to be grace.

Our objections can be expressed passively or aggressively, or both. They can be voiced wantonly and selfishly through our self-serving remarks and actions – even within the church – that disparage being obedient to our Lord's commission for fear that it will take away from our own needs or wants being met. Or, even more often, they can be expressed passively, through our failure to be obedient to what God has called us to do. The first century church needed to shed its objections – and the same is true for us today.

First, no human being is excluded from the saving grace of the gospel. No one is less deserving than another. We are ALL undeserving! No one is to be spurned, shunned, rejected, or despised because of his/her ethnic origin or race or culture or physical traits. Followers of Jesus should have no part in the kind of renewed racism that is cropping up around our nation today. Second, within every ethnic people group around the world, there are people being prepared by God to seek Him as they call out through prayer to a God who they do not yet know. Therefore, we are to go! We cannot stay where we are. For some of us, it will be to the other side of the world; for others of us, it will be to the other side of the street. Cornelius would not have been saved if no one had taken the gospel to him. And no one will be saved today without the gospel. Also, we must be full of hope and expectancy that God is still at work making connections between the "groping" of unreached peoples and those willing to take the gospel to them.

The Jewish believers who came with Peter stood in amazement as the gift of the Holy Spirit was poured out on the Gentiles. Peter asked them, *"Can anyone object to their being baptized?"*

We, too, can no longer object. God is still working wonders to bring the unreached to the gospel – and the gospel to the unreached. So, let us wash our minds and our mouths of all racial slurs and ethnic put-downs, and be done with all alienating behaviors. Let's be the Peter for some waiting Cornelius. Let's be the good Samaritan for some ethnic outcast. And, let's be the hands of Christ for some untouchable leper... until He returns.

* * *

32

THE LITTLE CHURCH THAT COULD

Meanwhile, the believers who had been scattered during the persecution after Stephen's death traveled as far as Phoenicia, Cyprus, and Antioch of Syria. They preached the word of God, but only to Jews. However, some of the believers who went to Antioch from Cyprus and Cyrene began preaching to the Gentiles about the Lord Jesus. The power of the Lord was with them, and a large number of these Gentiles believed and turned to the Lord. When the church at Jerusalem heard what had happened, they sent Barnabas to Antioch. When he arrived and saw this evidence of God's blessing, he was filled with joy, and he encouraged the believers to stay true to the Lord. Barnabas was a good man, full of the Holy Spirit and strong in faith. And many people were brought to the Lord. Then Barnabas went on to Tarsus to look for Saul. When he found him, he brought him back to Antioch. Both of them stayed there with the church for a full year, teaching large crowds of people. (It was at Antioch that the believers were first called Christians.) During this time some prophets traveled from Jerusalem to Antioch. One of them named Agabus stood up in one of the meetings and predicted by the Spirit that a great famine was coming upon the entire Roman world. (This was fulfilled during the reign of Claudius.) So the believers in Antioch decided to send relief to the brothers and sisters in Judea, everyone giving as much as they could. This they did, entrusting their gifts to Barnabas and Saul to take to the elders of the church in Jerusalem.
Acts 11:19-30

* * *

Saul had a hand in planting the church in Antioch – albeit unintentional. His persecution of the church in Jerusalem, and the stoning of Stephen, as he held the cloaks of the persecutors, led to the scattering, that led to the planting of this new church. It is a reminder that what the enemy intends for evil, God can use for good (Genesis 50:20). God was planting Antioch to be a strategic center that He would use for the advancement of the gospel throughout Asia.

The capital of Syria, three hundred miles north of Jerusalem, Antioch boasted a population of half a million people which made it the third largest city in the Roman Empire, surpassed only by Rome and Alexandria. A busy port and a center for luxury and culture, Antioch attracted all kinds of people, including wealthy retired Roman officials who spent their days chatting in the baths or gambling at the chariot races. With its large cosmopolitan population and its great commercial and political power, the general populace wanted for very little, including a Jewish Messiah. Antioch was also a very wicked city, perhaps eclipsed only by Corinth. Though all of the Syrian, Greek and Roman deities were honored in the city, the principal shrine was dedicated to Daphne, whose worship included immoral rituals. It was a city filled with every epicurean delight of the day.

Antioch presented to those scattered believers a very different field for evangelism, but they were armed with the Word of God on their lips and the Spirit of God in their hearts. As a result, *"a large number of these Gentiles believed and turned to the Lord."* The response was so significant that the elders of the church in Jerusalem commissioned Barnabas to go to Antioch to find out what was happening among the Gentiles. Gratefully the elders sent an encourager, one who was filled with faith and the Holy Spirit, so he did not go to control a mission, but to encourage a Spirit-filled movement. Through his encouragement, the church continued to grow and multiply, and there was now need for another shepherd to nurture and disciple this growing flock.

Barnabas could have easily sent word back to the elders in Jerusalem with a request for them to send someone to assist him. But Barnabas knew that God had commissioned Saul to minister to the Gentiles, so he didn't take the easy route of sending a messenger to Jerusalem, he took the "road" of greater effort and traveled personally to Tarsus. Remember, Barnabas had not seen Saul for seven years, and they had only actually been together for a few weeks in Jerusalem. Yet, he knew by faith that Saul was God's person for the job. God had used Barnabas to encourage and pour into

Saul's life in Jerusalem, and now the Lord was giving him more opportunity to do the same, as together they now co-labored in Antioch for a year.

Remember that Jesus had instructed Saul for three years in the wilderness of Arabia. He had equipped him as His apostle to make disciples of the Gentiles and to teach them to obey everything He commanded. For the past seven years, the Lord had continued that work of molding and shaping Saul as He prepared him now for this work in Antioch. Luke tells us that it was in Antioch *"that the believers were first called Christians."* In that day, it distinguished the believers as followers of Jesus. They became known as a people that sought after, followed and radiated Jesus. Unfortunately, due to our own actions, and those of many generations before us, the term "Christian" has lost a great deal of significance over the years, and now simply describes a culture, a tradition, a parentage or a religion, instead of a relationship with the One whose name we bear.

One of the first ways that the believers began to demonstrate their faith in Christ was through the giving of their financial resources to assist their persecuted brothers and sisters in Judea through an impending famine. They knew that to whom much has been given, much is required. They knew that the gospel had been given to them at a cost of great price – the shed blood of Jesus – and the message had been brought to them also at a cost of great price – the blood of the martyrs. They knew that whatever they gave paled in comparison to the price the Judean believers had given for them – so everyone gave as much as they could. And it is interesting to note one of the great ironies – that when they sent their gifts to Jerusalem, they did so through Barnabas and Saul (the one who was now bringing relief back to the very church that he had persecuted).

Most of us are by-products of that little church that could. Perhaps not of the financial relief that they sent to Judea, but definitely of the Good News that they sent throughout Asia and Europe. God used a handful of seeds that were sent out from a persecuted church that were, in turn, multiplied by a little church that could. God used them to touch a world for time and eternity. And He intends to do the same through us, if we too will be the little church that can… until He returns.

* * *

33

LORD, WHAT ABOUT HIM?

About that time King Herod Agrippa began to persecute some believers in the church. He had the apostle James (John's brother) killed with a sword. When Herod saw how much this pleased the Jewish people, he also arrested Peter. (This took place during the Passover celebration.) Then he imprisoned him, placing him under the guard of four squads of four soldiers each. Herod intended to bring Peter out for public trial after the Passover. But while Peter was in prison, the church prayed very earnestly for him. The night before Peter was to be placed on trial, he was asleep, fastened with two chains between two soldiers. Others stood guard at the prison gate. Suddenly, there was a bright light in the cell, and an angel of the Lord stood before Peter. The angel struck him on the side to awaken him and said, "Quick! Get up!" And the chains fell off his wrists. Then the angel told him, "Get dressed and put on your sandals." And he did. "Now put on your coat and follow me," the angel ordered. So Peter left the cell, following the angel.

But all the time he thought it was a vision. He didn't realize it was actually happening. They passed the first and second guard posts and came to the iron gate leading to the city, and this opened for them all by itself. So they passed through and started walking down the street, and then the angel suddenly left him…. At dawn there was a great commotion among the soldiers about what had happened to Peter. Herod Agrippa ordered a thorough search for him. When he couldn't be found, Herod interrogated the guards and sentenced them to death….
Acts 12:1-19

* * *

Several years ago, i participated in a wilderness safety, survival and security training in the mountains of Idaho with about thirty other people. Though i didn't know most of the folks going into the training, a shared experience like that creates a bond that sticks with you for the rest of your lives. Two of those folks – a husband and wife – and i were teamed together for several of the exercises. They – like the rest – will forever hold a special place in my heart. Over the years since then, i have seen God use this couple – Steve and Laura – in phenomenal ways in the advancement of the message of the Good News across the globe. He has ordered their steps and worked through them to have eternal impact for the Kingdom. In the midst of that activity, Steve was diagnosed with liver cancer. In recent months, he was in and out of the hospital – until one day the Lord delivered him from his frail body and took him home to heaven. The physical battle was intense – and while we prayed for healing, we also prayed for grace and strength, and restorative rest in the midst of the battle. One of their prayer requests was that God would grant Steve the time on this side of glory to finish a specific project that He had placed before him to do. By His grace, God granted Steve with that time, and he and his son were able to complete the project before God took him home.

In times like those, we tend to want to ask God, why them? Why are they having to walk through this difficult journey? And, if we were to be totally honest – and if we are walking through a difficult journey ourselves – we may sometimes want to ask God, why are we walking through this, while others are not seemingly needing to carry such a heavy burden? If you ask the latter question, you are in good company. You're asking the same question Peter asked Jesus.

You will recall that toward the end of the last chapter of John's Gospel, Jesus told Peter the manner in which he would die. It would be a painful and brutal death. Peter's immediate response was to direct the Lord's attention to John and ask, *"Lord, what about him?"* (John 21:21 CEV). This wasn't the first time, or the last, that followers of Jesus endeavored to compare themselves to other believers to determine whether they or the other person got the better deal. Peter wanted to know if his death was going to be in a manner that was more or less brutal than John's. Prior to this, the disciples often speculated as to which one of them would have the greatest position in the Kingdom. As the new church emerged, the widows were squabbling over who was receiving more attention or care from the apostles.

This idea of comparing ourselves to others didn't start with them. It started with Cain comparing the way God accepted Abel's offering to the way He refused to accept his. It continued with the competition that developed between Rachel and Leah for greater favor from God. And it didn't stop with them. How often do we compare ourselves to other followers of Jesus and ask:

- Why did Jesus heal him/her and not me?
- Why am i needing to walk through this betrayal and loneliness and others are not?
- Why am i walking through such great financial difficulty when others seem to be so much more successful?
- And so on.

Or allow me to frame the question in a slightly different way. But before i do, allow me to take a quick side road in Roman history. Tiberius was the Roman Emperor when Jesus was crucified. Upon his death in 37 A.D., Caligula became Emperor. His reign, however, was short-lived and he was assassinated in 41 A.D. There was a political struggle in Rome and Herod Agrippa backed the right man. Thus, when Claudius became the new Roman Emperor, he withdrew the current prefect (of which Pontius Pilate had been the fifth in a long line) from the rule of the Iudaean province, and replaced him with his ally Herod Agrippa. Soon after becoming the puppet King, Herod Agrippa arrested the apostles James and Peter in order to gain favor with the Jewish religious leaders.

Now, back to the question. James and Peter weren't doing anything illegal. As a matter of fact, they were doing exactly what Jesus had told them to do. They were both making disciples. The church in Jerusalem prayed for the release and safety of both men with equal fervency. But James was killed, while Peter was miraculously delivered from prison by an angel. Now where is the fairness or the equity in that? Does it mean that God loved Peter more than He loved James?

And what about us? One is miraculously healed of a terminal illness, and yet another suffers and dies? One seems to prosper in all that he/she does, and yet another who is working equally as hard can't seem to get ahead? Or why is one couple able to have children and another can't? The list of comparisons can be unending. And as we make those comparisons, it can often appear that God is very unfair.

. . .

In the case of Peter, John and James, the Father ordained for them to walk in very different paths. But you and i – and every follower since them – have been enriched by all three of their lives, their ministries and their testimonies. God was at work – and continues to be – through each one of their lives and through their very different paths.

It is imperative that we remember how Jesus responded to Peter, when he asked his question. Jesus replied, *"If I want him to remain alive until I return, what is that to you? As for you, follow Me"* (John 21:22 NLT). Jesus was acknowledging that all of our paths will be different. Even John's path would not be easy. But regardless of our path, we are to follow Him. And if we follow Him, we will end up right where He wants us to be. Paul encouraged the believers in Corinth when he wrote, *"…our Lord Jesus Christ … will sustain you to the end…"* (1 Corinthians 1:7-8 ESV). Take heart and strength in that promise! Our Lord Jesus Christ will sustain us. He will comfort us. He will enable us. He will encourage us. He will strengthen us. He will carry us. He will hearten us. To the <u>end</u>! And it will end. And it will end in His glory! His plan and purpose will be fulfilled. Trust His word. Trust His promise. Trust Him!

No matter what you are walking through today – good times or hardship – remember Jesus' words – *"As for you, follow Me!"* And remain faithful to do so… until He returns.

* * *

34

GOD DOESN'T SHARE HIS GLORY

Now Herod was very angry with the people of Tyre and Sidon. So they sent a delegation to make peace with him because their cities were dependent upon Herod's country for food. The delegates won the support of Blastus, Herod's personal assistant, and an appointment with Herod was granted. When the day arrived, Herod put on his royal robes, sat on his throne, and made a speech to them. The people gave him a great ovation, shouting, "It's the voice of a god, not of a man!" Instantly, an angel of the Lord struck Herod with a sickness, because he accepted the people's worship instead of giving the glory to God. So he was consumed with worms and died.
Acts 12:20-23

* * *

Just a few reminders – some of which are from our last chapter. Herod Agrippa was the grandson of Herod the Great. In 41 A.D., the new Roman Emperor Claudius rewarded Herod for his loyalty by placing him as puppet King over the Iudaean province, which included Judea, Samaria and Idumea (encompassing the lower two-thirds of what is the modern day nation of Israel). His grandfather had governed this region as a client kingdom under the authority of the Roman Emperor, as had Herod Archelaus, his uncle. Between Archelaus and Agrippa, a succession of seven Roman prefects had governed the region. Agrippa's rule only lasted for four years, but he was a cunning and ambitious ruler. He parlayed his favor with Caesar Claudius (and Caesar Caligula before him) to bring about the banishment of his uncle, Herod Antipas, and the merging of the provinces he had ruled (Galilee and Perea) into Iudaea. He was the last

Herodian to govern the region. Upon his death, the entire region returned to direct Roman rule.

The cities of Tyre and Sidon were not under the rule of Herod Agrippa. They were a part of the Phoenician province under the direct control of Rome. The Phoenician and Iudaean provinces enjoyed strong commercial relations with one another. Tyre and Sidon relied heavily on the corn, oil and wine that they imported from Iudaea. Apparently, Agrippa had become angry with the people of the two cities due to some perceived affront. Since both regions were under Roman rule, Agrippa was prohibited from seeking a military solution – but, he was free to pursue an economic one. He was threatening to withhold the vital food exports that the two cities needed. The two cities quickly resolved to seek peace with Agrippa over their affront by employing the tactic of flattery. The representatives knew that their plan would have better success if they sought out an ally within Agrippa's court. Apparently, they found one in Blastus, Herod's chamberlain and personal assistant – more than likely, by bribing him.

Josephus records that on the day of their appointment, Agrippa wore *"a garment made wholly of silver, of a truly wonderful texture...."* On the morning that he entered the theater where their audience was to take place, the risen sun reflected brilliantly off of the garment. *"There the silver of his garment, being illuminated by the fresh reflection of the sun's rays, shone out in a wonderful manner, and was so resplendent as to spread awe over those that looked intently upon him."* Apparently, the motivation of their mission, combined with the spectacle that he made through the garment that he wore, caused *"his flatterers to cry out, one from one place, and another from another, that he was a god."*

The men of Tyre and Sidon worshiped pagan gods. Though their statements and accolades were an abomination, they had no understanding of how they were profaning a Holy God. But Agrippa knew. He had been schooled in the Law given through Moses. He knew that only One was due worship, honor and reverence. He knew that to receive such flattery was sinful and blasphemous. Yet, he neither rebuked them nor rejected their impetuous and irreverent flattery. Instead, he received it unto himself and took pleasure in it. He arrogantly accepted worship that is only due to the Almighty God and, in so doing, attempted to keep it for himself. Instead of giving glory to God, he retained the glory for himself. But God will not be mocked. He will not share His glory with anyone else!

(Isaiah 48:11). Instantly, an angel of the Lord struck Herod, and five days later he died. It's interesting to note that God did not strike him dead because he was responsible for having the apostle James killed. Herod will be accountable for that act on the Day of Judgement, but he wasn't immediately put to death for that reason. He was struck dead because he attempted to rob God of His glory.

God is jealous for His glory! When we are jealous for our glory, it is the sin of our selfish pride. But it is not sinful for God to be jealous for His glory, because He alone is worthy of glory and all glory is due Him. We see God's zeal for His glory evidenced throughout all of Scripture:

- God chose His people for His glory (Ephesians 1:4-6).
- God created us for His glory (Isaiah 43:6-7).
- God called Israel for His glory (Isaiah 49:3; Jeremiah 13:11).
- God rescued Israel from Egypt for His glory (Psalm106:7-8).
- God raised up Pharaoh to show His power and glorify His name (Romans 9:17).
- God defeated Pharaoh at the Red Sea to show His glory (Exodus 14:4).
- God spared Israel in the wilderness for the glory of His name (Ezekiel 20:14).
- God gave Israel victory in Canaan for the glory of His name (2 Samuel 7:23).
- God did not cast away His people for the glory of His name (1 Samuel 12:20,22).
- God saved Jerusalem from attack for the glory of His name (2 Kings 19:34).
- God restored Israel from exile for the glory of His name (Ezekiel 36:22-23).
- Jesus sought the glory of His Father in all He did (John 7:18).
- Jesus told us to do good works so that God gets glory (Matthew 5:16).
- Jesus said that He answers prayer that God would be glorified (John 14:13).
- Jesus endured His final hours of suffering for God's glory (John 12:27-28).
- God gave His Son to vindicate the glory of His righteousness in forgiving us (Romans 3:25-26).
- God forgives our sins for the glory of His Name (Isaiah 43:25, Psalm 25:11).

- Jesus receives us into His fellowship for the glory of God (Romans 15:7).
- The ministry of the Holy Spirit is to glorify the Son of God (John 16:14).
- God instructs us to do everything for His glory (1 Corinthians 10:31).
- God tells us to serve in a way that will glorify Him (1 Peter 4:11).
- Jesus will fill us with fruits of righteousness for God's glory (Philippians 1:9, 11).
- All are under judgment for dishonoring God's glory (Romans 1:22-23; Romans 3:23).
- Jesus is coming again for the glory of God (2 Thessalonians 1:9-10).
- Jesus' ultimate aim for us is that we see and experience His glory (John 17:24).
- Even in wrath God's aim is to make known the wealth of His glory (Romans 9:22-23).
- God's plan is to fill the earth with the knowledge of His glory (Habakkuk 2:14).

Allow this to serve as a reminder for each one of us today. First, let us be mindful that all glory is due to God alone. The next time someone attempts to give the glory to you, pass it on to the One to whom it is due. It can be tempting to hold onto it and allow our egos to be stroked. But don't make the same mistake Agrippa made. We are but servants of the Most High God – all honor and praise is due to Him – and Him alone!

Second, remember that God created us for His glory. He redeemed us for His glory. He orders our steps for His glory. He has placed our feet on the path we are currently walking on for His glory. Even the wilderness that we may currently be walking in is ultimately for His glory. So, hold onto this truth, no matter where you are, or what is happening... until He returns:

For everything comes from Him and exists by His power and is intended for His glory. All glory to Him forever! Amen.
(Romans 11:36)

* * *

35

A SENDING CHURCH

Among the prophets and teachers of the church at Antioch of Syria were Barnabas, Simeon (called "the black man"), Lucius (from Cyrene), Manaen (the childhood companion of King Herod Antipas), and Saul. One day as these men were worshiping the Lord and fasting, the Holy Spirit said, "Appoint Barnabas and Saul for the special work to which I have called them." So after more fasting and prayer, the men laid their hands on them and sent them on their way.
Acts 13:1-3

* * *

The leaders of the church at Antioch gathered to fast, pray and worship – seeking clear guidance from the Lord. The church was at a point in their history when they needed a word from God about their next crucial step. i doubt that they realized what the Holy Spirit would say, and how monumental that step would be – God was about to use them to change the world forever.

And what a diverse group it was! Barnabas (the "son of encouragement") was a Levite from the island of Cyprus. Simeon was a dark-skinned Gentile believer from Africa. Lucius was probably a Cyrenian Jew who was one *"of the believers who went to Antioch from Cyprus and Cyrene"* {to begin} *"preaching to the Gentiles about the Lord Jesus"* (Acts 11:20-21). Manaen, who we will probe a little further in a moment, was raised in the luxury of the court of Herod the Great. Saul, a Jewish scholar from Tarsus in Cilicia, was a former persecutor of the church. None of them were originally from Antioch. All of them came from very different backgrounds. They were different ethnicities and races. They spoke different languages. They had very different "religious" backgrounds. They truly only had one thing in common – and that was that they were all followers of Jesus – who were prepared to go wherever He led. He had led them all to Antioch for this season and for His divine purpose. He had brought them together with a heart to follow Jesus and a heart to lead this newly-formed church in how to send out witnesses to places as diverse as the ones from which they had come. At least three of them would go out from this place – Barnabas and Saul, who we see being sent out in this passage – and Lucius, who we later read was with Paul in Corinth (Romans 16:21). We don't know what subsequently happened with Simeon and Manaen, though we know they had a heart to go because God had sent them to Antioch. God may have kept them there to shepherd this church that He was raising up to be a sending church – sending forth witnesses of His gospel to the ends of the earth.

We have already begun to probe the lives of Saul and Barnabas and seen how God had uniquely ordered their steps in preparation for what He was going to do through them in the years ahead. God had also been uniquely preparing the other three, through the twists and turns of their life journeys – twists and turns that no one could have ever imagined would lead to this place at this moment.

Let's look specifically at the life of Manaen. Historians of the early church tell us that when Herod the Great attained the summit of his power, he sought the counsel of an Essene by the name of Manaen, whom he had known as a boy. It is believed that through their friendship, Herod offered to be the patron of his son (or grandson), who also was named Manaen. It would have been a significant adjustment for Manaen to leave the stern purity of the life of the Essenes to now enter into the pomp and luxury of the court of Herod, and to be raised as the foster brother of Herod's sons – Antipas and Archelaus. This was followed by an even greater change when all three boys were sent to receive their educations in Rome. After receiving his education, Manaen continued to be attached to the royal household, having adopted the life and principles of those with whom he lived. The bond between Manaen and Antipas was apparently strong, so that when Herod the Great died, Manaen moved with Antipas as he became the client king over Galilee and Perea. Manaen appears to have turned a blind eye to Antipas' incestuous marriage to Herodias, but the teachings of John the Baptist apparently still had some effect on him. As time went on, several in the court of Antipas became disciples of John, and, soon after, others became disciples of Jesus. It would appear that the witness of these disciples had an ever-increasing influence on Manaen, as it did on others in the household. The imprisonment of John brought him into closer contact with those in the household of Antipas, who himself "heard John gladly." The turning point in Manaen's life may possibly have been the beheading of John. It is not known how much longer he remained in court after that event. Antipas was banished and exiled to Spain soon after Agrippa became King. But it is likely that Manaen left sometime before that – probably when he became a follower of Jesus. It could have been through the influence of Chuza, the manager of the Kings' household, and his wife, Joanna, prior to Jesus' crucifixion, or it may have occurred sometime soon after.

It is here in this passage in Acts that we have the first actual mention of Manaen. Though most of us would struggle to remember his name, we are recipients of his influence. He was one of the leaders of the church that God used to send out Barnabas and Saul with the witness of the gospel that was subsequently spread around the world – and at some point arrived to each one of us. He was a great encourager and supporter of Saul in that endeavor. There is a strong probability that Manaen's influential relationships with the Herodians and Romans proved to be beneficial in assisting Saul in his ministry and travels throughout the years. Luke's life as a follower of Jesus also appears to have begun at Antioch. (There are some who would go further and contend that Lucius and Dr. Luke are the same person.) Regardless, Manaen was more than likely Luke's source for many of the facts about the history of John the Baptist, and the details of multiple generations of Herodian rule, which he incorporated into his Gospel account.

We never know how God will use the experiences and relationships in our lives to further His purpose and plan through our lives. We must think of ourselves as an arrow being sent by the bow in the hands of the Master Archer. His aim is true. He always hits His target. He has shaped each of us uniquely as arrows, fittingly suited for the path and the target. We may have been designed for different purposes with different backgrounds, different ethnicities, different languages, and different races. But we have all been crafted as an "arrow" for His purpose. We have all been sent! None of us have been crafted to remain in the quiver. None of our churches have been planted to be permanent waiting rooms. These men led their church to lay their hands on Barnabas and Saul and "let them loose" (send them on their way). May that be true of each of our churches… and each of our lives… until He returns!

* * *

36

GREATER IS HE THAT IS IN US

Afterward they traveled from town to town across the entire island until finally they reached Paphos, where they met a Jewish sorcerer, a false prophet named Bar-Jesus. He had attached himself to the governor, Sergius Paulus, who was an intelligent man. The governor invited Barnabas and Saul to visit him, for he wanted to hear the word of God. But Elymas, the sorcerer (as his name means in Greek), interfered and urged the governor to pay no attention to what Barnabas and Saul said. He was trying to keep the governor from believing. Saul, also known as Paul, was filled with the Holy Spirit, and he looked the sorcerer in the eye. Then he said, "You son of the devil, full of every sort of deceit and fraud, and enemy of all that is good! Will you never stop perverting the true ways of the Lord? Watch now, for the Lord has laid his hand of punishment upon you, and you will be struck blind. You will not see the sunlight for some time." Instantly mist and darkness came over the man's eyes, and he began groping around begging for someone to take his hand and lead him. When the governor saw what had happened, he became a believer, for he was astonished at the teaching about the Lord.
Acts 13:6-12

* * *

When the Word of God is proclaimed, you can be assured that the enemy will send his representatives to try to oppose and pervert the truth, and try to discourage the proclaimer. That is a good reminder why God hasn't called us to be "Lone Ranger" followers. He has placed us within a body of believers and most often sends us out in teams of two or more, just as He did His disciples in Luke 10, so that we can encourage, exhort and uphold one another. But even more importantly, Jesus did not send us out alone. He gave us His Holy Spirit to dwell within us so that by Him we are empowered to be His witnesses (Acts 1:8). And John wrote to remind us: *"He who is in you is greater than he who is in the world"* (1 John 4:4 ESV). Jesus knows who and what we will encounter. He has known it since before the beginning of time and He has given us all that we need to overcome it.

Such was the case that day in Paphos. God in His sovereignty orchestrated that four men would encounter one another in the governor's court in this Roman capital of Cyprus. The first was a man named Joseph, who had become Barnabas. God had gifted him to be an encourager and an exhorter. Barnabas had the ability to enable those around him who were down to be lifted up. However, he wasn't "Pollyannaish", dispensing a hollow hope built on a substanceless foundation. He was an ambassador of the hope, assurance and encouragement that is built on the substantial Truth of God. It was that Truth that had given him the confidence to bring Saul before the apostles in Jerusalem when they feared him. It was that Truth that had enabled him to know that he was to bring Saul to Antioch to disciple those new believers. It was that Truth that now gave him the courage and the boldness to stand before a demon-filled sorcerer.

The second was a man named Saul, who in Paphos became known as Paul. The name "Paul" means "small or little". Some contend that he took that name as an act of humility, but all would agree he changed his name as a clear reminder to all that he was no longer Saul, the persecutor of the church, he was now Paul, servant of Christ. Paul was a student and a bold proclaimer of Truth. He had studied the Scripture at the feet of some of the best Jewish Scholars. He had travelled throughout the wilderness of Arabia being schooled by none other than Jesus Himself. And He had the Spirit of Christ dwelling within him. He could proclaim the Truth with confidence because he knew the One from whom it had come. He could proclaim the Truth boldly because he knew the One who had called him to carry it forth.

The giftedness of these two men complimented one another. The encouraging nature of Barnabas opened doors through which Paul was able to speak apostolic words of Truth. The prophetic nature of Paul provoked Barnabas to even greater understanding of the Truths of God which enabled him to be an even greater exhorter and encourager. God knew exactly what each of these two men needed and sovereignly brought them together for His purpose.

The third was a man named Bar-Jesus, who became known as Elymas. This instrument of deceit and fraud was a Jewish sorcerer. Talk about an oxymoron! The Jews were chosen and set apart by God to be His people, but this sorcerer – this dispenser of black magic – had chosen to be a servant of Satan. Apparently his assignment from the evil one was to keep the governor from ever accepting the Truth by blinding him and frustrating the attempts of Barnabas and Paul to proclaim the Truth to him. That continues to be Satan's strategy today.

The fourth was a man named Sergius Paulus, the governor of Cyprus. Sergius Paulus was a seeker of Truth. He had invited Barnabas and Paul to visit him because he wanted to hear and know the Truth. The enemy did not want that to happen. He never does! Elymas distracted the governor with his magic, his lies and his interruptions. But Satan knew that he was a defeated foe – and he remains a defeated foe. As the liar that he is, he had never told Elymas that his efforts would ultimately fail. Thus, his instrument, Elymas, was on the losing side of the battle. He may have appeared to be victorious for the moment, but his victory was short-lived. It always is! Satan will never prevail – no matter how dark things may look at the moment. Our Almighty God is the Sovereign Victor!

God, through His Spirit, enabled Paul to boldly confront the lies with Truth. As a result, the eyes of Sergius Paulus were opened, and the eyes of Elymas were blinded. God in His sovereignty even used the defeat of the deception of Elymas to bring Himself glory. What Satan had intended for evil, God used for His glory (Romans 8:28; Genesis 50:20). God still does – and He always will.

Are you being confronted by an "Elymas" who is spreading lies and attempting to defeat you today? Remember, *"He who is in you is greater...."* Has God brought a "Sergius Paulus" across your path who needs to hear God's Truth today? Be the "Barnabas" or the "Paul" that he/she needs to hear from, and remember, *"He who is in you is greater...."* And He will always be… until He returns.

* * *

37

THEY JUDGED THEMSELVES TO BE UNWORTHY

Paul and his companions then left Paphos by ship for Pamphylia, landing at the port town of Perga.... But Paul and Barnabas traveled inland to Antioch of Pisidia. On the Sabbath they went to the synagogue for the services. After the usual readings from the books of Moses and the prophets, those in charge of the service sent them this message: "Brothers, if you have any word of encouragement for the people, come and give it." So Paul stood, lifted his hand to quiet them, and started speaking. "Men of Israel," he said, "and you God-fearing Gentiles, listen to me. The God of this nation of Israel chose our ancestors and made them multiply and grow.... Then the people begged for a king, and God gave them... David.... And it is one of King David's descendants, Jesus, who is God's promised Savior of Israel! ....The people in Jerusalem and their leaders did not recognize Jesus as the one the prophets had spoken about. Instead, they condemned Him, ... but God raised Him from the dead! ...The promise was made to our ancestors, and God has now fulfilled it for us, their descendants, by raising Jesus.... We are here to proclaim that through this Man Jesus there is forgiveness for your sins. Everyone who believes in Him is made right in God's sight – something the law of Moses could never do." ...The following week almost the entire city turned out to hear them preach the word of the Lord. But when some of the Jews saw the crowds, they were jealous; so they slandered Paul and argued against whatever he said. Then Paul and Barnabas spoke out boldly and declared, "It was necessary that we first preach the word of God to you Jews. But since you have rejected it and judged yourselves unworthy of eternal life, we will offer it to the Gentiles...." When the Gentiles heard this, they were very glad and thanked the Lord for His message; and all who were chosen for eternal life became believers. So the Lord's message spread throughout that region.

Acts 13:13-49

*　*　*

In their day, it was the custom within the synagogues for Jews who were visiting from distant cities to bring a word of greeting and encouragement. Thus, those who were gathered that Sabbath day in the synagogue in Antioch of Pisidia were extending that customary courtesy to Paul and Barnabas. Paul began his message to those gathered in the synagogue in the same way that Stephen had (Acts 7), by recounting their history. He began with the ancestors – Abraham, Isaac and Jacob – and unfolded the history of the Chosen People of God. There were two primary truths in his message. The first truth was that everything in the history of Israel and the prophecies pointed to, and was leading up to, the coming of Jesus and the redemptive work that would be accomplished through His death and resurrection. The second truth in his message was that the underlying story throughout it all is God's story. Sixteen times in his message, Paul emphasized the truth that God is the central Actor in history. He was telling them that there is a great and glorious God. Know Him. Reckon with Him. Think about Him. He was saying that God is the main Worker in history. He is the explanation for, and the meaning of, everything!

We live in an age where most people do not believe that to be true. We have become a superficial and naive age. It is superficial and naive to discuss events and never acknowledge their most important connection – namely, their connection with God and His purposes. Let's look at it. Almost all news reports are superficial. Almost all history books are superficial. Almost all public education in America is superficial. Almost all editorial and news commentary is superficial. Why? Because of the complete disregard for God – who is the main Reality in the universe, <u>the</u> explanation behind everything, and without which all understandings are superficial. When we disregard the "Main Thing", we have made whatever it is superficial.

Someone may say, "Oh, that's just religion. You can't expect all news, or history, or education to be about religion." It's not religion. It's reality. If you want to be a Christian, it means believing that God is the main Actor in world events – that He is the most important Factor in all matters. Paul was talking to unbelievers here. He was evangelizing. And part of what he was trying to do was show them a way of looking at the world that sets the stage for the gospel – namely, that it is God's world. He made it. He owns it and everyone in it. He works in it. He is guiding it to His appointed purpose. Everything, without exception, has to do with God, and gets its main meaning and purpose from God.

One of the most amazing confirmations of the truth of the gospel is the way Jesus fulfilled so many prophecies made hundreds of years before His coming. In fact, to understand who Jesus Christ really is, we need to remember that He is not like a rabbit pulled out of a hat with no warning. He didn't just pop up in history with no meaning. Instead He is like a treasure chest of gold at the end of a centuries-long treasure hunt with lots of "clues" and markers pointing to Him along the way.

Let's look at a few of those "clues". In Genesis, God said to Abraham, "*All the families of the earth will be blessed through you*" (Genesis 12:3). So the earliest hope and expectation was that through the people of Israel some amazing blessing would come to the entire world. Three generations later, a promise was made to one of Abraham's great grandsons, Judah. "*The scepter will not depart from Judah, nor the ruler's staff from his descendants, until the coming of the One to whom it belongs; the One whom all nations will obey*" (Genesis 49:10). So the promise became more specific: the blessing will come to the world ("all the families") through a Ruler, and that Ruler will be of the house of Judah, one of Abraham's great grandsons.

Then several hundred years later. God gave a king to Israel, by the name of David, from the house of Judah. Before David died, God spoke to him through the prophet Nathan saying, "*When you die and are buried with your ancestors, I will raise up one of your descendants, your own offspring, and I will make His kingdom strong. He is the One who will build a house – a temple – for My name. And I will secure His royal throne forever*" (2 Samuel 7:12-13). God was not speaking of a temple built with hands, He was speaking of a temple – and a Kingdom – that would last forever. And the ruler to come, who would bring blessing to the nations, would be a Son of David and sit on the throne of David. Then came the prophet Isaiah who made the prediction even more specific: "*For a Child is born to us, a Son is given to us. The government will rest on His shoulders. And He will be called: Wonderful Counselor, Mighty God, Everlasting Father, Prince of Peace. His government and its peace will never end. He will rule with fairness and justice from the throne of His ancestor David for all eternity. The passionate commitment of the Lord of Heaven's Armies will make this happen!*" (Isaiah 9:6-7). Then the prophet Micah added that this Child, born of the house of David, would be born in Bethlehem and would have His origin from ancient days (Micah 5:2).

· · ·

How was this Ruler going to bring blessing to the entire world like God had said to Abraham? God revealed that answer through the prophet Isaiah seven hundred years before Jesus was born: *"He was pierced for our rebellion, crushed for our sins. He was beaten so we could be whole. He was whipped so we could be healed. All of us, like sheep, have strayed away. We have left God's paths to follow our own. Yet the Lord laid on Him the sins of us all"* (Isaiah 53:5-6). But that sounds like it's the end of Him – dying as a Sacrificial Lamb in the place of sinners so they could go free. How does He rule forever on the throne of David if He is dead? Isaiah goes on to make clear that He does not stay dead. God says, *"I will give Him the honors of a Victorious Soldier, because He exposed Himself to death. He was counted among the rebels. He bore the sins of many and interceded for rebels"* (Isaiah 53:12).

So hundreds of years before Jesus was born, we are told by God in the Scriptures that Jesus would be of the house of Judah. He would live a life of righteousness, but He would be accused with the transgressors. He would be put to death for the sins of many. He would rise from the dead and sit down on the throne of His father David at God's right hand. And He would rule there, spreading blessing to all the families of the earth until He is acknowledged as the Lord of all the nations. So when Jesus came onto the scene two thousand years ago, He was not like a rabbit out of the hat – a total surprise with no preparation, and nothing in history to give Him meaning. Instead He was like a treasure chest of gold at the end of a long treasure hunt with dozens of clues along the way of what He would be like and what He would mean.

And He really is the Treasure. To know Him and be known and loved by Him is worth more than all this world has to offer. And that's the way Paul spoke to his listeners. He used the Old Testament history and prophecy to show that the Messiah was to rise from the dead and reign as the Son of David and never die again. Then Paul proclaimed, *"through this Man Jesus there is forgiveness for your sins. Everyone who believes in Him is made right in God's sight."* He said you have been "made right" – acquitted, cleared, pardoned. Your condemnation has been lifted. You can become a clean slate. That's what Jesus means: He means freedom!

Those in the synagogue that day never expected that they would receive that message when they invited Paul to speak. It was as if their blinders had been removed. They had now heard the story behind the story. They had heard the substance and the connection. They were no longer left to view things superficially and naively. They had now heard the whole truth. Thus, there was only one thing left to do – accept it. The people begged them to return the following week. There must have been much discussion throughout the week, because almost the entire city turned out to hear them the following week.

But seeing the size of the crowd, the religious leaders became jealous. Crowds had never turned out like that to hear them teach! So they slandered Paul, disputed the truth and swayed the Jews to reject the truth. In their rejection, they judged themselves to be unworthy of the precious gift of eternal life. Eternal life was never a gift they could earn or merit. It is not a gift that any one of us will ever be worthy to receive. It is a gift given by God's grace. But by rejecting the truth – and by rejecting the gift – they adjudicated themselves to an eternity separated from God. They committed the one sin that can never be forgiven – they rejected Jesus. If we reject Jesus there is no eternal life with God. God's grace can overcome every sin except rejection of His grace. If we walk away from His grace and reject His Son, we have judged ourselves to be unworthy. And that is what many of the Jews did that day. But Luke tells us that many Gentiles believed that day, and the gospel spread throughout the region.

God has created all things for His redemptive purpose. He is at work in and through all things to draw His creation back to Himself. He is the reason and His purpose is behind all things – even those things that the enemy has intended for evil. None of us are worthy of His redemption. But by His grace, every event and circumstance has ultimately been permitted to point us to His redemptive purpose. At the end of the day, the only thing that will judge anyone as unworthy is rejection of Him and His truth. We have been called – like Paul and Barnabas – to point others to His truth. May He find us faithful to do so… until He returns.

* * *

38

FROM LAUDING TO LOATHING

When the crowd saw what Paul had done, they shouted in their local dialect, "These men are gods in human form!" They decided that Barnabas was the Greek god Zeus and that Paul was Hermes, since he was the chief speaker. Now the temple of Zeus was located just outside the town. So the priest of the temple and the crowd brought bulls and wreaths of flowers to the town gates, and they prepared to offer sacrifices to the apostles. But when the apostles Barnabas and Paul heard what was happening, they tore their clothing in dismay and ran out among the people, shouting, "Friends, why are you doing this? We are merely human beings – just like you! We have come to bring you the Good News that you should turn from these worthless things and turn to the living God, who made heaven and earth, the sea, and everything in them. In the past He permitted all the nations to go their own ways, but He never left them without evidence of Himself and His goodness. For instance, He sends you rain and good crops and gives you food and joyful hearts." But even with these words, Paul and Barnabas could scarcely restrain the people from sacrificing to them. Then some Jews arrived from Antioch and Iconium and won the crowds to their side. They stoned Paul and dragged him out of town, thinking he was dead. But as the believers gathered around him, he got up and went back into the town. The next day he left with Barnabas for Derbe.
Acts 14:11-20

* * *

The journey from lauding to loathing can be particularly painful. At one moment, everyone loves you (or so it would appear), and in the next, everyone seemingly despises you. Just ask Jesus. On Sunday, the crowd was cheering, *"Hosanna"*; then on Friday, they were shouting, *"Crucify Him!"* Or ask Paul. On one day, the crowd laid wreaths at his feet, then only a few days later, they left him for dead after stoning him. In neither instance had Jesus nor Paul done anything to warrant such a dramatic and violent change of opinion. Jesus deserved to be worshiped, but never deserved to be crucified. Paul didn't deserve to be worshiped (and he corrected the people for doing so), but he did not "deserve" to be stoned. It is amazing to see how quickly – and how easily – the crowd could be moved from emotive praise to relentless persecution and utter abandonment.

But then again, it isn't amazing. Jesus was never surprised. John writes this about Jesus, as He began His itinerant ministry: *"Now when He was in Jerusalem at the Passover Feast, many believed in His name when they saw the signs that He was doing. But Jesus on His part did not entrust Himself to them, because He knew all people"* (John 2:23-24 ESV). Jesus "knew all people": He knows what is in our hearts. He never sought the approval of men; He sought only the approval of the Father. Paul later wrote about himself: *"Obviously, I'm not trying to win the approval of people, but of God. If pleasing people were my goal, I would not be Christ's servant"* (Galatians 1:10). i have never experienced physical persecution, but i have experienced emotional abandonment. i have experienced the emotional withdrawal that felt like loathing, where previously there had been support, encouragement – and even praise. To that degree, i can relate to Paul's experience – and perhaps you can as well.

In the verses immediately preceding this passage, we are introduced to a man there in Lystra who had been crippled from birth. Paul saw the man and *"realized he had the faith to be healed"* (Acts 14:9). So Paul told him to stand up and walk. The crowd had just witnessed that miracle as we begin this passage in verse 11. The crowd went wild with excitement. They knew this man. He had been crippled all of his life. Miraculously, he was now able to walk. The crowd then made the mistake of attributing this man's healing to Paul and Barnabas. Upon seeing and hearing the crowd's reaction, Paul and Barnabas swiftly redirected the crowd's praise to the One who truly had healed the crippled man and was worthy of their praise and worship. They were careful to not make the mistake that too often we can make – and that is to allow some of that praise to fall on us. Paul and Barnabas knew that they were servants and instruments of the Most High God; they knew that anything praiseworthy was His work and not theirs.

. . .

Let's take an important sideroad: In the midst of his statement to the crowd, Paul says, *"In the past He permitted all the nations to go their own ways, but He never left them without evidence of Himself and His goodness."* How many of us have wondered about the salvation of those who do not have access to the gospel? What will happen to the people who have never heard the Name of Jesus? First, that question must compel us to go – just like Paul and Barnabas were doing – to tell the people who have not yet heard the Good News of the gospel. It has been my experience that those who accuse God of being heartless in condemning to death those who are dead in their sin and have not heard about Jesus are the very same people who are making the least effort to make Him known. Second, Paul is giving us insight into the work that God has already begun to draw them to Himself. This is not intended to keep us from going – rather, to encourage us to expedite our obedience. Well, if the people don't have the spoken word or the written Word, what do they have? God gave them a witness. What was it? I love this: "*... He sends... the rain and good crops and gives... food and joyful hearts.*" Do you know what that's known as? His providence. They're not excusable. You say, "But they don't have any written Word." That's all right. They have the word written in their hearts, and the visible creation and the providence of God. Every man in this world is responsible for the knowledge of God, for God has written it in his conscience. God has revealed it in the creation, and He continues to reveal it in His providence.

Back to the passage – soon after, some of the religious leaders who had stirred up the crowd in Antioch of Pisidia and Iconium did the same thing here in Lystra. They sowed seeds of discord through false accusations. Remember, those who were sowing the discord were truly seeking to maintain the status quo of their positional power. The gospel was a threat to their status quo. And regrettably the people were easily deceived. They stoned the one that only a few days earlier they had worshiped as if he was a god, dragged what they thought was his lifeless body out of town, and left him for dead. *"But as the believers gathered around him, he got up and went back into the town."*

That prompts two further sideroads: first, did Paul die or did the people only think he was dead? i believe he died. You should know that there are those who would disagree with me in that regard. But, in his second letter to the church in Corinth, Paul wrote, *"I was caught up to the third heaven fourteen years ago. Whether I was in my body or out of my body, I don't know – only God knows.... But I do know that I was caught up to paradise and heard things so astounding that they cannot be expressed in words, things no human is allowed to tell"* (2 Corinthians 12:2-4). i don't believe the crowd left him half-dead. i believe that he was dead, and as the believers gathered around him, God raised him from the dead! Why? Because he had not yet completed the assignment that God had for him on this earth. Which immediately prompts the second question – why, then, did God allow him to be stoned to the point of death? Paul answered that question in his letter to the Galatians: *"Don't be misled – you cannot mock the justice of God. You will always harvest what you plant"* (Galatians 6:7). Paul was permitted to harvest that which he had planted. He had ordered the stoning of Stephen and watched on as the evil deed was transacted. God permitted him to go through the same experience – but then brought him back to life and allowed him to live to tell about it. Why did he have to go through that pain even now after he had become a follower of Jesus and an apostle? Salvation guarantees that we will not suffer the eternal consequences of our sin, but it does not guarantee that we won't suffer the penalty for our actions on this side of eternity. As Paul wrote – what we sow, we reap. This was the temporal consequence for sin that he could not escape. And there was a continuing reminder of that sin through the lasting "thorn in the flesh" (2 Corinthians 12:7) from which Paul suffered for his remaining days. His "vision of paradise" and his "thorn in the flesh" were both born out of the stoning and the death that resulted. But God used even those things, in addition to raising him from the dead, to bring glory to His Name.

But as we close, let's come back to the lessons for us – because hopefully, you've never been a part of stoning anyone, and prayerfully you will never be stoned. You may however have the crowd turn against you – simply because you are being obedient to what the Father has directed you to do. The Son experienced death on the cross, and Paul experienced stoning. The Father gave them both the grace to endure for the sake of His mission. He never abandoned them. And even though both of them experienced a loathing to the point of death, He raised them both from the dead for His purpose. The bottom line for us is we need to trust Him. He will not forsake us. He will give us the grace and strength to walk through the pain. For most of us, it will have absolutely nothing to do with death – but it could include friends who walk away from us and relationships that are severed. We will feel betrayed and abandoned – and hurt. But if we know we have been faithful to do what God has told us to do – and have not sinned against "our neighbor" in any way – then we must trust God even in the outcome – even when it hurts. Our God who was able to raise Jesus and Paul from the dead is able to heal the pain of our hurt.

• • •

A mentor once told me, "Be sure to pass along all the praise to God when it comes, as well as all of the pain and criticism when it follows." When you are following Jesus, lauding can quickly become loathing. Pass them both on to Jesus and keep following Him… until He returns.

* * *

39

BE SURE TO REPORT THE PRAISES

Finally, they returned by ship to Antioch of Syria, where their journey had begun. The believers there had entrusted them to the grace of God to do the work they had now completed. Upon arriving in Antioch, they called the church together and reported everything God had done through them and how He had opened the door of faith to the Gentiles, too. And they stayed there with the believers for a long time.
Acts 14:26-28

* * *

The church at Antioch in Syria was Paul and Barnabas' sending church (chapter 35). Almost two years had passed since the church had commissioned them to go and sent them out. The church had provided the financial resources needed in order for them to go. They prayed for them throughout their journey – praying for divine opportunities for the spread of the gospel, for anointing in their preaching, for the nurture of new believers, for the new churches being planted, for safety and health in their travels, and so on. The church undergirded the work in every way. The church made it possible for them to go. The church was as much a part of the mission journey as if they had actually traveled with Paul and Barnabas. God's calling on Paul and Barnabas to go was also a calling on the church to send them and "go" with them. And now they had returned. They were two of the most beloved people in the life of the Antioch church. They looked a little worse for wear. Now the way they returned to the church and the way the church received them would be just as important – if not more – than the way they had been sent out.

• • •

Paul and Barnabas would have been the first to tell you that they could not have gone without the prayers and support of the Antioch church. The church had entrusted them to the grace of God. By His grace, God had called them to the journey. By His grace, He had gone before them to prepare hearts to receive the seeds of the gospel. By His grace, He had provided them with "people of peace" at each of the synagogues along the way who invited them to speak and thereby opened the door for them to be able to preach the Good News. By His grace, He gave them peace to continue when their traveling companion, John Mark, unexpectedly bailed out on them in Perga (Acts 13:13). By His grace, He gave them power to defeat Elymas, the sorcerer – the instrument of Satan. By His grace, He granted them favor with Governor Sergius Paulus, as they witnessed his personal salvation and thereafter experienced his favor as they continued to travel throughout the island. By His grace, He opened a wider door for the spreading of the Gospel among the Gentiles in Antioch of Pisidia and beyond. By His grace, He brought glory to His Name through the healing of the crippled man in Lystra. By His grace, He raised Paul from the dead after the stoning. By His grace, God raised up elders in every church that was planted. And by His grace, He permitted them to safely return to Antioch. In these ways, and in many others, the Spirit of God had gone before them in their travels and led them through each and every twist and turn.

The sending church needed to hear this report. They needed to know how their prayers had been answered. They needed to know how God had worked through them for the furtherance of His mission. They needed to have the opportunity to praise God and glorify Him through their worship and thanksgiving over the great things He had done. The sending church needed to love on Paul and Barnabas. They had "come home" weary from their travel. They had returned somewhat beaten and bruised. They had arrived back home with "empty tanks" having constantly been pouring into others. The church needed to be used by the Lord to fill them back up, to encourage them, to minister to their woundedness and their weariness. The church needed to be an oasis at the end of a long and vigorous journey.

Paul and Barnabas not only needed to share God's answers to prayer and to be ministered to themselves. They needed to pour from themselves into the church. They needed to use the experiences they had to better equip the church to reach the nations right there in Antioch. They needed to better equip the church in how to support and undergird those who would be sent out from her midst in the days to come. They needed to help the church better prepare the others that God was calling for them to send from within the body. They needed to help the church see her ever growing role in carrying out Christ's Great Commission to the nations.

"And they stayed there with the believers for…" over a year to do just that. They stayed and picked up their work of pastoring and discipling the people. It was during that time that Paul wrote his letter to the Galatians. And in that letter, he gives all the glory to God for what they had seen Him do.

As we close, let's look at a statement in the first part of the passage. They had been *"entrusted… to the grace of God to do the work they had now completed."* Note the last word – "completed". You know what that means? It means they did it. God said, "Go do it" and they did it. They completed it. All too often when God says, "Go do it", we don't do it. Or, if we start, we don't finish it. But there are some in the history of the church that God told to do it, and they did. Paul and Barnabas were two of them, They came back to report that the work – that specific portion for which they had been sent out – was completed!

When i come to the end of my life or the day that Christ returns – whichever comes first – and He says to me, "Ken, did you finish the course? Did you fight the good fight? Did you keep the faith? Did you complete the work that I called you to do? i pray that i will be able to say, "Yes, Lord, i completed the work that You gave me." And i pray that you will be able to say the same – for the honor and glory of God.

In the meantime – until He returns – let's be faithful to give Him praise as we bear witness and report on the great work He has done!

* * *

40

IT SEEMED GOOD TO THE SPIRIT

While Paul and Barnabas were at Antioch of Syria, some men from Judea arrived and began to teach the believers: "Unless you are circumcised as required by the law of Moses, you cannot be saved." Paul and Barnabas disagreed with them, arguing vehemently. Finally, the church decided to send Paul and Barnabas to Jerusalem, accompanied by some local believers, to talk to the apostles and elders about this question.... When they arrived in Jerusalem, Barnabas and Paul were welcomed by the... apostles and elders. They reported everything God had done through them. But then some of the believers who belonged to the sect of the Pharisees stood up and insisted, "The Gentile converts must be circumcised and required to follow the law of Moses." So the apostles and elders met together to resolve this issue.... Everyone listened quietly as Barnabas and Paul told about the miraculous signs and wonders God had done through them among the Gentiles. When they had finished, James stood and said, "Brothers, listen to me. Peter has told you about the time God first visited the Gentiles to take from them a people for himself.... And so my judgment is that we should not make it difficult for the Gentiles who are turning to God...." Then the apostles and elders together with the whole church in Jerusalem chose delegates, and they sent them to Antioch of Syria with Paul and Barnabas to report on this decision. The men chosen were two of the church leaders – Judas (also called Barsabbas) and Silas.
This is the letter they took with them:
"This letter... is written to the Gentile believers in Antioch, Syria, and Cilicia. Greetings! We understand that some men from here have troubled you and upset you with their teaching, but we did not send them! So we decided, having come to complete agreement, to send you official representatives... to confirm what we have decided concerning your question. For it seemed good to the Holy Spirit and

> *to us to lay no greater burden on you than these few requirements: You must abstain from eating food offered to idols, from consuming blood or the meat of strangled animals, and from sexual immorality. If you do this, you will do well...."*
> Acts 15:1-29

* * *

Whenever God is at work, there will always be people who attempt to put their mark on the work. They will endeavor to either add to, or take away from, the gospel. Often times, it is not an intentional attempt to distort the gospel; rather, it is borne out of our personal, cultural or traditional influences. In the case of the men from Judea, they believed that one could not be saved apart from the requirements of the law of Moses. Though they themselves had received salvation by believing in Jesus, they also believed that the laws they had followed since birth were a part of their salvation. They were mixing their personal religious experiences with salvation through Christ, and teaching a distorted gospel. You might say they were practicing syncretism by adding the gospel to their existing beliefs, instead of the gospel replacing their existing beliefs. In essence they were saying that a Gentile had to first become a Jew in order to become a Christian. Simply trusting in Jesus Christ wasn't sufficient; they also had to obey Moses.

Peter himself had learned that salvation is not determined by whether or not one eats meat, or whether one eats pork or doesn't eat pork. Salvation is not dependent upon whether we gather to worship on Sunday, or the Sabbath, or another day. It is not the result of keeping the Law, going through a ritual, or joining a church. We are all sinners before God, for whom Christ died on the cross. He was buried and rose again. He paid the price and extends His salvation to us by His grace which we receive through faith. There is one need, and there is but one gospel – with nothing to be added to or subtracted from it.

The church can still be guilty of trying to add to it today, particularly when we begin to elevate our traditions (whether old or new) to having equal importance to the gospel – i.e. what we wear when we gather to worship, our style of musical worship, the liturgical order of our worship gathering, and so forth. Allow me to use a missional example. For decades, the modern missionary movement from the western church exported a gospel heavily influenced by our western culture. We taught new believers that worship involved meeting in rectangular church buildings, sitting on uncomfortable benches, listening to a preacher that was flanked by notice boards that showed the hymns to be sung on one side, and last week's offering and attendance on the other side. And we built that rectangular building in the midst of villages surrounded by round mud huts, singing songs that were as foreign to the heart cries of the culture as our English language was. But we were convinced that all of that was a part of being a Christian church. We were teaching people from other cultures how to become a westerner in order to be a Christian. Gratefully, the Spirit of God awakened the realization that we must strip away our culture and traditions from the preaching and practice of the gospel as we are making disciples. Just as we have been freed from the Law of Moses, we are freed of the customs and traditions.

But also, whenever God is at work, there will be those who attempt to turn our focus away from the gospel and toward a myriad of other issues. Some will be as trivial as the color of the carpet in the church, the type of coffee we serve, or the Bible translation we use. Others will seek to turn our attention from the gospel to lesser doctrinal issues, such as the ongoing Calvinist-Arminian debate, or political issues – either inside or outside of the church – which cause us to shout at one another across the aisle either literally or figuratively.

The council in Jerusalem was seeking to resolve both an essential doctrinal issue, as well as a fellowship issue. At the conclusion of their deliberation, James stood up and summarized the council's understanding of what they believed God would have the church do. Just as a quick reminder: James was the half-brother of Jesus. He had not come to believe in Jesus until after He rose from the dead. James had grown up with Jesus. He had lived with Him as his brother for twenty-something years, and yet, he had rejected Him as Savior until the final days before Jesus ascended into heaven. In the eighteen years that had passed since His ascension, James had become a leader in the Church in Jerusalem. At the timeframe of this passage, he had already written the Epistle of James to the Jewish believers throughout the Roman provinces, exhorting them to endure in their faith. Now, on behalf of the council, he was speaking to the Gentile and Jewish believers, exhorting them to live out their lives in a way that signified their belief in Christ.

Gentile culture was characterized by idolatry and immorality – not unlike our world today. The early church leaders were admonishing the Gentile believers to walk in a manner worthy of the gospel, just as Paul himself did: *"Live as citizens of heaven, conducting yourselves in a manner worthy of the Good News about Christ"* (Philippians 1:27). That meant that they had to walk in the righteousness of Christ and abstain from any practice of idolatry or immorality -- or even the appearance of it. Thus, they should not even eat any food that had been presented to idols.

To the Jewish believers the council was saying: "God has not placed the burden of the Law upon the Gentiles – and you, as Jews, have no need to do so either." Jesus' blood had been shed for Jew and Gentile alike. One did not need to become like the other to partake in the grace of God. Rather, each needed to receive the gift of God by faith.

Further, just as the Jewish and Gentile believers were to walk in a manner worthy of the gospel, they were to walk in a manner that promoted unity within the body. The new church was a mixture of Jewish-background believers and Gentile-background believers. That church did a great deal of eating together and practicing hospitality. The idea that wherever two or more believers are gathered there is food, is not a new idea! The church leaders were calling upon the Gentile believers to make dietary concessions – to abstain from eating blood, as well as meat from animals that died by strangulation. Those concessions were for the purpose of promoting unity within the body, and presenting a united witness to a lost world.

Yes, we must continue to seek the Spirit and the Scriptures to make sure that we are not adding anything to, or taking anything away, from the gospel. We must come to the same place as those elders and apostles that *"it seem{s} good to the Holy Spirit and to us to lay no greater burden on you than"* this. At the same time, we would do well to learn that problems and differences of opinion will still arise within the church. Those differences can either be a point of dissension and division or an opportunity for growth in a healthy way. How many hurtful fights and church splits could be avoided if we took time to listen to the Spirit to hear "what seems good and right to the Holy Spirit"?

Jesus told us that the world would know that we are His disciples by the love we have for one another (John 13:35). God has opened a wide and effective door of ministry (1 Corinthians 16:9) for us to take the gospel of His grace to a condemned world. But there are forces at work in the church even today that want to close that door. They emphasize those things that would divide us and divert us. Let us learn from the early church in Jerusalem to listen only to God's Word and His Spirit that we might together continue to walk through that wide and effective door... until He returns.

* * *

41

WHO WAS RIGHT?

After some time Paul said to Barnabas, "Let's go back and visit each city where we previously preached the word of the Lord, to see how the new believers are doing." Barnabas agreed and wanted to take along John Mark. But Paul disagreed strongly, since John Mark had deserted them in Pamphylia and had not continued with them in their work. Their disagreement was so sharp that they separated. Barnabas took John Mark with him and sailed for Cyprus. Paul chose Silas, and as he left, the believers entrusted him to the Lord's gracious care. Then he traveled throughout Syria and Cilicia, strengthening the churches there.
Acts 15:36-41

* * *

John Mark was the son of a woman named Mary. It was their family's home in Jerusalem to which the apostle Peter went when the angel led him out of prison (Acts 12:12). Apparently theirs was an affluent family that employed servants – at least one (Acts 12:13). Peter appears to have had a close association with the family. The servant girl recognized his voice, and there was a group of believers gathered in the home at that very moment, praying for Peter's deliverance from prison. Peter subsequently refers to Mark as "my son" (1 Peter 5:13), indicating that he may have been the one who first led Mark to Christ. Peter was, without question, Mark's primary source for his Gospel account.

But, regrettably, to this point, as we move chronologically through Scripture, every time we have seen Mark, he is running away and abandoning those he is following. The first time was when he abandoned Jesus. Mark confesses his abandonment in his Gospel account. He writes, *"One young man following behind was clothed only in a long linen shirt. When the mob tried to grab him, he slipped out of his shirt and ran away naked"* (Mark 14:51-52). The unnamed young man is Mark himself. But in all fairness to him, all of Jesus' disciples abandoned Him in the garden and ran away. However, Mark is the only one that we are told *"ran away naked"*!

The next time we see him, he is accompanying Barnabas and Saul from Jerusalem to Antioch (Acts 12:25), and then as they are sent out by the church in Antioch on their first missionary journey. Mark was Barnabas' cousin (Colossians 4:10), and he journeyed with them as their assistant (Acts 13:5). When Saul (now Paul) and those traveling with him arrived in Pamphylia, we are told that Mark left them and returned to his home in Jerusalem (Acts 13:13).

Luke does not tell us why Mark abandoned them, but his departure came right after what appears to have been a fruitless time in Cyprus (Acts 13:4-12). To that point, they had seen a limited response to the gospel, and they had experienced strong demonic opposition through Elymas, the sorcerer. It is very possible that Mark was discouraged at the difficulty of the journey and decided to return to the comforts of his home. By the way, it is also very possible that God prompted him to return to Jerusalem to protect him from the persecution in Lystra that Paul and Barnabas would suffer. Perhaps God was protecting him for another day. Remember, we will seldom know all that God, in His sovereignty, has protected us from.

All of that brings us to where we are in this passage. Paul and Barnabas have agreed that they need to return to the cities in which churches were planted during their first missionary journey, in order to encourage the new believers. Barnabas wanted to forgive Mark's earlier failure and again bring him with them. His motivation was not only their family relationship, but more importantly, Barnabas, as we know, was an encourager. He was a nurturer. This "son of encouragement" (Acts 4:36) wanted to give Mark another opportunity to prove himself and serve the Lord. i, for one, am grateful for the "Barnabases" in my life who have not given up on me, but have been willing to go the second and third mile – and beyond – with me when i failed. Just as Barnabas had been willing to stand with Paul when it was unpopular to do so (Acts 9:27), he was insisting that they to do the same for Mark.

• • •

Paul, on the other hand, was just as adamant that they not take Mark. Pioneering missionary work requires dedication, resolve, and endurance. Paul saw John Mark as a risk to their mission. After all, he had deserted them on their prior journey and shown weakness. Paul believed their mission was too important, and the work too demanding, to bring someone along who had proven to be unreliable.

As the discussion continued, the two men "disagreed strongly", and neither one was willing to compromise. Here were two dedicated men who were both being used by God in great ways. As we saw in the last chapter, they had just helped bring about unity between the Jewish and Gentile believers; and yet, they could not settle their own disagreement. Their solution was for them to divide the territory and separate. Barnabas would take John Mark with him to Cyprus, and Paul would take Silas with him through Syria and Cilicia to encourage the believers in those churches.

So, who was right? That's probably the wrong question! It really doesn't make much difference. Perhaps both of them were right in some ways, and both of them were wrong in other ways. We know that John Mark ultimately did succeed in the ministry, and that Paul came to love and appreciate him. Paul later calls him a "fellow worker" (Philemon 1:24), and near the end of his life sends a request to Timothy from a Roman prison: *"Bring Mark with you when you come, for he will be helpful to me in my ministry"* (2 Timothy 4:11).

Where there had once existed one missionary team, there were now two! If God had to depend upon perfect people to accomplish His work, He would never get anything done. By His grace, He uses our limitations and imperfections for His good purpose – even our disagreements! Good and godly people in the church will disagree. Paul looked at Mark through the lens: "What can he do for God's work?" Barnabas, on the other hand, asked: "What can God's work do for him?" Both questions are right and important as we follow Jesus. But sometimes it is difficult to walk in that balance.

The key is that in our disagreement that we do not become disagreeable. There is no indication that either of these men – Paul or Barnabas – ever succumbed to "name-calling", or "talking trash" about the other. They did not separate to pout, or go their own way. They honored God even in their separation and, through it, the work was multiplied.

Regrettably, over the years, there have probably been more churches started as the result of church splits than there have been through intentional church planting – at least in the U.S. In too many instances, the splits have resulted in churches that were borne out of animosity, instead of a love for the gospel. When Paul and Barnabas went their separate ways, they did not do so with hearts filled with bitterness and hostility. Their passion for God and His work was never extinguished. They both earnestly sought to follow God with their whole hearts. And as they did, He led them to go their separate ways in a way that multiplied the work, rather than hurt the work.

Even in disagreement, they honored God. They were mature enough in their walk with God to know that the issue was not – "who was right?" – the issue was – "will you follow Me wherever I lead?" We would do well to learn that lesson and follow their lead. Disagreements will arise. Let's be faithful to seek the truth of God's Word in all things, to treat one another with love and respect, and to follow Jesus wherever He leads – even if our paths look different. If we do, we will be able to look back, as Paul later did, to see how God has worked it all for our good and His glory! And He has promised that He always will... until He returns.

* * *

42

WHO IS YOUR TIMOTHY?

Paul went first to Derbe and then to Lystra, where there was a young disciple named Timothy. His mother was a Jewish believer, but his father was a Greek. Timothy was well thought of by the believers in Lystra and Iconium, so Paul wanted him to join them on their journey. In deference to the Jews of the area, he arranged for Timothy to be circumcised before they left, for everyone knew that his father was a Greek. Then they went from town to town, instructing the believers to follow the decisions made by the apostles and elders in Jerusalem. So the churches were strengthened in their faith and grew larger every day.
Acts 16:1-5

* * *

It had been slightly more than two years since Paul and Barnabas had been in Lystra. It was there that Paul had been stoned and left for dead. They had returned to Lystra a few months later on their way back to Antioch, in order to encourage and strengthen the new believers. On one of those initial visits, Paul had met a young man by the name of Timothy, who had then come to faith in Christ. Timothy was the product of a mixed marriage – which was very common in that region. His mother Eunice was a Jew and his father was a Greek Gentile. Eunice and his grandmother Lois had also come to faith through the witness of Paul. In the ensuing two years, all three members of the family had grown in their walk as followers of Jesus and were esteemed by the other believers and well known for their faith. There is, however, no record that Timothy's father came to faith in Christ.

. . .

Seeing Timothy's spiritual growth and maturity, and hearing the good report from the churches, Paul invited him, now in his late teens or early twenties, to join Silas and him on this missionary journey. He would serve as their assistant, in a similar capacity to that which John Mark had served Paul and Barnabas. Perhaps this was another reason that God had led Paul and Barnabas to go their separate ways – so that Paul could disciple Timothy along the journey.

When Timothy decided to go with Paul and Silas, he was immediately confronted with a crisis of belief. That will often be true for us when we take a step of faith that God has placed before us. We will encounter something or be forced to make a decision that will reveal whether we truly believe what God has said. Timothy's crisis of belief stemmed from the fact that in order to join Paul on the trip, Timothy would need to be circumcised. Having been raised by a Greek father, he had not been circumcised as a boy.

An important question for us is – why did he need to be circumcised? Paul had only recently aided the elders and apostles at the Church in Jerusalem in coming to the decision that Gentile believers did not need to be circumcised in order to be saved. So, it was not an issue of salvation. But Paul's ministry was to both Jews and Gentiles – and he was shepherding the new believers to walk in unity with one another. He was nurturing Timothy to also serve in a shepherding role. If Timothy was to serve in that role, he would be working with both Jews and Gentiles in the churches. If Timothy was not circumcised, it would create contention among the Jewish believers. And obviously, contention would disrupt the unity of the body.

Paul described the principle behind this well in his first letter to the believers in Corinth:

"Even though I am a free man with no master, I have become a slave to all people to bring many to Christ. When I was with the Jews, I lived like a Jew to bring the Jews to Christ. When I was with those who follow the Jewish law, I too lived under that law. Even though I am not subject to the law, I did this so I could bring to Christ those who are under the law. When I am with the Gentiles who do not follow the Jewish law, I too live apart from that law so I can bring them to Christ. But I do not ignore the law of God; I obey the law of Christ. When I am with those who are weak, I share their weakness, for I want to bring the weak to Christ. Yes, I try to find common ground with everyone, doing everything I can

to save some. I do everything to spread the Good News and share in its blessings."
(1 Corinthians 9:19-23)

Timothy and Paul could have debated the issue with the Jewish believers that Timothy was not under the law of Moses. But those energies would have been expended to the detriment of the proclamation of the gospel and the nurturing of the church. In order to be a servant of Christ to all the believers, Timothy – under Paul's leadership – knew that it wasn't the law of Moses that he was under, but rather, the law of Christ. Timothy knew that he couldn't follow Christ – by following Paul – if he was not circumcised. He could not become a stumbling block and faithfully serve his Lord (Romans 14:13-15). As Warren Wiersbe writes, *"It is a wise spiritual leader who knows how and why to apply the principles of the Word of God – when to stand firm and when to yield."*

In later years Paul told Timothy, *"Work hard so you can present yourself to God and receive his approval. Be a good worker, one who does not need to be ashamed and who correctly explains the word of truth"* (2 Timothy 2:15). He counseled Timothy, his *"dear son"* (2 Timothy 1:2), from a heart of love, wanting Timothy to stand firm in his own faith and to lead others well.

In the years that followed, Timothy played an important role in the spread of the gospel, and the expansion and strengthening of the churches. He traveled with Paul and often served as his special ambassador to "trouble spots" in the work, such as Corinth. He became the shepherd of the Church in Ephesus, and joined Paul in Rome shortly before the apostle was martyred.

Paul invested his life into Timothy. He heeded his own counsel: *"What you have heard from me in the presence of many witnesses entrust to faithful men, who will be able to teach others also"* (2 Timothy 2:2). He entrusted truth to men like Timothy who in turn taught others. Men, all of us need to be investing our lives into "Timothys". Ladies, you need to be investing your lives into "Loises". Just as we have received from others, we are to give.

So who is your Timothy? Or, who is your Lois? Who are the ones that God has placed in your path to encourage, to mentor and disciple in the truth of God and the work of the ministry? You are never too young, and you are never too old. Continue to be faithful to do so… until He returns.

* * *

43

A MACEDONIAN CALL

Next Paul and Silas traveled through the area of Phrygia and Galatia, because the Holy Spirit had prevented them from preaching the word in the province of Asia at that time. Then coming to the borders of Mysia, they headed north for the province of Bithynia, but again the Spirit of Jesus did not allow them to go there. So instead, they went on through Mysia to the seaport of Troas. That night Paul had a vision: A man from Macedonia in northern Greece was standing there, pleading with him, "Come over to Macedonia and help us!" So we decided to leave for Macedonia at once, having concluded that God was calling us to preach the Good News there.
Acts 16:6-10

* * *

God orders our steps and our stops. Just ask Paul. Time and again Paul was either in the midst of a journey, or preparing to make one, when God stopped him in his tracks and redirected him. It started on the road to Damascus. He was headed there for one purpose, and God gave him a totally different mission. And that redirection changed the trajectory of his life from that point forward. Through those twists and turns this unlikely candidate became the apostle to the Gentiles. Now, the Holy Spirit was preventing him from going where he planned to go and redirecting him to the unplanned and the unforeseen. Paul was sovereignly prevented from entering into the provinces of Asia and Bithynia, and now found himself in the seaport town of Troas on the shore of the Aegean Sea. Paul had never planned to go to Troas – at least on that journey.

. . .

But then again, just ask Silas. He was a leader in the Church in Jerusalem. The elders of the church selected him and Judas Barsabbas to return with Paul and Barnabas to the Church in Antioch in Syria – to help bring the report from the Jerusalem Council (Acts 15:22). Little did he know that Barnabas and Paul would end up having a disagreement that would lead him to accompany Paul on this missionary journey. A brief trip that he thought would last for just a few weeks to a place just three hundred miles away would become a three-plus-year journey into Europe that would cover thousands of miles and result in the planting of churches in Philippi, Berea and Corinth. i sure hope he packed enough socks and underwear!

And we can also ask Timothy. Paul invited this "late-teen, early-twenty-something" to assist him and Silas in the work they would be doing in the churches in Galatia, Phrygia, Pamphylia and Asia. All of this was within a one hundred mile radius of his home. i'm fairly certain he had given some specific parameters for the trip to Timothy's mother Eunice. And those parameters wouldn't have included the Greek and Macedonian provinces of Europe. But then God redirected their steps, and we now have the letters written to encourage the churches that were planted as a result in Philippi, Thessalonica and Corinth – letters that the Spirit of God uses to encourage and teach us even to this day.

We can even ask Dr. Luke. The three men encountered Luke in Troas. They hadn't even planned to go to Troas. We don't know if Luke was already a follower of Christ, or if the physician became a follower as a result of the witness of Paul. But regardless, he became a "fellow laborer" (Philemon 1:24) and boarded the boat with them that took them to Neapolis (Acts 16:10). The Gospel of Luke and the Book of Acts represent twenty-five percent of the New Testament. Would we even have them, if Luke hadn't gotten on the boat? Before you quickly remind me that those Books were a part of God's plan – so, of course, we would have them – i merely want to point out that they were a product of Luke walking in "the steps and stops" that God set before him.

Their journeys had all looked different – and yet, God had ordered their steps for this moment to receive His call to Macedonia. And that day, after having closed so many other doors, God used a vision to redirect them to *"come over to Macedonia and help us!"*

. . .

None of it was "per chance". It was all the result of the activity of a sovereign God who had chosen them and called them – and set their feet in motion – long before they ever realized He had.

As i look back over my own life, i am reminded of significant redirections that i have seen God bring about in my personal journey, some of which pre-date my salvation. There are many, but i will name three specifically. The first is when he redirected me to attend a different university three weeks before classes were to begin. For months i had been enrolled to attend the University of Florida in Gainesville (Go Gators!). But at the last minute, He prompted me to enroll at Florida Atlantic University in Boca Raton (home to the Burrowing Owls!). Go figure! But unbeknownst to me, it was a redirect that would ultimately lead me to marry the help-mate that He had created specifically for me. Then twelve years later, God used my wife as a part of His work to bring me to faith in Him. Soon thereafter, God gave us a clarion call to serve Him in vocational ministry. i can tell you that was nowhere on my career plan! Then twelve years after that, He gave us our own Macedonian call to step out from where we were and join Him on a "Genesis 12 journey" that subsequently has led to the writing of this series of books. What would have happened if i had gone to Gainesville? i have no idea! But i know that this is the path God had for me.

You, too, can look back and see how God has ordered your steps and redirected your path. You can look back and see the twists and turns in the pathway. None of us can see the ones that are still up ahead. But we can be confident in the One who directed Paul, Silas, Timothy and Luke that day in Troas. He has a Kingdom purpose in mind. It is a journey that He will use to fulfill His purpose for our lives – and through our lives. Those men could no more imagine what God had in store for them, than we can today.

You may be at a place very similar to the one these men were just a few days prior to their arrival in Troas. Every door along your path seems to be closing. Every way you have turned has led you to a "dead end". You may be on the edge of discouragement. You may be saying, "God, I saw this going differently!" And you may be wondering if you can keep going on. Stay the course – Troas is just up ahead. And God has a Macedonia to which He is leading you. Keep your eyes on Him and the path He has set before you. Watch for His activity and His vision. He will make it clear. And He will be faithful to lead you all of the way… until He returns.

* * *

44

A MERCHANT BELIEVES

We boarded a boat at Troas and sailed straight across to the island of Samothrace, and the next day we landed at Neapolis. From there we reached Philippi, a major city of that district of Macedonia and a Roman colony. And we stayed there several days. On the Sabbath we went a little way outside the city to a riverbank, where we thought people would be meeting for prayer, and we sat down to speak with some women who had gathered there. One of them was Lydia from Thyatira, a merchant of expensive purple cloth, who worshiped God. As she listened to us, the Lord opened her heart, and she accepted what Paul was saying. She and her household were baptized, and she asked us to be her guests. "If you agree that I am a true believer in the Lord," she said, "come and stay at my home." And she urged us until we agreed.
Acts 16:11-15

* * *

This moment marks the beginning of a new epoch in the history of the gospel. Up to this point, the gospel had not gone further west than Asia Minor. In fact, on this journey, as we've already seen, Paul's original intention had been to stay in Asia, but God had changed his plans. As a result, Paul was able to witness the salvation of the first person in Europe. All of those who would subsequently come to faith over the centuries in Europe would in fact come after her. And as we'll see in a moment, her influence would not stop there.

. . .

Philippi was a Roman colony in Macedonia situated ten miles inland from the port of Neapolis. It had become the home to the Roman governor of the province, and was situated at the eastern end of the Via Egnatia. The highway was one of Rome's massive accomplishments, built on the backs of slave labor. It stretched 490 miles from the Adriatic Sea to the Aegean Sea – which created efficient access for the Roman military force and made it the major trade route over land from Italy to Asia. Thus, Philippi had become a strategic center – politically, commercially, militarily, and culturally.

Paul's first stop in any town or village was always the synagogue, but there does not appear to have been a synagogue in Philippi. Jewish custom required that there be at least ten men for the founding of a synagogue, so apparently there were not ten Jewish men that lived there. However, there was a group of Jewish women, or more than likely, Greek Gentile proselytes, that gathered for prayer along the riverbank. It would appear that Paul's call to Macedonia through the vision of a man, actually was God's response to the prayers of a gathering of women!

One of those women – Lydia – was a successful merchant from Thyatira. She was a seller of purple cloth. There is no mention of Lydia having a husband, so we can presume that she was either a widow, or a freeborn single woman. She had apparently moved to Philippi in order to ply her trade. Thyatira was the trade center for indigo dyes, situated in Asia Minor. It was one of the cities that the Holy Spirit had prevented Paul and Silas from visiting. Later in Scripture, we discover that a church was planted in Thyatira (Revelation 2:18). Though Paul was never able to visit the city in any of his missionary journeys, God apparently had a different plan to establish His church there. And that plan may possibly have included Lydia to be the one to bring the gospel back to her hometown.

God was already at work through His Holy Spirit drawing these women to Himself. Lydia had apparently already turned from the paganism of the world in which she lived, and was seeking to know and worship the one true God, even though she had not yet heard the gospel. This is another reminder like the Ethiopian eunuch (Chapter 22) and Cornelius (Chapter 30). If there is a pagan who in his/her heart honestly seeks to know God, He will reveal Himself in the fullness of the gospel to that individual. God knows exactly what He is doing, and He knows exactly where the seeking hearts are. He will never shut Himself off from a willing seeking heart. He will move heaven and earth to get to that seeking heart.

As God told Israel through Moses: "*If from there you seek the Lord your God, you will find Him if you seek Him with all your heart and with all your soul*" (Deuteronomy 4:29 NIV). God will always meet a seeking heart.

Lydia's salvation story is another great example of God's providence and His care for believers. God rerouted Paul and his traveling companions, while at the same time He also ensured that Lydia would be in the right place at the right time to encounter Paul and hear the Good News of Jesus. But Lydia not only sought the Lord, she listened.

Some people have ears but they don't hear. An example is the situation on the road to Damascus – Saul heard the voice of Jesus and fell down, whereas his traveling companions perceived a voice but did not hear. That's too often the case. People hear without listening. While Jesus was on earth He encountered the Pharisees often. They too heard, but they refused to listen. They were like people who choose to attend a concert or a great musical extravaganza wearing blinders and earplugs. They had no idea what was going on. They didn't see the truth when He stood in their presence and when He spoke they never listened to Him. But that's not the case with Lydia.

As Paul was speaking, Lydia heard the gospel of Jesus Christ, and *the Lord opened her heart*. As soon as she believed, Lydia was baptized, along with the rest of her household. She was obviously a woman of great influence – not only on others within her community, but upon her entire household as well. Whether "her household" refers only to her family, or if it included her servants, is unclear from the biblical account.

Seven years after this time in Philippi, Paul wrote a letter to the Church in Rome. He admonished the believers as to their behavior and told them not to be slothful in business, but rather to be fervent in spirit, and to serve the Lord (Romans 12:11). One can't help but wonder if he was thinking of Lydia when he wrote those words.

After Lydia's conversion and baptism, she insisted that Paul and his friends come stay at her home, if they judged her to be "*a true believer in the Lord*" (verse 15). Luke says that "*she urged us until we agreed,*" which indicates the fervency of her request. The missionaries did indeed judge Lydia to be a true believer, and her home became their place of lodging while they remained in Philippi. But her home became more than that – it also became the meeting place for that starting church. As we'll see in Chapter 46, Luke remained in Philippi to help nurture those that God was adding to this brand new church.

So, let's relook at the guiding hand and empowering work of the Spirit of God through all of this. God closed door after door to lead Paul and his traveling companions to this place – at just the right time. God worked in Lydia's life to bring her to Philippi, and began to work in her heart that she might seek Him. Out of that small prayer gathering, a church was formed in Lydia's home that became the launching pad for the gospel throughout Europe and beyond. Eleven years later, Paul would write this church, while he was imprisoned in Rome, with this admonition: *"I am certain that God, who began the good work within you, will continue His work until it is finally finished on the day when Christ Jesus returns"* (Philippians 1:6).

God began a good work in the life of a merchant who believed – and the ripple effects continue… until He returns.

* * *

45

A JAILER IS SET FREE

A mob quickly formed against Paul and Silas, and the city officials ordered them stripped and beaten with wooden rods. They were severely beaten, and then they were thrown into prison. The jailer was ordered to make sure they didn't escape. So the jailer put them into the inner dungeon and clamped their feet in the stocks. Around midnight Paul and Silas were praying and singing hymns to God, and the other prisoners were listening. Suddenly, there was a massive earthquake, and the prison was shaken to its foundations. All the doors immediately flew open, and the chains of every prisoner fell off! The jailer woke up to see the prison doors wide open. He assumed the prisoners had escaped, so he drew his sword to kill himself. But Paul shouted to him, "Stop! Don't kill yourself! We are all here!" The jailer called for lights and ran to the dungeon and fell down trembling before Paul and Silas. Then he brought them out and asked, "Sirs, what must I do to be saved?" They replied, "Believe in the Lord Jesus and you will be saved, along with everyone in your household." And they shared the word of the Lord with him and with all who lived in his household. Even at that hour of the night, the jailer cared for them and washed their wounds. Then he and everyone in his household were immediately baptized. He brought them into his house and set a meal before them, and he and his entire household rejoiced because they all believed in God.
Acts 16:22-34

* * *

The movement of the Holy Spirit at the riverbank was quickly followed by an attack of the evil one. He did not like "his territory" being invaded by the Spirit of God. In the verses immediately preceding this passage, we read that Paul and Silas repeatedly encountered a slave girl who was possessed by a demon (Acts 16:16-21). She earned a lot of money for her masters by telling fortunes. One day, Paul commanded the demon – in the name of Jesus Christ – to come out of the woman. Instantly it left her – and with it, so did her ability to tell fortunes – as did her ability to make money for her masters. The masters dragged Paul and Silas before the authorities to be punished. And as we read here, a mob quickly formed to do them bodily harm. In light of their own religious and racial prejudices the Roman officials acted rashly without investigating the matter fully. Remember – Paul and Silas were both citizens of Rome which meant that they could not be beaten or harmed until the matter had been properly adjudicated. But the officials failed to do so, and instead, ordered the jailer to severely beat them and throw them into prison.

Here is an important lesson for us. Paul and Silas were wrongfully accused, wrongfully judged and wrongfully punished. But instead of complaining or calling upon God to right these wrongs and judge their enemies, these men prayed and praised God – at the top of their lungs. They weren't shouting their complaints; they were declaring their praise. God responded by shaking the foundations of the prison, opening the doors and loosening their chains – not only those of Paul and Silas, but of every prisoner in the place. They could have all fled to freedom, but instead they all remained right where they were. An awe of God came over all of the prisoners and it overshadowed any fear that they had of their Roman captors. i can't help but wonder how many of the other prisoners came to faith in Christ that night.

But Paul's attention was fixed on the jailer – the one for whom Christ had placed them in the jail. Roman law stated that if a guard lost a prisoner, he would receive the same punishment the prisoner would have received. Potentially there could have been some pretty severe punishments awaiting that host of prisoners. So the jailer was prepared to take his own life instead of facing the shame and penalty of their escape. A hardhearted vindictive person could have easily justified taking vengeance on his persecutor by allowing the jailer to take his own life. But Paul rightly realized that the jailer was really the prisoner – imprisoned by his own sin. Paul was already the freed man – set free from the bondage of sin. Paul knew that he was no more worthy of the grace extended to him through the compassion of Christ on the Damascus road than this cruel jailer. So Paul shouted out, *"Don't kill yourself!"*

. . .

The power of God seized the jailer's attention, but it was the grace and compassion of God as expressed through His servants that brought the jailer to the recognition of his need for a Savior. It wasn't the supernatural power of the earthquake that God used to draw him to Himself; it was the spirit of humility, grace and kindness that drew him to the gospel. We would do well to remember that! Yes, God sometimes works in might and in power, but most often, He works through the fruit of His Spirit – love, joy, peace, patience, kindness, goodness, faithfulness, gentleness and self-control (Galatians 5:22-23) – that cannot be otherwise explained apart from Him.

Having witnessed the unexplainable, he asked, *"What must I do to be saved?"* Paul declared the simple truth of the gospel, and he believed. Then the members of his household heard and believed. And then all of them were baptized. An evening that had begun with the jailer subjecting Paul and Silas to severe beatings ended with him washing their wounds and caring for them.

How many of us would have anticipated that ending to this story? How many of us would have been that forgiving and compassionate toward the jailer? It's easy, as we read this, to get focused on the way God shook the jail and miss the gracious way that two men, under the control of the Holy Spirit, who were wrongfully beaten, graciously responded to those who had beaten them.

So here is what the jailer learned that day – and here is what Paul and Silas "preached" that day – not only through their words, but also through their actions:

- Being a Christian means recognizing that there is a great God who created all things and all persons for His glory – to display the greatness and beauty and power of who He is.
- Being a Christian means recognizing that every person exists to bring glory to God. This is our reason for being. This is the meaning of human life – to reflect back to God and to reflect to each other the glory of our Maker and all His attributes, by loving Him, trusting Him, thanking Him, and obeying Him.
- Being a Christian means recognizing that we have all failed to do this. We have all fallen short of living for His glory. We have exchanged it for other values we preferred, and so we have scorned His glory. The Bible calls it sin. And we are all guilty.

- Being a Christian means recognizing that we are all therefore condemned justly by God to eternal punishment for the infinite guilt of dishonoring an infinitely glorious God.
- Being a Christian means recognizing that the love of God moved Him to send His Son, Jesus Christ, into the world to provide eternal life for helpless sinners. When Jesus died for sinners, He became our ransom, our substitute, and the vindication of God's glory on our behalf.
- Being a Christian means we have gone beyond recognizing those truths, we have repented of our sin and turned to Jesus by faith, believing that all that He is, is all that we need.

Through the power of the gospel, the jailer was set free. But there are many who are still imprisoned in their sin, waiting to hear this powerful truth through our words – and through our actions… until He returns.

* * *

46

ARE WE TURNING THE WORLD UPSIDE DOWN?

Now when they had passed through Amphipolis and Apollonia, they came to Thessalonica, where there was a synagogue of the Jews. And Paul went in, as was his custom, and on three Sabbath days he reasoned with them from the Scriptures, explaining and proving that it was necessary for the Christ to suffer and to rise from the dead, and saying, "This Jesus, whom I proclaim to you, is the Christ." And some of them were persuaded and joined Paul and Silas, as did a great many of the devout Greeks and not a few of the leading women. But the Jews were jealous, and taking some wicked men of the rabble, they formed a mob, set the city in an uproar, and attacked the house of Jason, seeking to bring them out to the crowd. And when they could not find them, they dragged Jason and some of the brothers before the city authorities, shouting, "These men who have turned the world upside down have come here also, and Jason has received them, and they are all acting against the decrees of Caesar, saying that there is another king, Jesus." And the people and the city authorities were disturbed when they heard these things. And when they had taken money as security from Jason and the rest, they let them go.
Acts 17:1-9 (ESV)

* * *

The church in Philippi was continuing to grow. The household of Lydia, combined with the household of the jailer, had now formed the nucleus of a budding church. It was time for Paul, Silas and Timothy to continue on their journey to spread the gospel to other cities in Macedonia. It appears that Luke did not go with them, but remained in Philippi for a short period to shepherd those that God was raising up to be the leaders of the church.

Paul and company traveled to Thessalonica. The city was so named after the step-sister of Alexander the Great, and was another prominent city of its day. Three rivers flowed from the city into the Aegean which made it another major seaport for trade and transportation. It was a "free city" which meant that it had an elected citizens assembly and it had no Roman garrison stationed within its walls.

There were obviously more than ten Jewish men in Thessalonica because there was a synagogue in the city. Paul labored at his tentmaking trade through the week, but on the Sabbath, as was his practice, he went to the synagogue seeking out devout Jews and Gentiles, "God-seekers" and proselytes. He returned for two more Sabbaths, each time using the Scriptures to share the gospel message of Christ's death, burial and resurrection.

After three weeks of ministry, Paul saw a large number of people believe, especially Greek proselytes and women of influence. Among the men were Aristarchus and Secundus, who would later travel with Paul, as well as Jason, who welcomed Paul and company to lodge in his home. But seeing the spread of the gospel, the unbelieving Jews became envious, formed a mob and began to incite a riot against this infant church. They declared, *"These men who have turned the world upside down have come here also."*

The reputation of Paul and Silas – and more importantly the reputation of the gospel – preceded them. The only part of that statement that they got wrong was that truly the gospel was turning the world "right side up". A world that had become disoriented and blinded by sin had now been transformed by the Light of the world and was being turned to face heavenward and bring worship, honor and glory to God. And that work which had already begun in other cities in Europe and Asia was now taking place right here in Thessalonica!

The Jews sought to bring Paul and Silas before the city council under false accusations that were very similar to those used against Jesus. He had truly been the One to turn the world "right side up" that day when He rose from the grave. Now these two men who He was using to continue His work were also being falsely accused of disturbing the peace and promoting treason against Caesar.

Unable to find Paul and Silas, the Jews turned to Jason and some of the other new local believers and brought them before the council declaring them to be guilty of treason by virtue of their newly professed belief in Jesus. These believers were now in turn being accused of "turning the world upside down". Jason was forced to post a bond and guarantee that Paul and Silas would leave the city and not return. This was Satan's attempt through the unbelieving Jews to hinder the work that the Spirit of God had begun. But though Paul and Silas would be forced to leave, they all were soon to discover that what God begins, He continues and brings to completion (Philippians 1:6).

Paul himself wrote regarding these believers and their boldness despite the persecution:

> *So you received the message with joy from the Holy Spirit in spite of the severe suffering it brought you. In this way, you imitated both us and the Lord. As a result, you have become an example to all the believers in Greece – throughout both Macedonia and Achaia. And now the word of the Lord is ringing out from you to people everywhere, even beyond Macedonia and Achaia, for wherever we go we find people telling us about your faith in God. We don't need to tell them about it, for they keep talking about the wonderful welcome you gave us and how you turned away from idols to serve the living and true God. And they speak of how you are looking forward to the coming of God's Son from heaven – Jesus, whom God raised from the dead.*
> (1 Thessalonians 1:6-10)

So what about us – is anyone accusing us of turning the world upside down? Are the truth we are declaring and the actions we are demonstrating enough of an indictment of our belief in Christ to make the unbelieving world take notice and be in an uproar? Is that true in our own lives personally, like it was in Paul and Silas? Is that true in the witness of our church, like it was in the church of Thessalonica? Is that true in our witness as the larger body of Christ? It was true in the first century because the believers reflected the One who they followed. Does the world around us see Him in our lives? Or have we become content to blend in? Have we become more fearful of the world in which we live instead of the

One true God who is worthy of our reverent fear and awe? Have we become content in maintaining the status quo? Or are we truly committed to following the One who turned the world "upside down"?

The believers in the Church in Thessalonica are a part of that great crowd of witnesses that surrounds us (Hebrews 12:1). Will we become that same *"example to all believers"* that they were? Will *"the word of the Lord ring out from us to people everywhere"* as it did from them? Will others find that wherever they go, that *"people tell them about our faith in God, and how we serve the living and true God"*? Will the world *"speak of how we are looking forward to the coming of God's Son"*? Will the world even notice if we have been here? i pray that we will be found faithful in following the example of the church of Thessalonica as we follow Jesus in *"turning the world upside down"* – or rather, "right side up" – until He returns.

* * *

47

AN UNKNOWN GOD

While Paul was waiting for them in Athens, he was deeply troubled by all the idols he saw everywhere in the city. He went to the synagogue to reason with the Jews and the God-fearing Gentiles, and he spoke daily in the public square to all who happened to be there…. Then they took him to the high council of the city. "Come and tell us about this new teaching," they said…. So Paul, standing before the council, addressed them as follows: "Men of Athens, I notice that you are very religious in every way, for as I was walking along I saw your many shrines. And one of your altars had this inscription on it: 'To an Unknown God.' This God, whom you worship without knowing, is the one I'm telling you about. He is the God who made the world and everything in it….From one man He created all the nations throughout the whole earth…. His purpose was for the nations to seek after God and perhaps feel their way toward Him and find Him…. For in Him we live and move and exist…. And since this is true, we shouldn't think of God as an idol designed by craftsmen from gold or silver or stone. … Now He commands everyone everywhere to repent of their sins and turn to Him. For He has set a day for judging the world with justice by the man He has appointed, and He proved to everyone who this is by raising Him from the dead." When they heard Paul speak about the resurrection of the dead, some laughed in contempt, but others said, "We want to hear more about this later." That ended Paul's discussion with them, but some joined him and became believers. Among them were Dionysius, a member of the council, a woman named Damaris, and others with them.
Acts 17:16-34

* * *

After leaving Thessalonica, Paul preached the gospel in the city of Berea. News that the gospel had spread to Berea reached the Jews in Thessalonica and they traveled there to disrupt the work. Despite their disruption, there were many who believed in Jesus. But the new believers sensing the danger that Paul was in, encouraged him to leave the city. Some of the believers traveled with him as he departed from Berea and journeyed to Athens, while Silas and Timothy remained in Berea to disciple the new believers.

Paul was waiting for Silas and Timothy to arrive in Athens. While waiting, he went to the synagogue on the Sabbath and spent the remaining days in the market of the public square, probably selling tents, all the while sharing the Good News of Jesus. As he walked throughout the city, Paul witnessed their many objects of worship. He saw their altars, their idols and their temples. As a matter of fact, they even had an altar to the "Unknown God". The Athenians didn't want to leave anyone out. Everything and anything had become the object of their worship – except the One true God.

Paul saw the many objects of their worship because he was looking for them. A few years ago, a group of us gathered in New York City to discuss how believers in the U.S. can more effectively share the gospel with the growing number of people groups that God is leading to live in this country – people from most every language, tribe and nation. We were being challenged that Christ's Great Commission includes not only going to the ends of the earth, it also includes reaching out to those who are our immediate neighbors.

In the course of our gathering, we were challenged that we need to open our eyes, our ears and all of our senses as we walk through our cities and neighborhoods, and discover all of the many people – and different people groups – that God is placing within our regular traffic pattern. We were challenged that typically we walk through life with our heads down and our blinders on – we look but we don't see, and we hear but we don't listen. If we would truly be witnesses, we must first be open to witness all that is going on around us – and *who* is around us. When we remove the blinders, we begin to see and learn more about the people who are around us. We also begin to see the objects of worship of those around us – just like Paul did.

. . .

We need to be "seeing" literally. Just as Paul did. We need to open our eyes to see the literal altars, idols and temples that are around us, and gain insight into the beliefs of our neighbors, asking God to enable those insights to be a bridge to share the Good News. God enabled Paul to see the altar to the "Unknown God" in order that he might better understand the spiritual hunger of the Athenians and use the altar as a bridge to introduce them to the One true God.

But also, we need to be attuned to see figuratively. First, we are to watch for the altars. Altars are not the object of worship; they are a means of worship. We often think of an altar as a structure upon which an offering or sacrifice is made. Most Christian churches have a place or a structure that is referred to as the altar – and so do the Buddhists, the Hindus, the Jews and the Paganists – to name just a few. In Christian churches, it is often the place (most often at the front of the church) to which people are invited to come to pray or make a public commitment to Christ. But altars are not only physical structures or places, they can also be metaphorical. Altars can be those commitments in our lives that we are unwilling to give up regardless of the pain and destruction they may cause to others. For example, over the years i have encountered men and women engaged in ministry who became so wrapped up in the ministry that the activity of ministry became an altar on which their family and family relationships were sacrificed and destroyed. Causes of any kind, no matter how worthy, can become an altar, when we allow the pursuit of the cause to control us. Addictions can be altars. Far too many lives have been sacrificed and destroyed on the altar of addiction.

Second, we are to watch for the idols. They are the object of worship. Sometimes altars can become idols as well. In our walk with Christ, our service to Him can be an altar on which we express worship to Him. But we must guard making our service the object of our worship. That danger comes into play when we become focused on what we are doing, rather than the One who is the reason for what we are doing.

But there are many other idols we can worship. Money is "at" or "near" the top of the list for many. That is why Jesus spoke so often about money. Money is one of those things of which we can never have enough. When my wife and i were first married and starting out, we would frequently look at each other and say, "All we need is $10,000." Interestingly enough, once we had the $10,000, then all we needed was another $10,000, and so on!

. . .

Another common idol – which often goes hand-in-hand with money – is success. It can be success in anything – a career, a hobby, a pass-time (such as sports), a relationship, a possession, a goal, and so on. We have elevated anything to an idol when the pursuit of "it" has become all-consuming. There is only one object worthy of our worship and all-consuming pursuit – and that is the Almighty God. Anything that we have placed before Him has become an idol.

Third, we are to watch for the temples. They, too, can become the object of our worship. We can become so preoccupied with the temple that we lose sight of why it exists to begin with. We know that Paul wrote, *"Don't you realize that your body is the temple of the Holy Spirit, who lives in you and was given to you by God?"* (1 Corinthians 6:19) But we can lose sight of the continuation of that verse: *"…You do not belong to yourself,"* and become so focused on maintaining our bodies that we begin to worship them! Or – and i have seen this too many times – we elevate the place that we worship to the degree that it is all about the beautiful building, or the beautiful fixtures, or the wonderful programs – and totally miss the true object of our worship. Another example is creation itself. We see the beauty of God's creation and begin to worship it. That was a common practice among the Athenians, and it is still all too common today.

Most of those who heard Paul as he addressed the council did not believe. But Luke writes, *"some joined him and became believers. Among them were Dionysius, a member of the council, a woman named Damaris…."* The Holy Spirit used the "bridge" of the altar to the "Unknown God" to draw some of those who heard to faith in Jesus. The fact that Dionysius and Damaris are mentioned by name indicates that they were prominent in Athens and/or were somehow known to Luke's original readers in the early church. Some commentators assert that Damaris was the wife of Dionysius, but that is pure speculation.

As we close this chapter, let us be mindful to be watchful for the objects of worship of those who are all around us. And be watchful – and responsive – to the way the Holy Spirit would lead us to walk across the bridges that He has provided to share the Good News. Just as it was in Athens, there will be some who are just across the bridge waiting to hear… until He returns.

48

THE CORINTHIAN CHURCH

*Then Paul left Athens and went to Corinth. There he became acquainted with a
Jew named Aquila, born in Pontus, who had recently arrived from Italy with his
wife, Priscilla. They had left Italy when Claudius Caesar deported all Jews from
Rome. Paul lived and worked with them, for they were tentmakers just as he was.
Each Sabbath found Paul at the synagogue, trying to convince the Jews and
Greeks alike. And after Silas and Timothy came down from Macedonia, Paul
spent all his time preaching the word. He testified to the Jews that Jesus was the
Messiah. But when they opposed and insulted him, Paul shook the dust from his
clothes and said, "Your blood is upon your own heads – I am innocent. From now
on I will go preach to the Gentiles." Then he left and went to the home of Titius
Justus, a Gentile who worshiped God and lived next door to the synagogue.
Crispus, the leader of the synagogue, and everyone in his household believed in
the Lord. Many others in Corinth also heard Paul, became believers, and were
baptized. One night the Lord spoke to Paul in a vision and told him, "Don't be
afraid! Speak out! Don't be silent! For I am with you, and no one will attack and
harm you, for many people in this city belong to Me." So Paul stayed there for the
next year and a half, teaching the word of God. But when Gallio became governor
of Achaia, some Jews rose up together against Paul and brought him before the
governor for judgment. They accused Paul of "persuading people to worship God
in ways that are contrary to our law." But just as Paul started to make his
defense, Gallio turned to Paul's accusers and said, "Listen, you Jews, if this were
a case involving some wrongdoing or a serious crime, I would have a reason to
accept your case. But since it is merely a question of words and names and your
Jewish law, take care of it yourselves. I refuse to judge such matters." And he
threw them out of the courtroom. The crowd then grabbed Sosthenes, the leader of
the synagogue, and beat him right there in the courtroom. But Gallio paid no*

*attention. Paul stayed in Corinth for some time after that, then said good-bye to
the brothers and sisters and went to nearby Cenchrea.*
Acts 18:1-18

* * *

After Paul completed the work that the Holy Spirit had for him in Athens, he went to Corinth. Bear in mind that there would always be more work to be done in Athens. But God gave those assignments to others – like Dionysius and Damaris. Paul's part was completed. God orders our steps according to His purpose for His season. Those "seasons" have different durations. His work will continue until He returns – but our role in the work is to do what He has put before us to do for the season that He has placed us there to do so. When that season comes to an end, He will show us. As He does, we are to follow Him. That is exactly what Paul was doing.

Corinth's reputation for wickedness was known throughout the Roman Empire. With a population of 200,000 people, the city was the capital of the province of Achaia, and a center for trade – of all types – and travel. Money, vice, and philosophies of all varieties found a home in Corinth. There were many philosophers and teachers of false religions in Corinth preying on an easily swayed and superstitious population. When you live in a city built on the fulfillment of feelings and desires instead of truth, you'll fall for anything because you stand for nothing.

One way that Paul distinguished himself from the plethora of religious hucksters in the city was by supporting himself as a tentmaker. Soon after he arrived in the city, he met Aquila and Priscilla, who were also tentmakers. We don't know if they were already followers of Jesus when Paul met them, or if they surrendered their lives soon after. But they quickly became co-laborers with Paul – not only in tentmaking, but also in the spreading of the gospel in the city. With their hands, hearts and home, they dedicated themselves to the work of the Lord. When Silas and Timothy arrived from Macedonia, they brought with them financial aid from the church in Philippi (2 Corinthians 11:9), which enabled Paul to spend more of his time preaching the gospel.

As was Paul's practice, he had begun his teaching in Corinth in the synagogue. But many of the Jews opposed and insulted him. One notable exception was Crispus, the leader of the synagogue, who, together with everyone in his household, came to believe in Christ, and became a part of the new church of Corinth. Paul viewed the rejection by the Jews as a release from God to preach the gospel among the Gentiles.

God led Paul to a Gentile proselyte by the name Titius Justus who soon believed in Jesus and opened his home for the new believers to gather for the worship of God and the teaching of the gospel. Titius Justus lived right next door to the synagogue, so the Jews had a "ringside seat" to witness the many who were coming to faith and being baptized. Though Jewish opposition grew, God did not lead Paul to leave Corinth as He had in Thessalonica and Berea. God encouraged Paul and affirmed His direction for him to stand firm and remain faithful in that which He had placed before him: *"For I am with you, and no one will attack and harm you, for many people in this city belong to Me."*

So Paul stood firm for the next eighteen months – not only confident in the promise of God, but also in the presence of His Spirit. You and i would do well to heed that lesson. There will be times in our journey when circumstances will be pressing in on us. We may be tempted to throw in the towel and move on. But be mindful, we're not done until God says we're done. We must stand firm and rely on the promise and presence of God. Throughout my time in ministry, God has taken me to a word of admonition He directed me through when He first called me into vocational ministry. The word comes from the epistle that Paul wrote to the Colossians. As he closes the letter, he writes a "by-the-way-type" word of admonition to a man by the name of Archippus. He says, *"Take heed to the ministry which you have received in the Lord, that you may fulfill it"* (Colossians 4:17 NASB). My paraphrase is: "Stick with it until I tell you otherwise, that you may complete what I have called you to do."

Luke records one example of God's protection over Paul there in Corinth. Apparently, the arrival of a new governor from Rome, by the name of Gallio, gave the unbelieving Jews hope that Rome might declare this new "Christian sect" illegal. So they illegally assembled a mob and forcefully brought Paul before their new governor, making false accusations about him. But even before Paul was able to make any defense, Gallio turned to Paul's accusers and *"threw them out of the courtroom"*. Paul didn't need to raise a defense – his Defender raised up one to come to his defense! The crowd then turned on the new leader of the synagogue who had brought the charges – Sosthenes – and *"beat him right there in the courtroom."*

. . .

Before you grieve for Sosthenes – take heart. Sosthenes became a follower of Christ sometime soon after that beating. Sosthenes wrote the first letter to the new church in Corinth on Paul's behalf (1 Corinthians 1:1). So, he not only became a follower, but also a co-laborer. God truly does work in mysterious ways – and in ways we would never anticipate – or even ask or think (Ephesians 3:20).

Be mindful of these truths as you continue in your journey. The same God who protected Paul, who defended him, who encouraged him, and who directed him – goes before you – and He will be faithful to do so... until He returns.

★ ★ ★

49

WHAT DOES YOUR BAPTISM MEAN?

Now a Jew named Apollos, a native of Alexandria, came to Ephesus. He was an eloquent man, competent in the Scriptures. He had been instructed in the way of the Lord. And being fervent in spirit, he spoke and taught accurately the things concerning Jesus, though he knew only the baptism of John. He began to speak boldly in the synagogue, but when Priscilla and Aquila heard him, they took him aside and explained to him the way of God more accurately. And when he wished to cross to Achaia, the brothers encouraged him and wrote to the disciples to welcome him. When he arrived, he greatly helped those who through grace had believed, for he powerfully refuted the Jews in public, showing by the Scriptures that the Christ was Jesus. And it happened that while Apollos was at Corinth, Paul passed through the inland country and came to Ephesus. There he found some disciples. And he said to them, "Did you receive the Holy Spirit when you believed?" And they said, "No, we have not even heard that there is a Holy Spirit." And he said, "Into what then were you baptized?" They said, "Into John's baptism." And Paul said, "John baptized with the baptism of repentance, telling the people to believe in the one who was to come after him, that is, Jesus." On hearing this, they were baptized in the name of the Lord Jesus. And when Paul had laid his hands on them, the Holy Spirit came on them, and they began speaking in tongues and prophesying. There were about twelve men in all.
Acts 18:24 – 19:7

* * *

After his exoneration by Governor Gallio, Paul remained in Corinth for a short while before he departed, taking Timothy, Aquila and

Priscilla with him. Silas appears to have remained in Corinth for a short while after Paul's departure. (We then lose track of Silas for about ten years until he joins Peter in Rome.) Paul and his companions traveled across the Aegean Sea, departing from the port of Cenchrea and arriving in Ephesus. Paul remained there only a short while and then sailed to Caesarea Maritima, probably still accompanied by Timothy. Aquila and Priscilla, however, remained in Ephesus to disciple the new believers and assist the newly forming church (Acts 18:18-23).

About one year after Paul had departed from Ephesus, Apollos arrived. Ephesus, with its 300,000 inhabitants, was the capital city of the Roman province of Asia and an important commercial center. Thanks to its thriving harbor, the city grew wealthy on trade. Thanks to the temple of Diana, considered to have been one of the seven wonders of the world, the city attracted hosts of visitors. Cultic prostitution was an important part of temple worship, and hundreds of "priestesses" were available in the temple.

Apollos arrived in Ephesus from Alexandria, a center of education and philosophy with a large Jewish community. He had been well-schooled in the Scriptures (the Old Testament). He obviously had a boldness, a confidence and an eloquence in speech. He was well equipped to share the truths that he had learned. The only problem was that he did not yet know the whole gospel.

While Apollos was receiving his education in Alexandria, he had learned the truths that John the Baptist had proclaimed. John had preached about the coming salvation through the Messiah. He had even preached about a future baptism of the Holy Spirit (Matthew 3:11). But remember, none of those two prophecies had yet been fulfilled when John was beheaded. He believed by faith, but never witnessed it by sight – and at the time, neither had his disciples. So that was the message that Apollos had heard in Alexandria – and up until now, he had not yet personally heard the rest of the Good News himself. He had not yet believed in Jesus – because he had not yet heard about Jesus' redemptive work!

But God had arranged for him to encounter Priscilla and Aquila in Ephesus, that he might hear *"the way of God"* – *"more accurately"* and more completely. As a result, Apollos came to faith and truly believed. He was then baptized himself. Luke tells us that it then seemed good to the believers in Ephesus – and to the Holy Spirit – to send him to Corinth. Two of those believers who would have encouraged him to go to Corinth were Aquila and Priscilla. The new church in Corinth was close to their heart. They knew that Silas was no longer there. They probably believed that Apollos' understanding of the Scriptures would be of great help in the spiritual nurturing of that "very young" church. So off Apollos went.

Soon after Apollos left for Corinth, Paul returned to Ephesus – now on his "third missionary journey" through Asia and Europe. He encountered twelve men who had been discipled by Apollos before he himself had trusted in Jesus. When the men told Paul that they had not yet heard of the Holy Spirit, he knew that they had not yet truly been born again. They had been baptized and were seeking to be religious, but they had not yet heard the complete gospel of the saving work of Jesus. Therefore, they had not yet had an opportunity to fully receive the free gift of salvation.

In the first century, a person's baptismal experience was a clear indication of his or her spiritual condition. You had the baptism of John, which was a baptism of repentance under the Old Covenant, looking forward to the arrival of the coming Messiah. It had been important before the arrival of Jesus because it acknowledged the need for a Savior and the promise of His soon arrival.

Once Jesus began His earthly ministry, you then had the baptism being performed by His disciples, confirming Christ's arrival, but still looking ahead to the death, burial and resurrection of Christ, to be followed by the arrival of the Holy Spirit. Finally, you had the baptism that occurred on and following the Day of Pentecost, acknowledging the completed work of salvation through Christ and the indwelling presence of His Holy Spirit. The pattern was clearly established once the gospel made its way to the Gentiles, as recorded in Acts 10:43-48:

- sinners hear the Word of God,
- they repent of their sin and believe in Jesus Christ,
- they immediately receive the Holy Spirit, and
- they are baptized as a testimony of their salvation.

A person's baptismal experience today is also a clear indication of his or her spiritual condition. Baptism is not a part of salvation; it follows our salvation. There can be no salvation apart from the saving work of Jesus through His death, burial and resurrection (1 Corinthians 15:3-4). Then once we repent and believe by faith in Jesus, He seals our salvation by indwelling us with His Spirit (Ephesians 1:13-14). We then follow Christ in water baptism as an act of obedience – He told us to be baptized; and as an act of witness – bearing public testimony of the salvation we have already received by grace.

This account is an important reminder for us – not only for ourselves – but for those that God will lead us to disciple in the days ahead. It isn't sufficient for us to be passionate and bold in declaring only a portion of the gospel as Apollos was initially doing. In his enthusiasm, he led these twelve men to only have partial understanding – a partial understanding that still left them without a saving relationship with Jesus. Left in that condition, those men would have probably passed that *fatal* flaw – that incomplete truth – on to others. But God in His sovereignty brought Paul into their lives, so that they could hear the entire gospel.

We must be faithful to communicate the full story of salvation. Jesus told us, *"Go and make disciples of all the nations, baptizing them in the name of the Father and the Son and the Holy Spirit. Teach these new disciples to obey all the commands I have given you"* (Matthew 28:19-20a). Once they have become disciples, we must baptize them and teach them to obey ALL that He commanded. So that they in turn can do the same. And as we do, He told us we can be certain of this: *"I am with you always, even to the end of the age"* (Matthew 28:20b). Yes, He will be with us and empower us to bear witness to the full story of His salvation … until He returns.

* * *

50

THE EPHESIAN CHURCH

A solemn fear descended on the city, and the name of the Lord Jesus was greatly honored.... So the message about the Lord spread widely and had a powerful effect.... About that time, serious trouble developed in Ephesus concerning the Way. It began with Demetrius, a silversmith who had a large business manufacturing silver shrines of the Greek goddess Artemis. He kept many craftsmen busy. He called them together... and addressed them as follows: "Gentlemen, you know that our wealth comes from this business. But as you have seen and heard, this man Paul has persuaded many people that handmade gods aren't really gods at all.... I'm not just talking about the loss of public respect for our business. I'm also concerned that the temple of the great goddess Artemis will lose its influence and that Artemis... will be robbed of her great prestige!" ...Soon the whole city was filled with confusion. Everyone rushed to the amphitheater, dragging along Gaius and Aristarchus, who were Paul's traveling companions from Macedonia. Paul wanted to go in, too, but the believers wouldn't let him. ... Inside, the people were all shouting, some one thing and some another. Everything was in confusion. In fact, most of them didn't even know why they were there. The Jews in the crowd pushed Alexander forward and told him to explain the situation. He motioned for silence and tried to speak. But when the crowd realized he was a Jew, they started shouting again and kept it up for about two hours.... At last the mayor was able to quiet them down enough to speak. "Citizens of Ephesus," he said. "...You have brought these men here, but they have stolen nothing from the temple and have not spoken against our goddess. If Demetrius and the craftsmen have a case against them, ...they can be settled in a legal assembly. I am afraid we are in danger of being charged with rioting by the Roman government, since there is no cause for all this commotion." ...Then he dismissed them, and they dispersed.

Acts 19:17-41

* * *

Paul remained in Ephesus for three years. Throughout that time, he and the Ephesian church remained focused on the main thing – preaching the gospel and making disciples – through their words and their actions. The Lord Jesus was honored, the gospel spread widely and more were added to the Kingdom.

Paul did not arouse the opposition of the silversmiths by picketing the temple of Diana or staging anti-idolatry demonstrations. All he did was teach the truth daily and send out those who were coming to faith in Christ to do likewise to the lost in the city. Paul and the followers of "The Way" were declaring the true God, and pointing people to cleansing and purity through the free grace of God. And the Holy Spirit was drawing more people to faith each day.

Demetrius, the other craftsmen and sellers, as well as all of the leaders and purveyors of false religion, were promoting idolatry and immorality – motivated by greed and selfish ambition. As more and more people began to follow Christ, those who made a living from the worship of Diana began to see a decline in their income. The silversmiths were much more motivated by their concern for their jobs and declining incomes than they were about Diana and the temple. But they were cunning enough to not make that known; instead, they chose to use the art of manipulation. Demetrius made use of the two things the Ephesians loved the most – the honor of their city and the greatness of their goddess and her temple.

Demetrius was able to use those two passions to stir many in the city into an uproar – an uproar that became a riot. A crowd of about 25,000 shouting people began to make their way to the amphitheater. Along the way, they intended to seize Paul, but, being unable to find him, they seized two of his traveling companions – Gaius and Aristarchus, believers from Macedonia. When Paul learned what had taken place, he wanted to enter the amphitheater, but the believers, as well as some of the city leaders, wisely counseled him to stay away.

Most of the people in the amphitheater had no idea what was taking place or why they were there. They had been caught up in the emotion of the moment – and there is nothing more dangerous than an emotionally-charged, disoriented crowd.

Prior to this riot, the Jewish leaders had become envious of the popularity of Paul and The Way. They were losing adherents at a troubling rate which was, in turn, diminishing their bases of power and income. These leaders apparently saw this crowd as an opportunity for them to gain an upper hand over The Way. So they pushed one of their leaders – Alexander – forward to speak to the crowd. No doubt he wanted to tell the crowd that the Jews did not endorse Paul and The Way. They, too, wanted to see them stopped from making any further inroads into the city.

But Alexander's appearance only aroused the crowd even more, causing the deafening shouts to continue for two more hours. The crowd knew that the Jews also did not approve of the idols and did not honor Diana. The Ephesians saw the Jews as interlopers into their way of life, as much as, or maybe even more than, the followers of The Way. The only thing protecting the Jews was the Roman law that gave them freedom of religion.

Finally, it was the mayor of the city that was able to quiet down the crowd – and the mayor's interruption was motivated politically for his own self-preservation. Ephesus had been designated as a "free city" by Rome with its own elected citizens assembly. Rome extended that privilege merely as a concession, and would have welcomed any excuse to revoke that privilege. If Rome chose to do so, the mayor would be out of a job. So, he chose to use the same tactics to calm the crowd that Demetrius had employed to arouse them. He, too, reminded them of the greatness of their city and of their goddess.

The mayor declared that Paul and The Way were innocent of any crime. Rather, he accused Demetrius and the craftsmen of acting in an unlawful manner and admonished them to seek lawful remedy if there truly were any valid complaints.

The crowd was dismissed, and no doubt returned to their homes congratulating themselves for their success in defending their great city and their famous goddess. Regrettably, it is doubtful that the event caused many – or any – to question the truthfulness of their own beliefs, or the truths being preached by Paul. Jesus once said, *"You can enter God's Kingdom only through the narrow gate. The highway to hell is broad, and its gate is wide for the many who choose that way. But the gateway to life is very narrow and the road is difficult, and only a few ever find it"* (Matthew 7:13-14). All too often, it is much easier to believe a lie and follow the crowd, than to take a stand for the truth.

Today Ephesus is gone, and so is the world-wide worship of Diana. The city and the temple are gone, as is the silversmiths' guild. But the Good News of Christ lives on. And we are recipients of the truth that arose out of that Church in Ephesus. We have the Epistle to the Ephesians, as well as First and Second Timothy. Ten years after Paul left the city, the apostle John came to pastor the church. But the church subsequently drifted from its first love – Jesus (Revelation 2:1-7).

There are important lessons for us to glean from this church and this experience. The church thrived as they remained faithfully focused on their Lord and His gospel purpose. They didn't spend their time demonstrating against the immorality of the day; they spent their time sharing the gospel. They didn't spend their time debating the false religions of the day; they spent their time sharing the gospel. They didn't spend their time fighting off false attacks; they entrusted those to God and kept sharing the gospel.

In a day that we as the church have become better known for what we are against than what we are for, we too would be wise to heed the warning to return to our first love – Jesus. And share His gospel – in word and deed – until He returns.

* * *

51

EACH ONE RAN THEIR RACE – PART 1

When the uproar was over, Paul sent for the believers and encouraged them. Then he said good-bye and left for Macedonia. While there, he encouraged the believers in all the towns he passed through. Then he traveled down to Greece, where he stayed for three months. He was preparing to sail back to Syria when he discovered a plot by some Jews against his life, so he decided to return through Macedonia. Several men were traveling with him. They were Sopater son of Pyrrhus from Berea; Aristarchus and Secundus from Thessalonica; Gaius from Derbe; Timothy; and Tychicus and Trophimus from the province of Asia. They went on ahead and waited for us at Troas. After the Passover ended, we boarded a ship at Philippi in Macedonia and five days later joined them in Troas, where we stayed a week.
Acts 20:1-6

* * *

This passage is one of those sections of the Bible that would be easy for us to avoid, or even skip over – just another list of names and places, most of which are hard to pronounce. Yet, if we believe that every line of God's Word is not only inspired by Him, but is also a gift from Him, then there is treasure that He would have us glean from this travelogue. Let's take a few minutes to look at the eleven companions of Paul that are mentioned here.

<u>Timothy and Erastus</u>
While in Ephesus, Paul had received distressing news regarding the

church in Corinth. It prompted him to dispatch Timothy – with his pastoral heart -- to deliver a letter of correction (now known as 1 Corinthians). Timothy subsequently returned to Ephesus with continuing concerns about the Corinthian church, which included a significant personal offense against Paul and a challenge to his authority by one unnamed individual. When Timothy returned to Ephesus, he brought with him a man by the name of Erastus.

Erastus was the city treasurer in Corinth (Romans 16:23), and a new believer in Jesus Christ. Erastus was an influential man in the city. His duties likely included the upkeep of civic buildings, city streets, and city services, as well as the collection of public revenue. In that role, he also would have been called upon to settle public disputes. Erastus came to faith through Paul's second missionary journey (Chapter 48) and had become a leader within the Corinthian church. He apparently joined Timothy to bring further first hand witness to Paul of the continuing turmoil in Corinth.

In spite of his prominent rank, Erastus appears to have regarded ministry as his top priority. He left his work in Corinth to ask Paul to help bring healing to the division within the church, and then subsequently was used to spread the gospel into other lands. He did not, however, neglect his public duties, but rather, was a servant of the people, such as Paul describes in Romans 13:3-4.

While Paul was in Ephesus – before the riot – he felt compelled by the Holy Spirit that he must go to Jerusalem (Acts 19:21). In many respects, his face was set like flint toward Jerusalem, in much the same way that Jesus had set His face toward that city (Isaiah 50:7; Luke 9:51). The Father clearly had His purpose in mind. And though Paul, unlike Jesus, did not know all of what the Father's plan included in Jerusalem, he knew that he must be about the journey. He also knew, however, that he must first spend some time – a final time – with the churches that had been planted in Macedonia, Greece and Asia before going to Jerusalem. He sent Timothy and Erastus on ahead to Macedonia, while he concluded his time in Ephesus (Acts 19:22).

Titus and Trophimus
After the riot, Paul bid the Ephesian believers farewell and departed for Macedonia. He travelled through Troas, with the hope that he would

see Titus there. Titus, you will recall, was a Greek from Antioch. He was led to the Lord by Paul, whereupon he served as Paul's secretary and interpreter. Titus accompanied Paul to the council held in Jerusalem, regarding the implications of the Mosaic laws upon Gentile believers (Chapter 40). Although Paul had encouraged the circumcision of Timothy, in order to render his ministry acceptable among the Jews (Chapter 42), he did not encourage Titus to do the same, so as not to seem in agreement with those who would require it of Gentile believers.

In light of the concerns that Timothy and Erastus reported about the church in Corinth, Paul decided to send them another letter – referred to as his "severe letter" (2 Corinthians 7:8-9) – the contents of which we do not know. Paul decided to send this letter through a different courier this time. It would require someone with a different gifting than Timothy. God led Paul to send Titus to Corinth as the courier of the "severe letter" with the commission to strongly admonish the Corinthian saints.

Paul was hoping to meet Titus in Troas and get a full report of what had taken place in Corinth. But when Paul arrived in Troas, Titus was not there (2 Corinthians 2:12-13). So he decided to continue his travels on into Macedonia to catch up with Timothy and Erastus. Paul and Titus finally caught up with one another somewhere in Macedonia. Paul was overjoyed by Titus' report. The Corinthian church had responded with repentance, prompting Paul to write another letter to them (that we now know as 2 Corinthians). Titus couriered that letter to Corinth accompanied by a larger entourage. Paul would later join Titus in Corinth for three months. From Corinth, Paul then sent Titus to organize the collections of alms for the Christians at Jerusalem. Titus was a troubleshooter, a peacemaker, an administrator, and a missionary.

Trophimus was a Gentile believer from Ephesus. He, too, had come to faith through Paul's ministry, and had witnessed the activity of God throughout Paul's three years in that city. It is believed that he was one of the members of the entourage that accompanied Titus to Corinth, as together they delivered the letter of 2 Corinthians to the church. This would indicate Paul's high level of trust in Trophimus. He then traveled with Paul from Corinth through Macedonia, into Asia, and onward by sea to Jerusalem.

. . .

Paul apparently wanted the church leaders in Jerusalem to hear Trophimus' testimony about the work in Ephesus. As a result, the Jewish leaders in Jerusalem saw Paul and Trophimus in each other's company in the city, from which they fabricated the accusation that Paul had *"brought Greeks also into the Temple, and....defiled this holy place"* (Acts 21:28). That accusation is what led to Paul to be assaulted in the courts of the Temple by the Jewish mob, followed by his arrest and imprisonment by the Romans. Trophimus would rejoin Paul in his later journeys, after Paul was liberated from his first imprisonment in Rome.

Aristarchus

Aristarchus came to faith in Christ during Paul's trip to Thessalonica (Acts 17), and accompanied him on his third missionary journey. He was one of the two men seized by the crowd in Ephesus during the riot and placed before the mob in the amphitheater. Despite what had happened in Ephesus, Aristarchus continued with Paul through Macedonia and Achaia, and was there at Troas when the disciples came together, despite the attempts made by the Jews to stop the mission (Acts 20:3). Aristarchus remained close to Paul even after this, joining Paul in his voyage as a prisoner to Rome, after being locked up in Caesarea for two years (Acts 24:27). Aristarchus is mentioned as a "fellow prisoner" by Paul (Colossians 4:10; Philemon 24), showing his resolve to remain faithful no matter what trials came his way. He wasn't necessarily a great speaker, leader, or teacher. There's not even one recorded word from his mouth in Scripture. Yet, through these brief glimpses, we see a faithful follower of Christ, whose conduct can be an inspiration for the majority of us today. Let us not forget that a faithful Christian is not necessarily one who is remembered or recognized by the most men for their conduct and good works, but by God. While being a "Paul" is a great thing, let us be content with being an "Aristarchus", a Christian who didn't let trials and tribulations discourage him, but faithfully pressed toward the goal.

We'll pick up with the stories of the rest of these men in the next chapter. But in the meantime, we would do well to follow the lead of those that we have already seen and faithfully press toward that same goal – the upward calling of our Lord Jesus Christ... until He returns.

* * *

52

EACH ONE RAN THEIR RACE – PART 2

When the uproar was over, Paul sent for the believers and encouraged them. Then he said good-bye and left for Macedonia. While there, he encouraged the believers in all the towns he passed through. Then he traveled down to Greece, where he stayed for three months. He was preparing to sail back to Syria when he discovered a plot by some Jews against his life, so he decided to return through Macedonia. Several men were traveling with him. They were Sopater son of Pyrrhus from Berea; Aristarchus and Secundus from Thessalonica; Gaius from Derbe; Timothy; and Tychicus and Trophimus from the province of Asia. They went on ahead and waited for us at Troas. After the Passover ended, we boarded a ship at Philippi in Macedonia and five days later joined them in Troas, where we stayed a week.
Acts 20:1-6

* * *

Let's pick up from where we left off in the last chapter.

Secundus
Next on the list is Aristarchus' fellow countryman Secundus. Both men came from Thessalonica, but they were probably two very different men. Aristarchus' name was connected with aristocracy, the ruling class. It's likely that he came from a wealthy and powerful family. His is just the kind of name that would be given to a nobleman. We can suppose that he was a man of higher station. Secundus, on the other hand, was a common

name for a slave. It meant "Second." Slaves were often not called by their true names. The first-ranking slave in a household would have been called Primus; the second-ranking slave was often called Secundus. So, there they were - Aristarchus and Secundus, one probably a nobleman and the other probably a slave. Yet, side by side they served the Lord and the apostle Paul. This true fellowship between noblemen and slaves was a scandal to many in the Roman world; they found it hard to believe that they sat together and served together in church. Yet they did, because they both believed that who they were in Jesus Christ was more important than who they were thought to be in this world.

It has rightly been said that the ground is level at the foot of the cross. There is no one from such a high station of life that they don't need Jesus. There is no one from such a low station of life that Jesus can't lift them up. Everyone – both high and low – must humble themselves and come through the same gate of faith to Jesus. It doesn't matter if you are an Aristarchus or a Secundus – Jesus is your only way, and same way for all.

Sopater and Gaius

We know the least about Sopater. He was a Gentile background believer from Berea who traveled with this group back into Asia.

Another one of Paul's traveling companions was Gaius of Derbe. Derbe was a city in Galatia in Asia Minor. It is very probable that Gaius came to faith in Christ through Paul's first missionary journey. It seems that Gaius joined this traveling band while they were in Greece and assisted Paul throughout this journey through Asia.

Tychicus

Another one of Paul's companions on the way from Corinth to Jerusalem is Tychicus. He was a native of Asia Minor. Paul calls him a *"much loved brother"* and a *"faithful servant"* of the Lord (Ephesians 6:21). He is characterized as being an encourager (Ephesians 6:22), which is evidenced by the fact that he was with Paul during his first and second Roman imprisonments. He also was trustworthy; Paul entrusted him to deliver his epistles to the Ephesians and Colossians and to bring news of the apostle to those congregations (Colossians 4:7-8).

. . .

In traveling to Colossae, Tychicus accompanied Onesimus, the former slave who was returning to Philemon. No doubt, Tychicus, as a trusted companion to Paul, was able to emphasize the need for grace in receiving Onesimus back home (Philemon 17).

Tychicus also served as "interim pastor" in both Crete and Ephesus, so that Titus and Timothy, respectively, could visit Paul while he was in prison. It is believed that Paul was describing Tychicus when he wrote, *"a brother who has often proved to us in many ways that he is zealous, and now even more so because of his great confidence in you"* (2 Corinthians 8:22).

Silas and Luke

Lastly we see that Silas and Luke have reunited with the group. Silas rejoined Paul in Corinth, and they all reunited with Luke in Philippi. Then while the others all went ahead to Troas, Silas and Luke remained with Paul in Philippi for five more days until the Passover had concluded.

Like i said at the outset of the last chapter, it would be easy to skip over this list of names and places. But we need to see this unique group of men that God brought together for His purpose. They were men from Judea, Syria, Cilicia, Asia, Macedonia and Achaia. They were Gentiles and Jews. They were public officials, commoners, aristocrats and slaves. They represented a diversity of backgrounds, languages and cultures. But they all had three things in common.

First, they were all fully-devoted followers of Jesus. They were all sinners whose lives had been transformed by the saving grace of Christ – and they were completely sold out to Him.

Second, with the exception of Silas, they all appear to have come to faith through the ministry of Paul. And all of them – even now as co-laborers – have been discipled by Paul. Paul didn't forget about these men once they came to faith, he continued to pour his life into them. Each one of them were now being used by God to disciple others and extend His Kingdom throughout Europe and Asia. They were making disciples who were making disciples... who were making disciples.

· · ·

Third, each one, in obedience to God's direction in their lives followed Him without regard for personal safety, comfort or wealth. They were threatened by the Jews. They would soon be persecuted by the Romans. They dealt with disagreement and division within the church. And yet, they ran their race in such a way to obtain the prize (1 Corinthians 9:24).

We would do well to remember that God has also brought us together for His purpose. We come from different countries, cultures and languages – just like this group of eleven. Let's be faithful to follow their lead and run the race in such a way to obtain the prize… until He returns.

* * *

53

PERSUADED TO GO

The next stop after leaving Tyre was Ptolemais, where we greeted the brothers and sisters and stayed for one day. The next day we went on to Caesarea and stayed at the home of Philip the Evangelist, one of the seven men who had been chosen to distribute food. He had four unmarried daughters who had the gift of prophecy.
Several days later a man named Agabus, who also had the gift of prophecy, arrived from Judea. He came over, took Paul's belt, and bound his own feet and hands with it. Then he said, "The Holy Spirit declares, 'So shall the owner of this belt be bound by the Jewish leaders in Jerusalem and turned over to the Gentiles.'"
When we heard this, we and the local believers all begged Paul not to go on to Jerusalem. But he said, "Why all this weeping? You are breaking my heart! I am ready not only to be jailed at Jerusalem but even to die for the sake of the Lord Jesus." When it was clear that we couldn't persuade him, we gave up and said, "The Lord's will be done." After this we packed our things and left for Jerusalem. Some believers from Caesarea accompanied us, and they took us to the home of Mnason, a man originally from Cyprus and one of the early believers. When we arrived, the brothers and sisters in Jerusalem welcomed us warmly.
Acts 21:7-17

* * *

As we have already seen in Chapter 51, while Paul was in Ephesus the Holy Spirit compelled him to go to Jerusalem (Acts 19:21). It would be Paul's last journey to Jerusalem. And not unlike Jesus' last journey to Jerusalem, Paul stopped at multiple points along the way. He used the journey to encourage many of the churches that God had allowed him to be a part of planting. This journey had been about "watering" – and in some instances "pruning" – the churches that had already begun, more than it had been about "sowing" new seeds.

Along the way, he stopped in Miletus and invited the elders from Ephesus to come meet with him. When they arrived he declared, *"I am bound by the Spirit to go to Jerusalem. I don't know what awaits me, except that the Holy Spirit tells me in city after city that jail and suffering lie ahead.... And now I know that none of you to whom I have preached the Kingdom will ever see me again"* (Acts 20:22-23,25). He then encouraged them to shepherd the flock over which the Holy Spirit had appointed them as leaders. Having done so, they prayed together... and cried together – knowing they would not see one another again. Then they escorted him on his way (Acts 20:36-38).

Upon arriving in Tyre in Syria, he met with the local believers and stayed with them for a week. The believers there "kept on saying to him" that he should not set foot in Jerusalem (Acts 21:4). In Caesarea, a man named Agabus, who had the gift of prophecy, after having bound himself with Paul's belt, said to Paul, *"The Holy Spirit declares, 'So shall the owner of this belt be bound by the Jewish leaders in Jerusalem and turned over to the Gentiles'"* (Acts 21:11). Luke records that all of Paul's traveling companions – including Luke – as well as the local believers *"all begged Paul not to go to Jerusalem"* (Acts 21:12).

To which Paul responded: *"Why all this weeping? You are breaking my heart! I am ready not only to be jailed at Jerusalem but even to die for the sake of the Lord Jesus"* (Acts 21:13).

With few exceptions, most everyone was trying to persuade Paul to NOT go to Jerusalem. Most everyone included his closest companions like Luke and Silas. It included the elders of the churches. It included the evangelist Philip (Acts 21:8). It included Agabus the prophet. Most everyone was telling him not to go... EXCEPT the Holy Spirit. The Holy Spirit had clearly told Paul to go to Jerusalem.

So, what do you do when you know God has told you to do one thing and most everyone else – including those who are the closest to you – is telling you to do the exact opposite?

. . .

A number of years ago i read the book *"The Dream Giver"* by Bruce Wilkinson. It was a very timely read because, at the time, God was directing us to step out by faith on a journey into the unknown. It was unknown for us, but God clearly knew where the journey would lead.

Bruce Wilkinson writes in his book that when God leads you to leave your "Land of Familiar" – that place where you currently are, that place that is comfortable – and go to a new land – a "Land of Promise", you will pass through a Wilderness. That Land of Promise can be a gloriously inviting place – or it can be a difficult place. The key is that it is the place that you know God has told you to go – and to do anything less would be disobedience to God. That is exactly what Paul was doing – he was going to a place – physically and figuratively – that he knew God had told him to go.

As you take that journey and step into the Wilderness, Bruce writes that you will encounter three types of people along the way. You will encounter the "Bullies" who try to drive you back to Familiar, the "Buddies" who love you but are less than enthusiastic because they can't understand what you are doing, and the "Busters" who will encourage you each and every step along the way. Bullies and Buddies will always try to persuade you that there is another way – a better way. And they'll either try to bully you into submission, or sweet talk you into submission.

The Bullies are most often driven by a fear of what your journey of faith will do to them. They are concerned about the repercussions they will experience as a result of your decision. Or, they are driven out of grief. They are grieving a personal loss resulting from your journey. The Buddies are trying to save you heartache or difficulty. They have designated themselves to be your "holy spirit" because they believe they have your best interest in mind. They don't want you to go through the pain, and as your friend, they don't want to go through it either. An important distinction is that Bullies and Buddies do NOT have a word from God. They are leaning on their own understanding (Proverbs 3:5).

Busters, on the other hand, have sought the Lord with you. They may not like what they hear, but they know that they – like you – need to trust the One from whom they have heard it. They too have come to that place that to do anything different would be disobedience to God. Busters will do whatever they can to help you and encourage you along the way. Busters will also be your best prayer intercessors.

...

Over the years, we've encountered all three. Regrettably, the Busters stand in the minority – but what they lack in numbers they make up for in resolve. And i am grateful to God for each and every one that He has brought across our path! My prayer continues to be that i will be the Buster that God would have me be to others as they walk their personal faith journey. This series of books has in fact been written for that purpose.

Paul was not persuaded to depart from the path that God had set before him, because he had already been "persuaded" by God to walk that path. God had given him a clear word with a clear confirmation by His Spirit. i have intentionally used the word "persuaded" instead of the word "compelled". i have done so because i want it to be clear that Paul had a choice. He could have chosen to be disobedient to God and go his own way. The Bullies and Buddies would have supported that decision.

But Paul chose to walk by faith according to God's Word empowered by His Spirit. Paul himself later writes, *"For this reason I also suffer these things; nevertheless I am not ashamed, for I know whom I have believed and am persuaded that He is able to keep what I have committed to Him until that Day"* (2 Timothy 1:12 NKJ). Paul was "persuaded" to go because he knew that God was trustworthy and able to keep that which Paul had committed to Him – his own life – until the day of Christ's return. And He still is… and always will be… until He returns!

* * *

54

THE RIGHT CITIZENSHIP

The commander brought Paul inside and ordered him lashed with whips to make him confess his crime. He wanted to find out why the crowd had become so furious. When they tied Paul down to lash him, Paul said to the officer standing there, "Is it legal for you to whip a Roman citizen who hasn't even been tried?" When the officer heard this, he went to the commander and asked, "What are you doing? This man is a Roman citizen!" So the commander went over and asked Paul, "Tell me, are you a Roman citizen?" "Yes, I certainly am," Paul replied. "I am, too," the commander muttered, "and it cost me plenty!" Paul answered, "But I am a citizen by birth!" The soldiers who were about to interrogate Paul quickly withdrew when they heard he was a Roman citizen, and the commander was frightened because he had ordered him bound and whipped.
Acts 22:24-29

* * *

Paul's arrest had been precipitated by false accusations and misunderstandings. The *"whole city"* had been rocked by the accusations (Acts 21:30). A riotous crowd was trying to kill Paul when the Roman regiment arrived to bring order. The Jews had falsely accused Paul of bringing the Gentile Trophimus (Chapter 51) into the Temple, which he had not. The commander (Claudius) mistakenly thought Paul was an Egyptian rebel leader, which, of course, he was not. So Claudius ordered that Paul be bound in chains and taken to the fortress. Just before he was taken inside, Paul was granted permission to speak to the crowd. He spoke to them in Hebrew, so Claudius was unable to understand any of what Paul was saying.

. . .

The riotous crowd that was gathered in the courtyard of the fortress quieted down to listen as Paul told them the story of his conversion. They continued to listen while he told them that Jesus was the Messiah. But when he told the crowd that the Lord had told him to tell the Good News to the Gentiles, the crowd erupted. No devout Jew would have anything to do with the Gentiles! Had Paul not uttered that one word, he might have been released. Paul knew that, but he had to be faithful in his witness, no matter the cost. He knew that it was better for him to be a faithful prisoner than it would be for him to be a freed man who had failed to speak truth.

Claudius had no idea why the crowd was again rioting, but he ordered that Paul be taken inside and whipped, so that he might confess his crimes. That brings us to this particular passage in Acts. Claudius was about to have his soldiers commit a crime. A crime for which Claudius would have, at the very least, been discharged from his position. The soldiers would have themselves been beaten, if not also discharged from service. It was no small act to violate the rights of a Roman citizen.

Claudius, acknowledging his error, arranged to have Paul brought before his accusers – the Jewish high council. Claudius would ensure that this time there would be no riotous crowd. He wanted to know exactly what the trouble was all about so that he could officially charge Paul under his rights as a Roman citizen. Secondly, Claudius needed to have official charges so that he could support the action he had already taken against Paul. (He needed to cover his back against any possible repercussions!)

As Paul stood before the high council, the members quickly divided – Pharisees versus Sadducees – over whether Paul stood accused of anything. Quickly Claudius realized that no one was expressing any crime for which Paul should be charged. But as the debate became more animated, Claudius was afraid they would tear Paul apart. *"So he ordered his soldiers to go and rescue him by force and take him back to the fortress"* (Acts 23:10).

Later that night the Lord appeared to Paul in his jail cell and said, *"Be encouraged, Paul. Just as you have been a witness to me here in Jerusalem, you must preach the Good News in Rome as well"* (Acts 23:11). God had just given

Paul an irrefutable word. He was going to Rome! He would preach the Good News in Rome! He may have currently been sitting in a jail cell in Jerusalem, but the Lord God was going to move heaven and earth to accomplish His purpose through Paul. From that moment until he "preached in Rome", Paul became invincible. There wasn't a power on earth – or outside of this earth – that could keep him from accomplishing God's purpose. God did not give Paul a *conditional* word; He gave him an *absolute* word.

There would be numerous times between that moment in the jail cell and the moment that he would first preach in Rome that Paul would have good reason to question whether that, in fact, was going to take place! But on each of those occasions all Paul would need to do was remember the word God had given him. That is as true for us as it was for Paul. When God gives you a promise, hold onto it! Write it down! God is not a man that He should lie (Numbers 23:19). Nothing and no one can keep God from fulfilling His promise!

God's promise was to be tested in Paul's life as soon as the next morning. A group of more than forty men made an oath before the leading priests and elders that they would not eat or drink until they had killed Paul. They sought the assistance of the priests by requesting that a message be sent to Claudius to bring Paul back before the council. They planned to kill Paul along the way. But Paul's nephew learned of the plot and informed Claudius. Claudius wisely directed two of his officers to take Paul that very evening, under an armed guard of almost five hundred soldiers, to Caesarea. (Acts 23:12-24). Think about it – when God makes a promise He backs it up with all the resources that are needed to bring it about. He arranged for Claudius to provide five hundred soldiers to protect Paul! And He also provided a horse so he wouldn't have to walk! (Acts 23:24).

Claudius sent Paul together with a letter to the Governor of the Iudaean province – Marcus Antonius Felix. (By the way, Felix was the seventh governor over Iudaea after Pilate, and the fourth after Agrippa (Chapter 33). No one seemed to be able to hold that job for very long.) The letter said, *"This man was seized by some Jews, and they were about to kill him when I arrived with the troops. When I learned that he was a Roman citizen, I removed him to safety. Then I took him to their high council to try to learn the basis of the accusations against him. I soon discovered the charge was something regarding their religious law – certainly nothing worthy of imprisonment or death. But when I was informed of a plot to kill him, I immediately sent him on to you. I have told his accusers to bring their charges before you"* (Acts 23:27-30).

We'll pick up with the story in the next chapter. But here's what we need to see thus far. Throughout his ministry – and even now as he began this leg of his journey that would subsequently lead to Rome – God demonstrated that He had uniquely equipped Paul to be the missionary to the Roman Empire. Even Claudius came to realize that Paul was a remarkable man. He was a learned man who spoke Greek. He was not the common crook or rebel leader that Claudius first thought. His Greek training had given him a global worldview. His Hebrew training in the Mosaic Law and prophecies had prepared him to interpret the law in the light of Christ and His redemptive death and resurrection. His Roman citizenship opened doors throughout the empire and ultimately these doors to Rome.

God has uniquely prepared and equipped each and every one of us for the mission He has set before us. You may not speak Greek, Hebrew, Aramaic or Latin – but you speak the language that you will need to accomplish God's purpose. You may not have formal training in the Scriptures, but you have the knowledge that you will need to communicate the gospel and fulfill the mission God has for you. You may not have Roman citizenship, but you have just the citizenship that you will need – you're a citizen of the Kingdom! As a result, the same Holy Spirit who dwelt within Paul dwells within you. Yes, you have all of the ability that you need to accomplish God's purpose through the indwelling presence of His Holy Spirit (Acts 1:8). And you have the same mandate that Paul had – to go and make disciples.

Nothing can prevent us from accomplishing that purpose – except ourselves. We're citizens of the Kingdom. So let's take a pointer from Paul and trust our God to lead us, protect us, empower us and direct us – each and every step of the way… until He returns.

* * *

55

THE CASE FOR THE PROSECUTION

"I will hear your case myself when your accusers arrive," the governor told him. Then the governor ordered him kept in the prison at Herod's headquarters. Five days later Ananias, the high priest, arrived with some of the Jewish elders and the lawyer Tertullus, to present their case against Paul to the governor. When Paul was called in, Tertullus presented the charges against Paul in the following address to the governor: "You have provided a long period of peace for us Jews and with foresight have enacted reforms for us. For all of this, Your Excellency, we are very grateful to you. But I don't want to bore you, so please give me your attention for only a moment. We have found this man to be a troublemaker who is constantly stirring up riots among the Jews all over the world. He is a ringleader of the cult known as the Nazarenes. Furthermore, he was trying to desecrate the Temple when we arrested him. We would have judged him by our law, but Lysias, the commander of the garrison, came and violently took him away from us, commanding his accusers to come before you. You can find out the truth of our accusations by examining him yourself." Then the other Jews chimed in, declaring that everything Tertullus said was true.
Acts 23:35 – 24:9

* * *

Marcus Antonius Felix had been the Roman governor of Iudaea for approximately six years. He was said to have the disposition of a slave and the power of a tyrant. Emperor Claudius had appointed Felix governor in about 52 AD. He governed Iudaea until about 60 AD when he was recalled to Rome to answer for disturbances in the province and irregularities in his rule. Felix's home base was Caesarea Maritima, just like the kings, prefects and procurators of that province before him.

Affairs between the Jewish people and their Roman rulers deteriorated under Felix's governorship. He was well known for his cruelty and licentious behavior. His predisposition to receiving bribes further led to a great increase in corruption and crime throughout the province. The years of his rule were marked by internal feuds and disturbances, which he was known to put down with brutal severity.

In general, the Iudaean populace mistrusted him. There had been a Sadducee by the name of Jonathan, who had been instrumental in helping Felix secure his appointment as governor. Initially Jonathan was a counselor and confidant to Felix, helping him navigate relations with the Jews. When the High Priest Ananias was sent to Rome in 52 AD, Felix named Jonathan to replace him. In his role as High Priest, Jonathan continued to counsel Felix to change his ways if he wanted peaceful relations with the people and favor from Rome. Jonathan truly wanted Felix to succeed and feared that the governor's actions would cause the Jewish leaders to complain to Caesar. But Felix tired of Jonathan's criticism. As a result, he persuaded one of Jonathan's most faithful friends to kill him. Soon thereafter, Ananias returned to the role of High Priest.

In fairness, Felix had little experience ruling when he was originally given the position. He was born a slave, became a freedman, then was quickly elevated to a high government official. Felix's brother Pallas was one of Emperor Claudius' most trusted ministers and probably obtained the governorship for Felix. While governor, Felix fell in love with Drusilla, the beautiful daughter of King Agrippa. At the time of their meeting, she was the wife of Azizus, king of Emesa. She and Felix conspired together for her to divorce Azizus so that the two of them could marry.

Ananias was the High Priest in Jerusalem from 47-52 and 53-59 AD. In 52 AD he was sent to Rome by Quadratus, legate of Syria, to answer a charge of oppression brought by the Samaritans, but Emperor Claudius acquitted him. On his return to Jerusalem, he resumed the office of high priest which had just been vacated by Jonathan's untimely demise. He was a typical Sadducee – wealthy, haughty, unscrupulous, fulfilling his sacred office for purely selfish and political ends, anti-nationalist in his relation to the Jews, and friendly to the Romans. He would later die an ignominious death, being assassinated by the popular zealots at the beginning of the last Jewish war.

Tertullus was a well-known "prosecuting attorney" in the province. He had certainly argued in Roman court many times before. The Jews had employed him to state their case before Felix. More than likely, he was a Hellenistic Jew. The high council had not needed a lawyer to try Paul in their own court, but after Claudius had secretly moved Paul to Caesarea, they had no choice. They required an expert in Roman law to present their case accordingly. With only a matter of days to prepare, Tertullus was their choice.

After dispensing with the customary – and completely baseless – flattery, the lawyer set forth his unjust charges. First, he charged that Paul was creating disturbances among Romans throughout the empire to stir up sedition – an offense against the Roman government. Second, he charged that Paul was the ringleader of a rebellious sect known as the Nazarenes. It is interesting to note that the lawyer did not refer to the "sect" as Christians. That term was already being used in many parts of the province, but for Tertullus to do so would imply that the Jews' were acknowledging Jesus as the Christ (the Messiah). Third, he charged that Paul had attempted to profane the Temple (by bringing a Gentile into it), a crime that the Jews themselves were permitted to punish.

Additionally, Tertullus included subtle insinuations against Claudius Lysias, intended to imply that the Romans had unnecessarily escalated the matter. He was intimating that if Claudius had handled the situation properly Felix would never have had to be called upon to adjudicate this disturbance. But now that it had been escalated, he clearly indicated that the charges against Paul had implications for the entire empire. When he was done, *"the other Jews chimed in, declaring that everything Tertullus said was true."* He lied… and they swore to it!

It was a formidable attack against Paul. On one side stood an unscrupulous religious leader represented by a crafty attorney, presenting their case before a crooked judge who was ultimately looking for a bribe. On the other side was a near-blind missionary who had been falsely accused. The cards were stacked in favor of the prosecution – or so they thought. Because no one in the room, except Paul, had the spiritual eyes to see that God was on his side!

. . .

Paul was His ambassador on His mission, journeying according to His plan. The outcome of this trial had been settled long ago. God had already declared His verdict. "My servant Paul is going to Rome to preach My gospel" (Acts 23:11). No "trumped up" charges were going to change that. No eloquence on the part of the attorney was going to make any difference. And Ananias and Felix were impotent to do anything about it.

You may be in a place right now that feels like that "court room" did for Paul. You may feel like the cards are stacked against you. Follow Paul's lead. God is right there with you. Hold onto the promise He has given you and trust Him to lead you through all of the details. He's the Judge… and the Jury. This is all going to end according to His verdict and His plan. Watch Him work… and trust that He will… until He returns.

* * *

56

A DIVINE DELAY

…Paul said, "I know, sir, that you have been a judge of Jewish affairs for many years, so I gladly present my defense before you. You can quickly discover that I arrived in Jerusalem no more than twelve days ago to worship at the Temple. My accusers never found me arguing with anyone in the Temple, nor stirring up a riot in any synagogue or on the streets of the city. These men cannot prove the things they accuse me of doing. But I admit that I follow the Way, which they call a cult. I worship the God of our ancestors, and I firmly believe the Jewish law and everything written in the prophets…. Ask these men here what crime the Jewish high council found me guilty of…." At that point Felix, who was quite familiar with the Way, adjourned the hearing and said, "Wait until Lysias, the garrison commander, arrives. Then I will decide the case." He ordered an officer to keep Paul in custody but to give him some freedom and allow his friends to visit him and take care of his needs. A few days later Felix came back with his wife, Drusilla, who was Jewish. Sending for Paul, they listened as he told them about faith in Christ Jesus. As he reasoned with them about righteousness and self-control and the coming day of judgment, Felix became frightened. "Go away for now," he replied. "When it is more convenient, I'll call for you again." He also hoped that Paul would bribe him, so he sent for him quite often and talked with him. After two years went by in this way, Felix was succeeded by Porcius Festus. And because Felix wanted to gain favor with the Jewish people, he left Paul in prison.
Acts 24:10-27

* * *

Tertullus had accused Paul of treason – but there were no witnesses and there was no evidence to support such a charge. If Paul was guilty of treason, he should be put to death. But once Felix had heard the charges against Paul as presented by Tertullus (Acts 24:2-9), he clearly saw that there was no basis for those charges. Legally Felix should have let Paul go free right there and then. He didn't even need to hear Paul's defense. The prosecution had failed to make its case!

But Felix, above all else, had learned how to be a politician. He did not want to needlessly antagonize the religious leaders. In order to retain his position as governor of the province, he needed to keep peace with the Jews. And in order to keep peace with the Jews, he needed the religious leaders to see him as an ally – at least in this matter – and not as an adversary. He was more concerned about doing what was politically expedient than he was about doing what was right. He was quite content to keep Paul unjustly imprisoned because it fulfilled his end purpose. Though he said that he wanted to hear from Claudius Lysias before he made any decision about Paul, there is no indication that Claudius was ever asked to give such a report at any time over the two years that followed.

Over the course of the next two years, Paul repeatedly had opportunity to preach the Good News to Felix and Drusilla. But on each occasion Felix would put off making any decision until "the next time". As Luke writes, particularly as time went on, part of the reason for Felix continuing to keep Paul imprisoned was his hope that Paul would give him a bribe. He even made it easy for Paul to arrange a bribe by allowing his friends *"to visit him and take care of his needs."* But no bribe every materialized, so Paul remained a prisoner.

It would have been customary for Felix to release Paul from prison when he was turning over rule of the province to Porcius Festus. But even on that occasion, Felix was more concerned about the political capital he was earning by keeping Paul imprisoned than he was with doing the right thing.

But if we read all of this at face value and attribute Paul's extended imprisonment to the decisions of Felix, we will have missed the whole point. This was God's plan, not Felix's. This delay was a part of the plan that the Holy Spirit confirmed when He told Paul that he would *"preach the Good News in Rome"* (Acts 23:11). Paul would not only preach to Romans in Rome; he would preach to Romans along the way.

In Chapter 22, we looked at divine appointments, but here we witness a divine delay. Divine delays are not necessarily momentary – though they can be. The divine delays that i'm talking about are those seasons that appear to go on for what feels like an eternity. Often, there is no apparent reason for what is causing the delay.

Scripture is full of people who were delayed by God. Abraham and Sarah waited twenty-five years for the son God promised to give them. Jacob worked for Laban for fourteen years in order to receive the hand of Rachel in marriage. Joseph waited thirteen years to rise from the pit of his imprisonment to the throne room of Pharaoh. The Israelites wandered in the wilderness for forty years before they entered the Promised Land. Fifteen years passed between the time that David was anointed king and the time he actually ascended to the throne. The one hundred twenty disciples waited eight days in the upper room for the Holy Spirit to be poured out upon them. And Paul remained imprisoned for two years by Felix.

What are we to do while we wait in that waiting room of delay? i know the simple answer is "trust God". But what more has God shown us through the life of Paul and others in Scripture.

First, embrace the promise God has given you. And if you don't have a promise, ask Him for one! God is at work through every detail of our lives to bring glory to His Name. We have the tendency to live with the myopic view that everything is about us. It isn't! God created the heavens and the earth and all of us who dwell within it for His purpose – not ours. Everything we have is from Him. Our very lives belong to Him. Every person that i mentioned from Scripture received a promise from God – Abraham and Sarah were told they would have a son, Jacob was promised that his descendants would be as numerous as the dust of the earth, Joseph was promised that his family would bow before him, the Israelites were promised a land in which they would worship God, David was promised the throne, the disciples were promised the Helper, and Paul was told he would preach in Rome. Keep God's promise before you and don't let go of it.

. . .

Second, remember that a delay is not inactivity. We must walk in obedience, doing all that God has placed before us to do, while we are awaiting the fulfillment of His promise. For Abraham, it included rescuing his nephew. For Joseph, it included being a faithful steward in prison. For David, it included slaying the giant Goliath. For the disciples, it included worshiping in the Temple under the watchful eyes of the very leaders who had arranged to have Jesus crucified. For Paul, it involved preaching to Felix and Drusilla. Delays are rarely times to just sit back; more often they are a time to press forward in what we know God has called us to do. There is always a temptation to step out on our own to try and find a shortcut around the delay. Abraham and Sarah attempted to do that. Their efforts resulted in the birth of Ishmael, when God's promise was Isaac. Don't sit idly by. Take the path God puts before you. But make sure it is His path.

Third, acknowledge that His timing is perfect. God is at work in ways we will never know to accomplish His purpose in His perfect timing. We all know that the Holy Spirit came upon the disciples in that upper room on the Day of Pentecost – but, as we already saw in chapter 6, let's remember why it was significant that the Holy Spirit came on that day. Pentecost is a Greek name. The Jews called it the "Festival of the Harvest". The festival celebrated the first fruits of the harvest season. With the arrival of His Holy Spirit on the "Festival of the Harvest", God was signifying that the harvest of the first fruits of salvation had now begun. Three thousand were baptized that day. The church was birthed. His harvest had begun – on the "Festival of the Harvest". A word that the Lord gave me years ago is *"I am the LORD; in its time I will hasten it"* (Isaiah 60:22 ESV). His timing is perfect. He will delay until then, and He will hasten it on the day.

There is an end to the delay. It ends with His promise being fulfilled and Him being glorified. No matter how much time it takes, no matter how long you have been delayed in the waiting room, remember He will complete what He has begun! Hold onto that promise… until He returns.

* * *

57

AN APPEAL TO CAESAR

Three days after Festus arrived in Caesarea to take over his new responsibilities, he left for Jerusalem, where the leading priests and other Jewish leaders met with him and made their accusations against Paul. They asked Festus as a favor to transfer Paul to Jerusalem (planning to ambush and kill him on the way). But Festus replied that Paul was at Caesarea and he himself would be returning there soon. So he said, "Those of you in authority can return with me. If Paul has done anything wrong, you can make your accusations." About eight or ten days later Festus returned to Caesarea, and on the following day he took his seat in court and ordered that Paul be brought in. When Paul arrived, the Jewish leaders from Jerusalem gathered around and made many serious accusations they couldn't prove. Paul denied the charges. "I am not guilty of any crime against the Jewish laws or the Temple or the Roman government," he said. Then Festus, wanting to please the Jews, asked him, "Are you willing to go to Jerusalem and stand trial before me there?" But Paul replied, "No! This is the official Roman court, so I ought to be tried right here. You know very well I am not guilty of harming the Jews. If I have done something worthy of death, I don't refuse to die. But if I am innocent, no one has a right to turn me over to these men to kill me. I appeal to Caesar!" Festus conferred with his advisers and then replied, "Very well! You have appealed to Caesar, and to Caesar you will go!"
Acts 25:1-12

* * *

It had been two years, but the Jewish leaders still wanted to kill Paul. He may have been out of sight, but he hadn't been forgotten. It appears that at their first meeting with the new governor, Porcius Festus, the Jewish leaders told him their accusations against Paul.

It is noteworthy to see how the priests and elders interacted with their new governor. First, they asked him to transfer Paul to Jerusalem. They were hopeful that as a new governor, Festus would acquiesce to their request as a sign of good faith for future relations, and they would be able to successfully execute their original plan to kill Paul. Second, after the first attempt failed, they followed Festus back to Caesarea requesting that he immediately convene a trial. But no mention is made of a lawyer accompanying them. Apparently they felt that Tertullus' representation before Felix had proven to be inadequate and ineffective, so they were confident that they could do no worse representing themselves before their new governor.

Very quickly, as the religious leaders made their accusations against Paul, it became obvious to Festus, just as it had been to Felix, that Paul wasn't guilty of any crime under Roman law. So here he was – just like Pontius Pilate and Felix before him. Festus' assignment from Rome was to maintain peaceful control over this occupied nation. He was directed by his superiors in Rome to not do anything that could disrupt the peace or make the Roman occupation more tenuous. Before him stood the religious leaders of the occupied people pressuring him to find a man guilty of baseless charges. If he found in favor of Paul, he would alienate the Jews and potentially disrupt the peace of what was already a tenuous occupation. If he found Paul to be guilty, he would be sentencing a man to death that he knew wasn't guilty of any crime. At that moment, he blamed Felix for having left him with that "no-win" dilemma.

Since no Roman law was broken, Festus' resolution was that Paul should be returned to Jerusalem to be tried in the Temple court. Though that remedy would not provide the religious leaders with the legal means to execute Paul, it would enable them to arrange to have him killed while he was being transported back to Jerusalem. So Festus' solution was more than acceptable to the Jews.

But Paul's response to Festus' resolution totally caught the new governor off guard. He appealed to Caesar! As we saw in Chapter 54, Roman citizenship came with various perks. One of those perks was that citizens had the right to appeal a decision to a higher authority. And the decisions of governors, such as Festus, could be appealed to Caesar himself. Decisions appealed to local authorities could often take as long as one to two years due to administrative backlogs. As you can imagine, the Emperor's backlog was even greater.

Once a citizen had requested an appeal to a higher authority, the process could not be negated by a lower authority. So, for example, once Paul appealed to Caesar, Festus was powerless to do anything further. He could no longer require that Paul be taken to Jerusalem. He was powerless to do anything regarding Paul, other than keep him under guard awaiting transport to Rome.

In many respects, Paul's appeal to Caesar provided Festus with the best solution to his "no-win" dilemma. He was now powerless to make any decision regarding Paul – therefore he no longer was compelled to do anything to this innocent man for fear of how the Jews would respond. And the Jews could no longer hold him responsible, because he was powerless to make a decision!

But it's important for us to remember that this wasn't Festus' plan. It wasn't even Paul's plan. This was God's plan. Long before there was a Caesar, and long before there was a Paul, God had orchestrated that Paul would have the ability to appeal unto Caesar. He had put all the mechanisms in place for Paul to be able to make that appeal. And it wasn't simply for the protection of Paul; it was for the furtherance of God's plan – that Paul preach the Good News in Rome!

God has promised that He will make a way where there seems to be no way. The prophet Isaiah wrote:

> *I am the Lord, who opened a way through the waters,*
> *making a dry path through the sea…*
> *I will make a pathway through the wilderness.*
> *I will create rivers in the dry wasteland.*
> (Isaiah 43:16,19)

He will do whatever it takes to accomplish His purpose in and through our lives. He'll make a dry path across a Red Sea, or He'll use an unsuspecting Caesar and a process of appeal.

If you find yourself in one of those situations where you're not sure how or where to turn, allow God to lead you in the path that He has set before you – your equivalent of an appeal to Caesar… or a dry pathway through a sea… or a river in a dry wasteland. He's already prepared it. And He will continue to do so… until He returns.

* * *

58

I AM ALMOST PERSUADED

A few days later King Agrippa arrived with his sister, Bernice, to pay their respects to Festus. During their stay of several days, Festus discussed Paul's case with the king. "There is a prisoner here," he told him, "whose case was left for me by Felix.... I was at a loss to know how to investigate these things, so I asked him whether he would be willing to stand trial on these charges in Jerusalem. But Paul appealed to have his case decided by the emperor. So I ordered that he be held in custody until I could arrange to send him to Caesar." "I'd like to hear the man myself," Agrippa said. And Festus replied, "You will – tomorrow!" So the next day Agrippa and Bernice arrived at the auditorium with great pomp, accompanied by military officers and prominent men of the city. Festus ordered that Paul be brought in. Then Festus said, "King Agrippa and all who are here, this is the man whose death is demanded by all the Jews, both here and in Jerusalem. But in my opinion he has done nothing deserving death. However, since he appealed his case to the emperor, I have decided to send him to Rome. But what shall I write the emperor? For there is no clear charge against him. So I have brought him before all of you, and especially you, King Agrippa, so that after we examine him, I might have something to write. For it makes no sense to send a prisoner to the emperor without specifying the charges against him!" Then Agrippa said to Paul, "You may speak in your defense." So Paul, gesturing with his hand, started his defense.... Agrippa interrupted him. "Do you think you can persuade me to become a Christian so quickly?" Paul replied, "Whether quickly or not, I pray to God that both you and everyone here in this audience might become the same as I am, except for these chains." Then the king, the governor, Bernice, and all the others stood and left. As they went out, they talked it over and agreed, "This man hasn't done anything to deserve death or imprisonment." And Agrippa said to Festus, "He could have been set free if he hadn't appealed to Caesar."

Acts 25:13 – 26:32

* * *

King Agrippa II was the great grandson of King Herod the Great. His father, King Agrippa I had ruled the Iudaean province from 41 to 44 AD. So Agrippa II had been a teenage boy in this palace in Caesarea when his father ruled. Agrippa II was now the client ruler over several cities in Galilee, Perea and four smaller territories, while Festus, as governor, was the ruler over the Iudaean province. Though the two men had different titles, they held equal rank in the hierarchy of Roman rule.

This was a cordial visit by Agrippa II to welcome the new governor of Iudaea. His sister (and incestuous lover), Bernice, accompanied him on the visit. It was a very timely visit in light of Paul's imprisonment. Coming from Rome, Festus was not knowledgeable about the religious beliefs of the Jews. His predecessor Felix had the advantage that his wife, Drusilla, was a Jew and therefore was able to counsel him as to Jewish beliefs. By the way, she was the sister of Agrippa II and Bernice. They were the fourth generation of their family to live in this region – and all of the generations were well-versed in Judaism though their practice of those beliefs varied. They used that understanding to curry favor with the people, while more often choosing to personally embrace Greco-Roman culture and religion. Festus knew that Agrippa and Bernice would be able to provide him with an insight into Jewish beliefs that he lacked.

Festus was struggling with what explanation he should give to Caesar for sending Paul to him. He truly wanted to understand why the Jews were trying to kill Paul. But he also knew that he would look foolish before the Emperor if he was unable to provide official charges for a trial in Rome. Thus, he seized the opportunity to ask Agrippa for his advice.

Festus arranged to have Paul present his case in the amphitheater. In honor of Agrippa and Bernice, it was arranged with great pomp, including military officers and prominent men from the city. The amphitheater was filled with people – more for Agrippa's sake than Paul's – but still, it provided a great audience to hear Paul's message.

Paul acknowledged Agrippa's understanding of these matters by saying, *"I know that you are an expert on all Jewish customs and controversies"* (Acts

26:3). He then proceeded to explain that he had been a Pharisee and a persecutor of those who followed the Way until he encountered Jesus on the Damascus road. Paul told Agrippa what Jesus had said to him: *"For I have appeared to you to appoint you as My servant and witness. Tell people that you have seen Me, and tell them what I will show you in the future. And I will rescue you from both your own people and the Gentiles. Yes, I am sending you to the Gentiles to open their eyes, so they may turn from darkness to light and from the power of Satan to God"* (Acts 26:16-18). Then Paul said, *"And so, King Agrippa, I obeyed that vision from heaven…. I teach nothing except what the prophets and Moses said would happen – that the Messiah would suffer and be the first to rise from the dead, and in this way announce God's light to Jews and Gentiles alike"* (Acts 26:19, 22-23).

At that point, Festus interrupted Paul because it all sounded like craziness to him. *"But Paul replied, 'I am not insane, Most Excellent Festus. What I am saying is the sober truth. And King Agrippa knows about these things. I speak boldly, for I am sure these events are all familiar to him, for they were not done in a corner! King Agrippa, do you believe the prophets? I know you do!'"* (Acts 26:25-27) Agrippa interrupted him, saying, *"You almost persuade me to become a Christian"* (Acts 26:28 NKJ). Paul then replied, *"Whether quickly or not, I pray to God that both you and everyone here in this audience might become the same as I am, except for these chains."*

Agrippa, Bernice, Festus and all the others then stood and walked out saying, *"This man hasn't done anything to deserve death or imprisonment. He could have been set free if he hadn't appealed to Caesar."*

Sadly, they had heard, but they had not listened. Paul was more than likely the only "free" man in the amphitheater that day. He had turned to Jesus on that Damascus road and received forgiveness for his sins. He had been redeemed from sin and death. His was not the plight to be pitied. But Agrippa, Bernice, Festus and, more than likely, all of the others were walking out of that place still under the bondage of their sin.

Agrippa had "almost" been persuaded. But "almost" is what had prevented him from being set free. Paul wasn't the prisoner; the rest of them were. Prayerfully we will one day learn that some of those assembled that day did surrender their lives to Christ, but there is no indication that any of them did so – on that day, or any day thereafter. But here's the thing, Paul wasn't responsible for how anyone responded. His responsibility rested with being obedient to the "heavenly vision" – to proclaim the Good News.

That day wasn't about Paul being set free; it was about the others being given the opportunity to be set free spiritually. God had promised that Paul would preach the Good News in Rome, and the journey had begun with the opportunity to preach it to an amphitheater full of Romans in Caesarea. As we continue in our journey, it would be good for us to be mindful – and obedient – to proclaim the Good News so that the captives we encounter are set free. Let's be found faithful to that heavenly vision… until He returns.

* * *

59

EVEN THOUGH THE SHIP MAY GO DOWN

When the time came, we set sail for Italy.... Aristarchus, a Macedonian from Thessalonica, was also with us.... The next day when we docked at Sidon, Julius was very kind to Paul and let him go ashore to visit with friends so they could provide for his needs. Putting out to sea from there, we encountered strong headwinds that made it difficult to keep the ship on course, so we sailed north ... landing at Myra, in the province of Lycia. There the commanding officer found an Egyptian ship from Alexandria that was bound for Italy, and he put us on board.... We struggled along the coast with great difficulty and finally arrived at Fair Havens, near the town of Lasea. ...The weather was becoming dangerous for sea travel because it was so late in the fall, and Paul spoke to the ship's officers about it. "Men," he said, "I believe there is trouble ahead if we go on – shipwreck, loss of cargo, and danger to our lives as well." But the officer in charge of the prisoners listened more to the ship's captain and the owner than to Paul. ...The terrible storm raged for many days, blotting out the sun and the stars, until at last, all hope was gone. ...Finally, Paul called the crew together and said, "Men, you should have listened to me in the first place and not left Crete. You would have avoided all this damage and loss. But take courage! None of you will lose your lives, even though the ship will go down. For last night an angel of the God to whom I belong and whom I serve stood beside me, and He said, 'Don't be afraid, Paul, for you will surely stand trial before Caesar! What's more, God in His goodness has granted safety to everyone sailing with you.' So take courage! For I believe God. It will be just as He said. But we will be shipwrecked on an island." ...So everyone escaped safely to shore.
Acts 27:1-44

* * *

Paul wasn't the only prisoner being transported to Rome in the charge of a Roman centurion named Julius. But it would be safe to assume that he was the only prisoner who was a Roman citizen. The others were more than likely prisoners who were being sent to Rome to become gladiators. Rome's lust for blood was insatiable. Romans found armed combat to the death to be very entertaining, so the need for new gladiators was endless. They were brought to Rome from the far corners of their empire. They were men without hope headed to their deaths in the Colosseum at the hands of other gladiators or in the jaws of wild beasts. This was a group that needed to hear about the grace of God – and before the journey was done, they would witness it first-hand.

Paul was also accompanied by two companions – Dr. Luke and Aristarchus from Thessalonica (Chapter 51). Both of these men would have also been Roman citizens – which afforded them the right to be able to travel with Paul on this journey. As citizens, however, their passage would not have been paid for by Rome; the three of them (including Paul) would have needed to pay their own way. Given Paul's unique circumstance, the centurion granted him the freedom to go ashore in Sidon to visit friends and obtain the needed financial provisions – not only for the voyage, but also for expenses he would incur when he subsequently arrived in Rome. Whether Julius' kindness was motivated by compassion or the financial gain that would result from Paul's visit ashore is not clear.

After sailing to Myra, Julius arranged passage for all of them on an Egyptian vessel bound for Rome. Delays in the journey pushed them into late fall, well past the ideal season for sailing to Rome. It was Paul that expressed safety concerns to the ship's officers, recommending that they find a safe harbor to weather the winter. But the ship's owner and captain, motivated by personal avarice, assured Julius that the journey could be made. Given the option of listening to experienced sailors or a Jewish tentmaker, Julius opted for the former.

Ultimately the ship was battered by gale-force winds that raged for days *"blotting out the sun and the stars, until at last, all hope was gone."* Even the experienced seamen had now lost hope. It was then that Paul gathered all the men on the ship – seamen, prisoners, soldiers and companions – telling them to take courage. God had again reminded Paul that he would *"surely stand trial before Caesar"* and *"God in His goodness"* had promised the *"safety to everyone sailing with"* Paul. Everyone who stayed on the ship would be saved. The One who can still the waves and the storm had assured them that they would not perish.

This moment reminds me of the night when Jesus and the disciples were crossing the Sea of Galilee and a storm arose.[1] The disciples had learned that night, as must we, that storms are a part of the journey. If God is sovereign over all things – which He is – then the storms of our life, at the very least, have been permitted by Him, and in some instances have been orchestrated by Him. All for the purpose that He desires to accomplish in and through our lives for His glory.

There is an important difference between that night for the disciples on the Sea of Galilee and this journey for Paul and his companions on the Mediterranean Sea that gives us added insight. God had given those now journeying on the Mediterranean Sea an opportunity to escape the storm. Paul had warned the ship's captain and owner not to sail on – but they had made the decision to go ahead despite the warning. On the Sea of Galilee, the disciples didn't have any choice. On the Mediterranean Sea, Paul and the prisoners didn't have a choice, but the others did – and they had chosen poorly. Jesus stilled the storm on the Galilean Sea. This group had to weather the storm on the Mediterranean Sea. Their actions had caused them to endure the storm – even the "innocent ones" like Paul.

But still God extended His grace to everyone – all two hundred seventy-six on board – even those who had chosen poorly. They experienced two weeks of a violent storm, as well as damage to the ship and cargo, that all could have been avoided. But no one perished – they all made it safely to shore.

So it is worthwhile to repeat these truths that we must always remember when we find ourselves in the midst of a storm.

1. **Hold onto the promise that God gave you before you encountered the storm (or while you were in the midst of the storm)**. God had promised Paul the safety of everyone who remained on the ship. We must hold on to the promise He gave us before the storm, in the midst of the storm, and after the storm has passed. He is trustworthy! What He says will be accomplished!

· · ·

You may be going through a storm right now. It may be health-related… or financial… or you may find that you are unemployed. Whatever the storm is, hold on to His promise. It may not be a storm of your making – it may in fact be a storm that has arisen because of your obedience to God. Hold to His promise. If He has not given you a specific promise about this particular storm – whatever it is – Jesus has promised you that He will never fail you or abandon you! (Hebrews 13:5)

If you find that you are in a storm because of your disobedience, repent and turn to Him. Trust Him to lead you out of the storm to safe shores – though perhaps somewhat bruised

2. **Take comfort in His presence in the midst of the storm**. Now granted, we can only take strength from that fact if we are truly walking in His presence, and we haven't headed off doing our own thing. In those times, it's difficult to take comfort in His presence – because we have probably walked away from Him. But the good news is, if we repent of our disobedience and seek His forgiveness, we have then entered back into His presence. And we not only have the assurance of His promise, we have the assurance of His presence.

3. **Your Master is more powerful than your storm**. There is not anything outside of His view. There is not anything taking place in our lives that is beyond His *capacity* to know what needs to be done to make it right. AND, there is nothing beyond His *capability* to make it right. Every storm we will ever encounter will ultimately experience defeat at the hands of God.

4. **Your Master will use your storm to bring Himself glory**. More than likely, He will not still your storm in the way you expected – or perhaps in the way you would have preferred. But one fact stands above all the rest – He will still the storm and bring you to safety in the way that brings Him the greatest glory! And we may not understand what that is on this side of heaven. But hold to His promise that He *"causes everything to work together for the good of those who love God and are called according to His purpose for them"* (Romans 8:28).

Even though the ship may go down, trust the faithfulness of God. Encountering His faithfulness will often involve storms! Why? Because in the storms we come to realize our total dependence upon Him. And at the end of the day, that's a good place to be – totally dependent upon Him – even if the ship goes down.

---

1. Walking With The Master, Ch. 29, Mark 4:35-41

60

EVEN THE SNAKE WAS POWERLESS

Once we were safe on shore, we learned that we were on the island of Malta. The people of the island were very kind to us. It was cold and rainy, so they built a fire on the shore to welcome us. As Paul gathered an armful of sticks and was laying them on the fire, a poisonous snake, driven out by the heat, bit him on the hand. The people of the island saw it hanging from his hand and said to each other, "A murderer, no doubt! Though he escaped the sea, justice will not permit him to live." But Paul shook off the snake into the fire and was unharmed. The people waited for him to swell up or suddenly drop dead. But when they had waited a long time and saw that he wasn't harmed, they changed their minds and decided he was a god. Near the shore where we landed was an estate belonging to Publius, the chief official of the island. He welcomed us and treated us kindly for three days. As it happened, Publius's father was ill with fever and dysentery. Paul went in and prayed for him, and laying his hands on him, he healed him. Then all the other sick people on the island came and were healed. As a result we were showered with honors, and when the time came to sail, people supplied us with everything we would need for the trip. It was three months after the shipwreck that we set sail on another ship that had wintered at the island – an Alexandrian ship with the twin gods as its figurehead.
Acts 28:1-11

* * *

Two hundred seventy-six people arrived safely on shore that day in the midst of a torrential rain, clinging onto planks or debris from the broken up ship. Remember that many were prisoners being sent to Rome for punishment. Yet the people of the island greeted them all with open arms of kindness and compassion.

It was early to mid-November. It was biting cold and those that had washed up on the shore were soaked. The first order of business was to build a fire for warmth. Many hands made light work as everyone – those who had been shipwrecked, together with those who lived on the island – searched for and gathered dry wood for the fire. As Paul added his armful of sticks to the pile, a poisonous snake crawled out of the fire, biting him and affixing itself to his hand. The residents, believing Paul to be a criminal, concluded that justice was seeking its revenge. *"A murderer, no doubt!"*

They expected Paul to fall dead as a victim of his "crimes". These pagan people, uninitiated in the gospel, uninformed about Christianity in any sense, and having no idea of the revelation of God, had a sense of right and wrong. They had a sense of justice and a sense that sin gets punished. They were thinking, "Aha, if he dies, look, he must be a murderer." In other words, there is a right and a wrong, and when you are wrong there are consequences.

They had a sense of morality. They had an understanding of sin – and the penalty for sin. Where did that come from? Paul would later write to the believers in Rome, *"God shows His anger from heaven against all sinful, wicked people who suppress the truth by their wickedness. They know the truth about God because He has made it obvious to them"* (Romans 1:18-19). Their sense of morality and sin was God-given.

God has also planted a sense of goodness and kindness in a man's heart (such as what the Maltese expressed to those who washed ashore), as well as a sense of morality. The residents on Malta had an understanding of goodness and evil even though they did not yet know God. It began for them, just as it did for everyone, when Eve and Adam took a bite of the fruit in the garden and received the knowledge of good and evil. That's why God would hold the Maltese people – and all people – responsible for their activities and their actions. *All have sinned – and all have fallen short of the glory of God* (Romans 3:23). And the people knew clearly that *the wages of sin is death* (Romans 6:23). They already knew that! They didn't need to be told that! But now they were about to hear and experience the Good News – that *the gift of God is eternal life through Christ Jesus* (Romans 6:23).

This shipwreck was all a part of God's plan and grace to bring the message of the gospel to that island.

The people watched, as Paul shook off the snake. They fully expected his hand to swell up and for him to fall over dead at any moment. Usually such a snake bite would create a panic and the person who had been bitten would be running around and flailing in horror. But Paul was calm – and as they watched, they saw that he was unharmed. The only death to occur was that of the snake being burned up in the fire. Seeing that Paul was unharmed by the snake bite, the residents decided that he was no ordinary man. They were wrong when they thought him to be a god, but they were right that he was no ordinary man – he was a redeemed man.

Here was the picture for them – and for us. Paul was a criminal – he was a sinner – just like each and every one of us. And the guaranteed outcome of sin is death. BUT, God in His grace made a way for us to be redeemed through the shed blood of His Son. If we have received His gift of grace by believing in His Son by faith, our sins have been forgiven and the consequence of death has been defeated. Sin no longer has power over us. Regrettably, we still have a capacity to sin, but God has assured us that *if we confess our sins to Him, He is faithful and just to forgive us of our sins and cleanse us from all unrighteousness* (1 John 1:9).

The picture of the snake – a reminder of that serpent in the Garden of Eden -- being shaken off and burned in the fire is a reminder that Satan is a defeated foe. And one day he will be burned up in the fire. We do not live in fear of him or in panic over his power over us. He is powerless over us – not because of anything we can do – but because we have been redeemed by the blood of the Lamb, and we are indwelt by His Holy Spirit.

Over the next three months, the residents of the island – as well as the survivors of the shipwreck – all had more opportunity to hear and witness the power of the gospel as Paul, Luke and Aristarchus preached and lived it out. But nothing was more powerful in communicating that truth than that first day when they witnessed that the snake was powerless.

The same is true for us. A watching world will be most attuned to listen to the gospel when they see for themselves that sin and Satan are powerless

over us. Live out the gospel through your action – and then add words…
until He returns.

* * *

61

PROCLAIM THE GOOD NEWS BOLDLY

The brothers and sisters in Rome had heard we were coming, and they came to meet us at the Forum on the Appian Way. Others joined us at The Three Taverns. When Paul saw them, he was encouraged and thanked God. When we arrived in Rome, Paul was permitted to have his own private lodging, though he was guarded by a soldier. Three days after Paul's arrival, he called together the local Jewish leaders. He said to them, "Brothers, I was arrested in Jerusalem and handed over to the Roman government, even though I had done nothing against our people or the customs of our ancestors. The Romans tried me and wanted to release me, because they found no cause for the death sentence. But when the Jewish leaders protested the decision, I felt it necessary to appeal to Caesar, even though I had no desire to press charges against my own people. I asked you to come here today so we could get acquainted and so I could explain to you that I am bound with this chain because I believe that the hope of Israel – the Messiah – has already come." They replied, "We have had no letters from Judea or reports against you from anyone who has come here. But we want to hear what you believe, for the only thing we know about this movement is that it is denounced everywhere." So a time was set, and on that day a large number of people came to Paul's lodging. He explained and testified about the Kingdom of God and tried to persuade them about Jesus from the Scriptures. Using the law of Moses and the books of the prophets, he spoke to them from morning until evening. Some were persuaded by the things he said, but others did not believe. And after they had argued back and forth among themselves, they left with this final word from Paul: "... I want you to know that this salvation from God has also been offered to the Gentiles, and they will accept it." For the next two years, Paul lived in Rome at his own expense. He welcomed all who visited him, boldly proclaiming the

Kingdom of God and teaching about the Lord Jesus Christ. And no one tried to stop him.
Acts 28:15-31

* * *

The day arrived when their ship docked in Italy at the port of Puteoli, one hundred twenty-five miles southeast of Rome. After remaining in the port town for a week and regaining their "land legs", Julius and his soldiers led Paul and the rest of the company by foot to Rome along the Appian Way. About forty-three miles outside of Rome, they encountered a group of believers looking for Paul. Apparently word had already reached the believers in Rome that Paul was coming. After traveling another ten miles they encountered a second group. The journey from Jerusalem to Rome had taken slightly less than three years, including Paul's two-year imprisonment in Caesarea. After all of the difficulties he had experienced along the way, seeing these believers as he approached Rome was a great encouragement to Paul.

One does have to wonder about the centurion Julius, as well as the rest of the soldiers. They had been traveling with Paul, Luke and Aristarchus – in very close quarters and through very difficult circumstances – for more than six months. But through it all, Paul and his companions had remained confident in God's promise and steadfast in His mission. The soldiers had heard the gospel preached a countless number of times – and they had seen it lived out minute-by-minute for many months. They had witnessed God's healing power at work through Paul, and God's miraculous protection when the snake bit him. Scripture does not tell us whether Julius, any of the other soldiers, or any of the other prisoners came to faith during their time together. But one thing we know for certain is that if they did not come to faith, it was not for lack of witness or opportunity.

After arriving in Rome, Paul stayed in his own private lodging for two years. God graciously provided the resources for him to be able to do so. Throughout the time, he preached the Good News – first to the Jews and then to the Gentiles. He received anyone who wanted to discuss the things of the Kingdom of God. Throughout the time, he was chained to a guard who was relieved every six hours. The guards had no choice but to listen to Paul as he preached, taught, and prayed. It would be no surprise to one day learn that some of them entered into the Kingdom as a result (Philippians 1:13-14).

. . .

Throughout his time in Rome, Paul was surrounded by men that he continued to pour his life into – Timothy, John Mark, Luke, Aristarchus, Epaphras, Justus and Demas. And he discipled the churches from a distance as he wrote his letters to the Philippians, Ephesians and Colossians, as well as his letter to Philemon.

Luke's account concludes before Paul's case was heard by Caesar. Apparently he was released and was able to resume his ministry travels – back to Greece, Macedonia, Asia and Crete, as well as into Spain (Romans 15:24). Wherever he went, he was faithful to preach the Good News to all. Five years after his release from Rome, he was again arrested – this time in Troas – and transported back to Rome. Scripture is silent as to the specific details surrounding this arrest.

But we do know that this time he did not live in his own lodging; he was chained in a prison and treated like a criminal (2 Timothy 1:16; 2:9). This time he was not surrounded by believers (2 Timothy 4:9-16); they appear to have abandoned him, except for Luke. And this time, his imprisonment didn't end in his being released; it ended in death. Because he was a Roman citizen, Paul was not crucified on a cross, but he was beheaded by orders of Emperor Nero.

The Holy Spirit did not inspire Luke to write the Book of Acts that we might simply know the early history of the church. He gave us this Book to encourage the church, in every age, to be faithful to the Lord to carry the gospel to the ends of the earth.

Jesus commissioned us to go boldly and proclaim the Good News throughout Jerusalem, Judea, Samaria and the ends of the earth. The early church took that mandate seriously and went – with all boldness – to wherever the Holy Spirit led them. Which brings us, most importantly, back to the promise that Jesus made, just before He ascended to sit at the right hand of the Father. It is the promise that James, Stephen, Peter, Paul and so many others carried with them until their last breath –

> *"Be sure of this: I am with you always, even to the end of the age."*
> (Matthew 28:20)

Wherever you are in your journey, hold onto that promise. Whatever circumstance, whatever trial or whatever battle you are walking through, walk according to that promise. Whether you are surrounded by others who are encouraging you, or you have been abandoned and are walking alone, do not let go of that promise. Stay the course. Finish the race. Fulfill the ministry He has given you… until He returns!

* * *

PLEASE HELP ME BY LEAVING A REVIEW!

i would be very grateful if you would leave a review of this book. Your feedback will be helpful to me in my future writing endeavors and will also assist others as they consider picking up a copy of the book.

To leave a review, go to:
  amazon.com/dp/1732867070

Thanks for your help!

* * *

THE COMPLETE LESSONS LEARNED IN THE WILDERNESS SERIES

* * *

There are lessons that can only be learned in the wilderness experiences of our lives. As we see throughout the Bible, God is right there leading us each and every step of the way, if we will follow Him. Wherever we are, whatever we are experiencing, He will use it to enable us to experience His Person, witness His power and join Him in His mission.

Each of the six books in the series contains 61 chapters, which means that the entire series is comprised of 366 chapters — ***one chapter for each day of the year.*** *The chapters have been formatted in a way that you can read one chapter each day or read each book straight through. Whichever way you choose, allow the Master to use the series to encourage and challenge you in the journey that He has designed uniquely for you so that His purpose is fulfilled, and His glory is made known.*

* * *

The Journey Begins (Book #1)

God's plan for our lives is not static; He is continuously calling us to draw closer, to climb higher and to move further. In that process, He is moving us out of our comfort zone to His land of promise for our lives. That process includes time in the wilderness. Many times it is easier to see the truth that God is teaching us through the lives of others than it is through our own lives.

"*The Journey Begins*" is the first book in the "*Lessons Learned In The Wilderness*" series. It chronicles those stories, those examples and those truths as revealed through the lives and experiences of the Israelites, as recorded in the Book of Exodus in sixty-one bite-sized chapters.

Available through Amazon

The Wandering Years (Book #2)

Why did a journey that God ordained to take slightly longer than one year, end up taking forty years? Why, instead of enjoying the fruits of the land of milk and honey, did the Israelites end up wandering in the desert wilderness for forty years? Why did one generation follow God out of Egypt only to die there, leaving the next generation to follow Him into the Promised Land?

In the journeys through the wildernesses of my life, i can look back and see where God has turned me back from that land of promise to wander a while longer in the wilderness. God has given us the wilderness to prepare us for His land of promise, but if when we reach the border we are not ready, He will turn us back to wander.

If God is allowing you to continue to wander in the wilderness, it is because He has more to teach you about Himself – His Person, His purpose and His power. "**The Wandering Years**" chronicles through sixty-one "bite-sized" chapters those lessons He would teach us through the Israelites' time in the wilderness as recorded in the books of Numbers and Deuteronomy.

Available through Amazon

Possessing the Promise (Book #3)

The day had finally arrived for the Israelites to possess the land that God had promised. But just like He had taught them lessons throughout

The Complete Lessons Learned In The Wilderness series 253

their journey in the wilderness, He had more to teach them, as they possessed the promise.

And so it is for us. Possessing the promise doesn't mean the faith adventure has come to a conclusion; rather, in many ways, it has only just begun. Possessing the promise will involve in some respects an even greater dependence upon God and the promise He has given you.

"**Possessing the Promise**" chronicles the stories, experiences and lessons we see recorded in the books of Joshua and Judges in sixty-one "bite-sized" chapters.

Available through Amazon

Walking With The Master (Book #4)

Our daily walk with the Master is never static – it entails moving and growing. Jesus was constantly on the move, carrying out the Father's work and His will. He was continuously surrendered and submitted to the will of the Father. And if we would walk with Him, we too must walk surrendered and submitted to the Father in our day-to-day lives.

Jesus extended His invitation to us to deny ourselves, take up our cross and follow Him. "**Walking With The Master**" chronicles, through "sixty-one" bite-sized chapters, those lessons the Master would teach us as we walk with Him each day, just as He taught the men and women who walked with Him throughout Galilee, Samaria and Judea as recorded in the Gospel accounts.

Available through Amazon

Taking Up The Cross (Book #5)

What does it mean to take up the cross? In this fifth book of the *Lessons Learned In The Wilderness* series, we will look at the cross our Lord has set before us as we follow Him. The backdrop for our time is the last forty-seven days of the earthly ministry of Jesus, picking up at His triumphal entry into Jerusalem and continuing to the day He ascended into heaven to sit at the right-hand of the Father.

We will look through the lens of the Gospels at what taking up the cross looked like in His life, and what He has determined it will look like in ours. He doesn't promise that there won't be a cost – there will be! And He doesn't promise that it will be easy – it won't be! But it is the journey He has set before us – a journey that will further His purpose in and through our lives – and a journey that will lead to His glory.

Available through Amazon

Until He Returns (Book #6)

Moments after Jesus ascended into heaven, two angels delivered this promise: "Someday He will return!" In this sixth and final book of the *Lessons Learned In The Wilderness* series, we will look at what that journey will look like *Until He Returns*. No matter where we are in our journey with Him – in the wilderness, in the promised land, or somewhere in between – He has a purpose and a plan for us.

In this book, we will look through the lens of the Book of Acts at what that journey looked like for those first century followers of Christ. Like us, they weren't perfect. There were times they took their eyes off of Jesus. But despite their imperfections, He used them to turn the world upside down. And His desire is to do the same thing through us. Our journeys will all look different, but He will be with us every step of the way.

Available through Amazon

* * *

For more information, go to
wildernesslessons.com or kenwinter.org
or my author page on Amazon

ALSO BY KENNETH A. WINTER

THROUGH THE EYES
(a series of biblical fiction novels)

Through the Eyes of a Shepherd (Shimon, a Bethlehem shepherd)
Through the Eyes of a Spy (Caleb, the Israelite spy)
Through the Eyes of a Prisoner (Paul, the apostle)

* * *

THE EYEWITNESSES
(a series of biblical fiction short story collections)

For Christmas/Advent
Little Did We Know – the advent of Jesus — for adults
Not Too Little To Know – the advent – ages 8 thru adult

For Easter/Lent
The One Who Stood Before Us – the ministry and passion of Jesus — for adults
The Little Ones Who Came – the ministry and passion – ages 8 thru adult

* * *

THE CALLED
(a series of biblical fiction novellas)

A Carpenter Called Joseph (Book 1)
A Prophet Called Isaiah (Book 2)
A Teacher Called Nicodemus (Book 3)
A Judge Called Deborah (Book 4)
A Merchant Called Lydia (Book 5)
A Friend Called Enoch (Book 6)
A Fisherman Called Simon (Book 7)
A Heroine Called Rahab (Book 8)
A Witness Called Mary (Book 9)
A Cupbearer Called Nehemiah (Book 10)

* * *

THE PARABLES

(follow the Fearsithe family in this series of christian fiction novels)

An Elusive Pursuit (Book 1) - releasing October 2023
A Belated Discovery (Book 2) - releasing Spring 2024

* * *

For more information, go to
wildernesslessons.com or kenwinter.org
or my author page on Amazon

ALSO AVAILABLE AS AUDIOBOOKS

THE CALLED

(the complete series)

A Carpenter Called Joseph
A Prophet Called Isaiah
A Teacher Called Nicodemus
A Judge Called Deborah
A Merchant Called Lydia
A Friend Called Enoch
A Fisherman Called Simon
A Heroine Called Rahab
A Witness Called Mary
A Cupbearer Called Nehemiah

* * *

Through the Eyes of a Shepherd

* * *

Little Did We Know

Not Too Little to Know

* * *

ABOUT THE AUTHOR

Ken Winter is a follower of Jesus, an extremely blessed husband, and a proud father and grandfather – all by the grace of God. His journey with Jesus has led him to serve on the pastoral staffs of two local churches – one in West Palm Beach, Florida and the other in Richmond, Virginia – and as the vice president of mobilization of an international missions organization.

Today, Ken continues in that journey as a full-time author, teacher and speaker. You can read his weekly blog posts at kenwinter.blog and listen to his weekly podcast at kenwinter.org/podcast.

* * *

And we proclaim Him, admonishing every man and teaching every man with all wisdom, that we may present every man complete in Christ. And for this purpose also I labor, striving according to His power, which mightily works within me.
(Colossians 1:28-29 NASB)

PLEASE JOIN MY READERS' GROUP

Please join my Readers' Group in order to receive updates and information about future releases, etc.

Also, i will send you a free copy of *The Journey Begins* e-book — the first book in the *Lessons Learned In The Wilderness* series. It is yours to keep or share with a friend or family member that you think might benefit from it.

It's completely free to sign up. i value your privacy and will not spam you. Also, you can unsubscribe at any time.

Go to kenwinter.org to subscribe.

Or scan this QR code using your camera on your smartphone:

* * *

www.ingramcontent.com/pod-product-compliance
Lightning Source LLC
Chambersburg PA
CBHW061634040426
42446CB00010B/1412